Public Health Palliative Care and Public Palliative Care Education

Public Health Palliative Care and Public Palliative Care Education

Editors

Georg Bollig
John Rosenberg

MDPI

Basel • Beijing • Wuhan • Barcelona • Belgrade • Novi Sad • Cluj • Manchester

Editors
Georg Bollig
Department of Palliative Medicine
University of Cologne
Cologne
Germany

John Rosenberg
School of Health
University of the Sunshine Coast
Queensland
Australia

Editorial Office
MDPI
St. Alban-Anlage 66
4052 Basel, Switzerland

This is a reprint of articles from the Special Issue published online in the open access journal *Healthcare* (ISSN 2227-9032) (available at: www.mdpi.com/journal/healthcare/special_issues/Public_Health_Palliative_Care_Public_Palliative_Care_Education).

For citation purposes, cite each article independently as indicated on the article page online and as indicated below:

Lastname, A.A.; Lastname, B.B. Article Title. *Journal Name* **Year**, *Volume Number*, Page Range.

ISBN 978-3-0365-9047-9 (Hbk)
ISBN 978-3-0365-9046-2 (PDF)
doi.org/10.3390/books978-3-0365-9046-2

Contents

About the Editors vii

Preface ix

Georg Bollig and John P. Rosenberg
Public Health Palliative Care and Public Palliative Care Education
Reprinted from: *Healthcare* **2023**, *11*, 745, doi:10.3390/healthcare11050745 1

Evelyn Mueller, Georg Bollig, Gerhild Becker and Christopher Boehlke
Lessons Learned from Introducing Last Aid Courses at a University Hospital in Germany
Reprinted from: *Healthcare* **2021**, *9*, 906, doi:10.3390/healthcare9070906 5

Erika Zelko, Larisa Vrbek and Melita Koletnik
Last Aid Course—The Slovenian Experience
Reprinted from: *Healthcare* **2022**, *10*, 1154, doi:10.3390/healthcare10071154 15

Leah Macaden, Kirsten Broadfoot, Clare Carolan, Kevin Muirhead, Siobhan Neylon and Jeremy Keen
Last Aid Training Online: Participants' and Facilitators' Perceptions from a Mixed-Methods Study in Rural Scotland
Reprinted from: *Healthcare* **2022**, *10*, 918, doi:10.3390/healthcare10050918 26

Georg Bollig, Mariam Safi, Marina Schmidt and Hermann Ewald
Is There a Need for Cultural Adaptation of the Last Aid Course?—A Mixed-Methods Study across the Danish-German Border
Reprinted from: *Healthcare* **2022**, *10*, 658, doi:10.3390/healthcare10040658 45

Chantal Giehl, Nino Chikhradze, Georg Bollig, Horst Christian Vollmar and Ina Otte
"I Needed to Know, No Matter What I Do, I Won't Make It Worse"—Expectations and Experiences of Last Aid Course Participants in Germany—A Qualitative Pilot Study
Reprinted from: *Healthcare* **2023**, *11*, 592, doi:10.3390/healthcare11040592 61

Silvia Librada Flores, Sonia Herminia Roa Trujillo, Nurlian Torrejano Gonzálex, María del Pilar García Buitrago and Miguel Ángel Lucas Díaz
A Survey of Attitudes and Beliefs about Care, Compassion and Communities Networks in Palliative Care. A Preliminary Study for the Development of a Compassionate University
Reprinted from: *Healthcare* **2021**, *9*, 946, doi:10.3390/healthcare9080946 71

Samar M. Aoun, Robyn Richmond, Leanne Jiang and Bruce Rumbold
Winners and Losers in Palliative Care Service Delivery: Time for a Public Health Approach to Palliative and End of Life Care
Reprinted from: *Healthcare* **2021**, *9*, 1615, doi:10.3390/healthcare9121615 85

Lena Kroik, Carol Tishelman, Krister Stoor and Anette Edin-Liljegren
A Salutogenic Perspective on End-of-Life Care among the Indigenous Sámi of Northern Fennoscandia
Reprinted from: *Healthcare* **2021**, *9*, 766, doi:10.3390/healthcare9060766 98

Chia-Jen Liu, Sheng-Jean Huang and Samuel Shih-Chih Wang
Implementation of Compassionate Communities: The Taipei Experience
Reprinted from: *Healthcare* **2022**, *10*, 177, doi:10.3390/healthcare10010177 113

Su Hyun Bae and Yeo Hyang Kim
The First Step to Initiate Pediatric Palliative Care: Identify Patient Needs and Cooperation of Medical Staff
Reprinted from: *Healthcare* **2022**, *10*, 127, doi:10.3390/healthcare10010127 . . . . **123**

Max Kleijberg, Rebecca Hilton, Beth Maina Ahlberg and Carol Tishelman
Play Elements as Mechanisms in Intergenerational Arts Activities to Support Community Engagement with End-of-Life Issues
Reprinted from: *Healthcare* **2021**, *9*, 764, doi:10.3390/healthcare9060764 . . . . **131**

Bruce Rumbold and Samar M. Aoun
Palliative and End-of-Life Care Service Models: To What Extent Are Consumer Perspectives Considered?
Reprinted from: *Healthcare* **2021**, *9*, 1286, doi:10.3390/healthcare9101286 . . . . **147**

About the Editors

Georg Bollig

Georg Bollig MD MAS PhD DEAA is a physician and researcher. After medical studies at the universities of Cologne (Germany), Vienna (Austria) and Seattle (USA), he became a specialist in anaesthesiology, pain therapy and palliative care. He received a Master's Degree in Palliative Care and Organisational Ethics from the University Klagenfurt/IFF Vienna. His PhD at the University of Bergen, Norway was about Palliative Care, ethical challenges and end-of-life decision-making in nursing homes. Georg has done scientific work in various fields and has published books and scientific articles on anaesthesiology, pain therapy, emergency medicine, nursing home medicine, palliative care and ethics. He has been a board member of the Norwegian Palliative Association from 20092016 and is speaker of a working group on Palliative Care in long-term care facilities of the Hospiz- und Palliativverband Schleswig-Holstein and a member of a working group of the German association for palliative medicine on palliative medicine for non-cancer patients. From 2016 to 2022, he has been working as a senior consultant in Palliative Medicine at the University hospital of Southern Jutland and as Associate Professor in Palliative Care at the University of Southern Denmark. Currently, he works as senior consultant in palliative medicine and head of Palliative Medicine at the Academic teaching hospital Helios Klinikum Schleswig in Germany. In addition to his clinical work, Georg is a research fellow at the Department of Palliative Medicine, University of Cologne, Faculty of Medicine and University Hospital, Cologne, Germany. Georg has first published the idea of a Last Aid Course as measure of public palliative care education (PPCE) and is the leader of the International Last Aid working group. His main research interests are public palliative care education (PPCE), Last Aid Courses and tele-palliative care.

John Rosenberg

John Rosenberg RN BN MPallC PhD FPCNA is a Registered Nurse and health care academic. His clinical background is in community-based palliative care, conducted in Melbourne and Brisbane, Australia. He has a Master's Degree in Palliative Care from Flinders University and was awarded a PhD from Queensland University of Technology in 2007 for the first ever doctoral study of Health Promoting Palliative Care. John is a longstanding contributor to the advancement of Public Health Palliative Care, including the Death Literacy Index and partnering methodologies for collaboration between health care services and communities. John was President of Public Health Palliative Care International from 2019 to October 2023. Currently, he is a Senior Lecturer in the School of Health at the University of the Sunshine Coast in Queensland, Australia, where his teaching, research and engagement portfolios focus on palliative care for older people, aged care, and community development approaches to Compassionate Communities. John is a Foundation Fellow of Palliative Care Nurses Australia.

Preface

Today, palliative care is seen as an essential part of public health care. The provision of palliative care in the community is a public duty. Palliative care and end-of-life care at home for all in need can only be done as a cooperation of healthcare professionals and citizens. The Compassionate Communities approach introduced by Kellehear and others has led to the recognition of palliative care as everyone's business and an important public health topic. Unfortunately, death literacy is not yet common among the public. Public awareness of palliative care is low, and public palliative care education is rarely implemented in most communities. Nevertheless, some educational programs for public palliative care education, for example, the Last Aid Course, do exist in some countries in Europe, Brazil and Australia.

There are many open questions concerning public health palliative care and public education. Activation of citizens is needed to enable them to participate in palliative care and end-of-life care provision. Cultural aspects of public health palliative care must be explored and included in future public palliative care education programs.

The goal of this reprint on "Public Health Palliative Care and Public Palliative Care Education" is to highlight recent advances and challenges in public health palliative care and education. It includes original research, reviews and other papers that address these challenges and has collected chapters that cover a broad range of topics, including social and cultural aspects and experiences with public health palliative care and public palliative care education in the communities.

The reprint will be of interest to researchers and clinicians from various fields and to policymakers, officials, and politicians who make public health decisions and policies for the future, facing demographic changes and an increased need for palliative care and end-of-life care in the community.

The COVID-19 pandemic has shown the importance of a broad implementation of palliative care in all communities and societies. Public palliative care education and participation of volunteers and the public in cooperation with community health care and specialized palliative care services can help to ensure palliative care for all in need in the future.

We want to thank all authors who have contributed to the work published in this reprint. Their contributions are described in more detail in the first chapter. We are grateful for the support from our families, colleagues and the whole team from healthcare that helped to make this possible.

Georg Bollig and John Rosenberg
Editors

healthcare MDPI

Editorial

Public Health Palliative Care and Public Palliative Care Education

Georg Bollig [1,2,*] and John P. Rosenberg [2,3]

[1] Department of Anesthesiology, Intensive Care, Palliative Medicine and Pain Therapy, HELIOS Klinikum, 24837 Schleswig, Germany
[2] Last Aid Research Group International (LARGI), 24837 Schleswig, Germany
[3] School of Health, University of the Sunshine Coast, Caboolture, QLD 4510, Australia
* Correspondence: georg.bollig@helios-gesundheit.de

This Special Issue, "Public Health Palliative Care (PHPC) and Public Palliative Care Education (PPCE)", highlights recent advances and challenges in PHPC and PPCE. The articles demonstrate the breadth and diversity of local responses from across the globe, including Europe, Asia, Australia and South America. The COVID-19 pandemic clearly shows how collaboration between healthcare services and communities is an essential component of public health. This collaboration, initially described in the *Ottawa Charter for Health Promotion* [1] and the growing body of literature about public health approaches to palliative and end-of-life care, demonstrates the importance of the broad implementation of palliative care in all communities and societies.

If most people want to die at home, the public must take a role in the support of seriously ill and dying people. The participation of the public is essential to enable more people to die at home. According to Allan Kellehear's "95% rule" [2], seriously ill and dying people spend little more than 5% of their final year of life in the direct care of healthcare services; the other 95% relies upon relatives, friends or others without healthcare backgrounds to provide support. Public health palliative care (PHPC) and public palliative care education (PPCE) approaches attempt to address this provision of support.

However, public awareness of palliative care is generally low, and although public education has been recommended by a number of authors, PPCE is rarely implemented in most communities [3–7]. Often, this education—like clinical care—is provided by healthcare services with familiarity with the issues of dying, death and loss. Although this is not unreasonable, it is more consistent with the principles and practices of PHPC to provide such education in partnerships between services and communities, demonstrating responses to local needs.

Five papers highlight different aspects and experiences of the implementation of the Last Aid Course (LAC) from different countries and settings. LACs demonstrate a standardised approach to PPCE that has been implemented in 20 countries worldwide, including Germany, Switzerland, Scotland, Lithuania, Australia, Canada and Brazil. LAC was introduced in 2014 to educate the public about death, dying and end-of-life care, to encourage and to empower people to participate in end-of-life care at home, and to enhance the public discussion about these themes [3,8].

Mueller and colleagues report on LACs in a German university hospital [9], where they were very well accepted by the whole staff (both healthcare and non-healthcare professions) in general, but healthcare staff sought extended content and opportunity for group discussions. These findings led to the formation of an extended "LAC Professional" for healthcare professionals comprising ten teaching hours [10]. In Slovenia, Zelko et al. demonstrate that web-based delivery is very well received and favourably rated by LAC participants [11]. They recommend that the LAC should also address the cultural diversity and characteristics of local settings and populations; they describe early experiences with

check for updates

Citation: Bollig, G.; Rosenberg, J.P. Public Health Palliative Care and Public Palliative Care Education. *Healthcare* **2023**, *11*, 745. https://doi.org/10.3390/healthcare11050745

Received: 24 February 2023
Accepted: 27 February 2023
Published: 3 March 2023

an LAC for deaf people. Macaden at al. report from Scotland that LAC could serve as the foundational core training to promote death literacy in communities to enhance personal knowledge, skills and confidence of community members [12].

In a cross-border pilot study from Denmark and Germany, Bollig et al. showed that LAC participants find individual differences more important than cultural differences in end-of-life care [13]. They describe differences in regulations and organisation of services across the border that people need to be informed about; some suggest the topics of organisation and support across the border, religions and cultures, and supporting people in grief could be added to the LAC. This pilot study has influenced the work of the revision of LAC content during the 3rd International Last Aid Conference in Maribor, 2022. Interviews with German participants of the LAC presented by Giehl et al. inform us about the effects that LAC can have on palliative care provision at home and empowerment of participants [14]. The LAC helps to provide knowledge, guidance and recommendations for action in palliative care situations.

These articles on LACs add to our understanding of the impact of LAC training of both the public and professionals. They show that the LAC concept is feasible in different settings in a range of countries. Indeed, LAC may contribute to increased death literacy in communities, where the development of personal skills to strengthen community action underpins PHPC [15]. In the context of Compassionate Communities, LACs can be seen as practical support offered by fellow citizens to relieve suffering.

Recognition of palliative care as everyone's responsibility also enables universities to play a role in the development of Compassionate Communities. Librada Flores et al. recognise that, with minimal death awareness in universities, a university that sensitises, trains and mobilises students and professionals to develop care networks around people at the end of life is highly beneficial [16]. Including universities as partners in Compassionate Communities may contribute to social change with the sensitisation of future leaders educated there.

Aoun and her colleagues report on a large community-focused study of bereaved and current carers, and patients, of palliative care [17]. They observe that those with the greatest awareness of palliative care are the 'winners' in receiving best quality care and the 'losers' were the opposite; however, in both cases, wider social networks are key to providing appropriate support. The importance of communities supporting their members in times of need is very clear, and this reiterates the necessity of public awareness. This is perhaps most clear in communities with a strong, shared cultural identity. Kroik et al. explore this in the indigenous Sámi of Fennoscandia [18]. Where community coherence is high, capacity for well-functioning palliative and end-of-life care is increased; yet the greatest challenge lies in the establishment of supportive interactions with healthcare services. Developing meaningful care relies upon this partnership.

The implementation of the Compassionate Cities charter [19] in downtown Taipei, Taiwan, guided the development of a compassionate community in a local district [20]. A culturally sensitive and holistic program was developed using health and social services, universities and community representatives, which enabled a sustainable approach to community connection and greatly increased awareness of palliative and end-of-life care issues. In South Korea, Bae and Kim also demonstrate the importance of regional knowledge in designing appropriate responses to local needs [21].

Interestingly, this clear sense of common purpose can be created between previously disparate groups. Kleijberg and his colleagues explored the application of the arts to intergenerational groups where community partners, children and older adults were drawn together for intentional 'play' [22]. These activities engaged with end-of-life issues, and illustrate a powerful alternative to didactic pedagogy in building knowledge and connections.

Rumbold and Aoun's review of the literature provides an informative overview of the consumer experience of palliative care, including consumer contribution to service and policy design [23]. Arguably, it is from a community where citizens' engagement with palliative and end-of-life care issues is high that these experiences are more positive; however, this review demonstrates minimal use of consumer perspectives in the models of palliative care. This is true not only in the low usage of generalised evidence but also in the notable absence of community representation in the co-creation of services.

This Special Issue adds to the growing body of knowledge, based on practice, theory and research, about PHPC and PPCE. It is clear that global perspectives of PHPC are best expressed through both international, national and local activities including PPCE, such as Last Aid. Partnerships between healthcare services, civic organisations and communities are essential to increase awareness, skills and practice. It is evident that PHPC and PPCE are needed to improve palliative care support by the public in communities. These examples show that encouraging work on this important theme is ongoing worldwide, although more effort for implementation and research is needed.

Author Contributions: Both authors have contributed equally. All authors have read and agreed to the published version of the manuscript.

Conflicts of Interest: The authors declare no conflict of interest.

References

1. World Health Organization. *The Ottawa Charter for Health Promotion*; WHO: Geneva, Switzerland, 1986.
2. Kellehear, A. The social nature of dying and the social model of health. *Oxf. Textb. Public Health Palliat. Care* **2022**, 22–29.
3. Bollig, G.; Bauer, E.H. Last Aid Courses as measure for public palliative care education for adults and children: A narrative review. *Ann. Palliat. Med.* **2021**, *10*, 8242–8253. [CrossRef] [PubMed]
4. Gopal, K.S.; Archana, P.S. Awareness, knowledge and attitude about palliative care, in general, population and health care professionals in tertiary care hospital. *Int. J. Sci. Study* **2016**, 3 (Suppl. S10), 31–35.
5. McIlfatrick, S.; Slater, P.; Beck, E.; Bamidele, O.; McCloskey, S.; Carr, K.; Muldrew, D.; Hanna-Trainor, L.; Hasson, F. Examining public knowledge, attitudes and perceptions towards palliative care: A mixed method sequential study. *BMC Palliat. Care* **2021**, *20*, 44. [CrossRef]
6. Westerlund, C.; Tishelman, C.; Benkel, I.; Fürst, C.J.; Molander, U.; Rasmussen, B.H.; Sauter, S.; Lindqvist, O. Public awareness of palliative care in Sweden. *Scand. J. Public Health* **2018**, *46* (Suppl. S4), 478–487. [CrossRef]
7. Kozlov, E.; McDarby, M.; Reid, M.C.; Carpenter, B.D. Knowledge of Palliative Care among Community-Dwelling Adults. *Am. J. Hosp. Palliat. Care* **2018**, *35*, 647–651. [CrossRef]
8. Bollig, G.; Brandt Kristensen, F.; Wolff, D.L. Citizens appreciate talking about death and learning end-of-life care: A mixed-methods study on views and experiences of 5169 Last Aid Course participants. *Prog. Palliat. Care* **2021**, *29*, 140–148. [CrossRef]
9. Mueller, E.; Bollig, G.; Becker, G.; Boehlke, C. Lessons learned from introducing Last Aid Courses at a university hospital in Germany. *Healthcare* **2021**, *9*, 906. [CrossRef]
10. Bollig, G.; Schmidt, M.; Aumann, D.; Knopf, B. Der Letzte Hilfe Kurs professionell—Erste Erfahrungen mit einem eintägigen niedrigschwelligen Palliative Care Fortbildungsangebot für Personal aus dem Gesundheitswesen. *Z. Palliativmed* **2023**, *24*, 31–39. [CrossRef]
11. Zelko, E.; Vrbek, L.; Koletnik, M. Last Aid Course—The Slovenian Experience. *Healthcare* **2022**, *10*, 1154. [CrossRef]
12. Macaden, L.; Broadfoot, K.; Carolan, C.; Muirhead, K.; Neylon, S.; Keen, J. Last Aid Training online: Participants' and facilitators' perceptions from a mixed-methods study in rural Scotland. *Healthcare* **2022**, *10*, 918. [CrossRef]
13. Bollig, G.; Safi, M.; Schmidt, M.; Ewald, H. Is there a need for cultural adaptation of the Last Aid Course? A mixed-methods study across the Danish-German border. *Healthcare* **2022**, *10*, 658. [CrossRef]
14. Giehl, C.; Chikhradze, N.; Bollig, G.; Vollmar, H.C.; Otte, I. "I needed to know, no matter what I do, I won't make it worse"—expectations and experiences of Last Aid Course participants in Germany—A qualitative pilot study. *Healthcare* **2023**, *11*, 592. [CrossRef]
15. Mills, J.; Rosenberg, J.P.; Bollig, G.; Haberecht, J. Last Aid and Public Health Palliative Care: Towards the development of personal skills and strengthened community action. *Prog. Palliat. Care* **2020**, *28*, 343–345. [CrossRef]
16. Librada Flores, S.; Roa Trujillo, S.H.; Torrejano Gonzálex, N.; García Buitrago, M.d.P.; Lucas Díaz, M.Á. A survey of attitudes and beliefs about care, compassion and communities networks in palliative care. a preliminary study for the development of a compassionate university. *Healthcare* **2021**, *9*, 946. [CrossRef]
17. Aoun, S.M.; Jiang, L.; Rumbold, B. Winners and losers in palliative care service delivery: Time for a public health approach to palliative and end-of-life care. *Healthcare* **2021**, *9*, 1615. [CrossRef]
18. Kroik, L.; Tishelman, C.; Stoor, K.; Edin-Liljegren, A. A salutogenic perspective on end-of-life care among the Indigenous Sámi of Northern Fennoscandia. *Healthcare* **2021**, *9*, 766. [CrossRef]
19. Kellehear, A. *Compassionate Cities*; Routledge: London, UK, 2012.

20. Liu, C.-J.; Huang, S.J.; Wang, S.S.-C. Implementation of Compassionate Communities: The Taipei experience. *Healthcare* **2022**, *10*, 177. [CrossRef]
21. Bae, S.H.; Kim, Y.H. The First Step to Initiate Pediatric Palliative Care: Identify Patient Needs and Cooperation of Medical Staff. *Healthcare* **2022**, *10*, 127. [CrossRef]
22. Kleijberg, M.; Hilton, R.; Ahlberg, B.M.; Tishelman, C. Play elements as mechanisms in intergenerational arts activities to support community engagement with end-of-life issues. *Healthcare* **2021**, *9*, 764. [CrossRef]
23. Rumbold, B.; Aoun, S.M. Palliative and end-of-life care service models: To what extent are consumer perspectives considered? *Healthcare* **2021**, *9*, 1286. [CrossRef] [PubMed]

healthcare

Article

Lessons Learned from Introducing Last Aid Courses at a University Hospital in Germany

Evelyn Mueller [1], Georg Bollig [2,3,4], Gerhild Becker [1] and Christopher Boehlke [1,*]

1 Medical Center, Department of Palliative Medicine, Faculty of Medicine, University of Freiburg, 79106 Freiburg, Germany; evelyn.mueller@uniklinik-freiburg.de (E.M.); gerhild.becker@uniklinik-freiburg.de (G.B.)
2 Palliative Care Team, Medical Department Sønderborg/Tønder, South Jutland Hospital, 6400 Sønderborg, Denmark; georg.bollig@rsyd.dk
3 Palliative Care Research Group, Medical Research Unit, Institute of Regional Health Research, University of Southern Denmark, 6200 Aabenraa, Denmark
4 Last Aid International, 24837 Schleswig, Germany
* Correspondence: christopher.boehlke@uniklinik-freiburg.de

Abstract: In recent years, so called "Last Aid courses", concerning end-of-life care for people dying, have successfully been established in community settings in several European countries, Australia, and South-America. To date, they have not been evaluated in hospital settings, where educational needs (concerning care of the dying) are especially high, and may differ from the general population. To evaluate if Last Aid courses are feasible in hospital settings, and if informational needs of hospital staff are met by the curriculum, we introduced Last Aid courses at a university hospital. Five courses were offered; participants of courses 1 and 2 completed surveys with open-ended questions; the answers were used to develop the evaluation questionnaire employed in courses 3–5. In these three courses, 55 of the 56 participants completed an evaluation survey to explore their learning goals and obtain feedback. Courses were fully booked; participants were heterogeneous with regard to their professional background. The most prevalent learning goals were "preparation for emotional aspects in care of dying" (65.5% ratings "very important"), "preparation for medical/care aspects in care of dying" (60.0%), and "knowledge of supportive services and facilities" (54.5%). Overall, the evaluation showed that Last Aid courses were more suitable to educate non-medical hospital staff about care of the dying. Medical staff, in contrast to non-medical staff, more often requested courses with an extended curriculum in order to meet their learning goals. Last Aid courses were well accepted and helped to reduce information deficits on care of the dying in a heterogeneous population of hospital staff.

Keywords: Last Aid course; palliative care; hospital staff; education; survey

Citation: Mueller, E.; Bollig, G.; Becker, G.; Boehlke, C. Lessons Learned from Introducing Last Aid Courses at a University Hospital in Germany. *Healthcare* **2021**, *9*, 906. https://doi.org/10.3390/healthcare9070906

Academic Editor: Robbert Gobbens

Received: 31 May 2021
Accepted: 11 July 2021
Published: 16 July 2021

1. Introduction

Estimations of individuals in need of general palliative care at the end-of-life exceed 60% [1,2]; numbers will increase in the decades to come due to expected demographic changes [3]. While the medical needs of seriously ill and dying people must be met by professionals, many needs (e.g., practical and emotional support) can be supported by citizens and compassionate communities [4]. Citizens of a compassionate community care for the old, sick, and dying people in their midst; "death" is integrated as a part of life in society. However, the public is often not aware of the needs of dying people and their relatives, or people are inadequately educated or prepared to support them [5].

The Last Aid course curriculum was created by an international working group to educate citizens about the care of the dying and palliative care; it was successfully implemented in community settings in several countries [6–8]. Furthermore, a special Last Aid course curriculum was developed for children and teenagers, and is well accepted by them [9].

Hospital staff (medical and non-medical) face death and dying in various ways; thus the need for information on palliative care is possibly even higher than for the general population. At the same time, professional courses on palliative care are not common in many medical disciplines, and are not intended for non-medical professions. We therefore implemented Last Aid courses with only four teaching hours (45 min each) in a hospital setting, and asked if the courses were suited for the needs of the staff. We investigated the participants' reasons for course attendance, their professional and private burdens (concerning death and dying), general feedback on the course, and suggestions for improvements.

2. Materials and Methods

We implemented Last Aid courses in a tertiary university hospital in Germany in 2018. Each course was open to 20 participants. The courses were announced for non-medical staff on the hospital's intranet platform. However, courses were open to all employees (including medical staff) of the hospital and no participation fees applied. The curriculum was comprised of four sessions, 45-min, named, "dying as a normal part of life", "planning ahead", "relieving suffering", and "final goodbyes". Teaching methods included lectures, group discussions, and practical exercises (for details, see [6]). Overall, five courses took place. Each course was fully booked and 17–20 persons participated. The interest in the courses was high—another five courses could have been held without need for additional announcements, but courses were paused due to time constraints of the teachers (two physicians, three nurses). Courses were taught in teams of two (physician and nurse).

2.1. Pre-Survey and Item Development

In the first two courses, participants were asked to complete a pre-survey of mainly open questions, so researchers could collect information for item development for the survey in courses 3–5. The pre-survey was completed by 33 participants (n = 4 medical staff; n = 29 non-medical staff; n = 27 female, n = 2 male, n = 2 no answer; age: m = 49.6 (sd = 10.2)). The pre-survey resulted in written descriptions on various topics, e.g., their goals and concerns (see Appendix A), as well as their burdens, due to death and dying. The answers were categorized by clustering similar descriptions and formulating subcategory labels by C.B. and E.M. For goals and expectations, five subcategories were identified. The subcategory descriptions formed the basis for the item wording of the "goals and concerns before attending the course" in the survey, of courses 3–5 (see Appendix B; item 8). For "burden due to death and dying", only generalized items on burdens in professional work and private life were included (see Appendix B; items 4 and 5). A range of other items was developed based on information from literature and the pre-survey (see Appendix B; not all results reported).

All newly developed items were pre-tested regarding face validity, suitability of Likert scales for questions, and comprehensibility through three cognitive interviews (physician, nurse, social worker), and modified by a team of three experts in the field (palliative medicine, psychology, and psychometrics). As the sample size in the pre-survey and cognitive interviews was limited, we included open-ended questions in the questionnaire in courses 3–5, ensuring participants could add new aspects, if they were not reflected in the pre-survey.

2.2. Evaluation Survey

In courses 3–5, the actual evaluation survey was conducted, the results of which are reported here. Participants were informed that the evaluations—aimed at further development of the course and data collection, analysis, and reporting—were anonymous. They were asked to complete the survey immediately after the course or send the form back via mail. The questionnaire is included in Appendix B. The survey comprised: (a) sociodemographic and occupational characteristics of participants; (b) items for evaluation of course contents, extent of new information, recommendation, and comprehensibility (drawn from standard evaluation questionnaires); (c) the specially developed items on goals and concerns, as well as burden due to death and dying. The items employed Likert-scales as answer options and open-ended questions. Additionally, participants could include comments and suggestions in an open-ended question.

2.3. Data Analysis

For analysis, medical expertise levels were obtained by classification of reported professions into four levels: 0 non-medical professions; 1 therapeutic and medical assistance staff; 2 nurses and midwifes; and 3 physicians. Furthermore, burden due to death and dying was asked both for work and for private context. Within a summarized category of "overall burden", any person reporting medium, high, or very high burden in at least one of the contexts was classified as "burdened by death and dying".

Missing data were not imputed. Explorative data analysis included calculation of descriptive statistics as well as correlations (Kendall Tau-b); the Friedman test was employed to test for differences in ratings between the four modules; due to the explorative approach of the analysis, alpha level was not adjusted and was 5 % (two-tailed) for all tests. SPSS 24 was used for statistical analysis.

3. Results

Courses 3–5 were fully booked (n = 60), and 56 staff members attended the course; 55 of the 56 (98.2%) participants completed the evaluation survey. Characteristics of the sample are reported in Table 1. The sample was heterogeneous with regard to age, profession, and extent of patient contact. A total of 90.9% (n = 50) of the participants were female. The participants covered the full range of professions in a hospital, from hairdressers, or laboratory and administrative staff (with no medical expertise) to nurses and physicians. The majority of participants (67.3% (n = 37)) was non-medical staff. A total of 36.4% (n = 20) of the participants reported care or support for dying relatives in the private context.

Table 1. Characteristics of participants of the Last Aid course (n = 55).

	N (%)
Age:	
20–29 years	9 (16.4%)
30–39 years	4 (7.3%)
40–49 years	5 (9.1%)
50–59 years	19 (34.5%)
≥60 years	12 (21.8%)
No answer	6 (10.9)
Sex:	
Male	3 (5.5%)
Female	50 (90.9%)
No answer	2 (3.6)
Medical Competence:	
Non-medical staff	
Non-medical professions	21 (38.2%)
Therapeutic and medical assistance staff	16 (29.1%)
Medical	
Nurses and midwifes	16 (29.1%)
Physicians	1 (1.8%)
No answer	1 (1.8%)

Table 1. *Cont.*

	N (%)
Contact with patients:	
Never	17 (30.9%)
Rarely	8 (14.5%)
Sometimes	7 (12.7%)
Often	3 (5.5%)
Very often	20 (36.4%)
Support of dying relatives:	
Yes	20 (36.4%)
No	35 (63.6%)

3.1. Motivation to Participate in Last Aid Courses and Burden by Death and Dying

To understand the motivation of participants, we asked the participants of courses 1 and 2 for their reasons to attend the course. For examples of open-ended answers in the pre-survey categorization, see Appendix A. We deducted categories from the answers, formulated items on that basis, and asked the participants in the main survey how important these goals were (Figure 1). "Preparation for emotional aspects in care of dying", "preparation for medical/care aspects in care of dying", and "knowledge of supportive services and facilities" were rated as "very important" by the majority of participants. Less often rated as "very important" were "reduction of own anxiety and insecurity when dealing with the subject of death" and "contribution to the social discussion on the subject of dying". However, all learning goals were rated as "very/rather important" by more than 60% of participants (Figure 1).

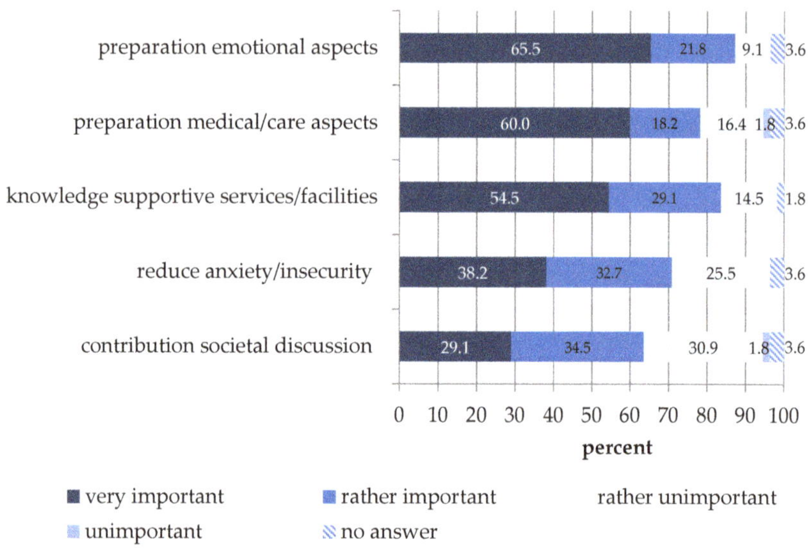

Figure 1. Goals and concerns before attending the course (n = 55).

As perceived burden by death and dying might be a reason for attendance, we asked if participants felt burdened by "death and dying" at work and at home (Table 2). Summarizing it in "overall burden", 33 of the 55 participants (60.0%) reported medium/high or very high burden by death and dying in at least one of the contexts (at home/at work).

Table 2. Burden because of death and dying (n = 55).

	At Work N (%)	At Home N (%)
At work		
No burden	16 (29.1%)	13 (23.6%)
Low burden	20 (36.4%)	16 (29.1%)
Medium burden	14 (25.5%)	19 (34.5%)
High burden	2 (3.6%)	4 (7.3%)
Very high burden	1 (1.8%)	2 (3.6%)
No answer	2 (3.6%)	1 (1.8%)

The burden by the topic "death and dying at work" correlated with the extent of patient contact (Chi2 (df = 16) = 28.8; p = 0.03, Figure 2), participants reporting more frequent contact were more likely to report burden. Furthermore, we found associations of burden of participants and their learning goals: more burdened participants were likely to indicated a higher importance of "knowledge of supportive services and facilities" (Kendall tau r = −0.41; p = 0.00), "preparation for emotional aspects of death and dying" (r = 0.28; p = 0.02), and "preparation for medical/care aspects" (r = −0.25, p = 0.03). Thus, burdened participants reported another pattern of informational needs than participants who did not feel burdened by death and dying.

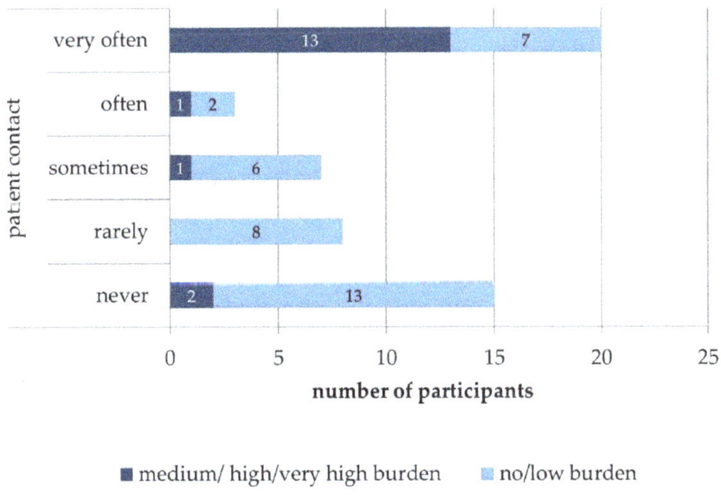

Figure 2. Burden by the topic death and dying at work in relation to the extent of patient contact (n = 53).

3.2. Evaluation of Last Aid Courses by Medical and Non-Medical Staff

The four modules of the course were mostly rated "good" to "very good" with only a small subset of participants rating the modules "not so good", with none rating the courses being "unsatisfactory". The best-rated module 3 "relieving suffering" was rated "very good" by 70.9% of the participants (Figure 3).

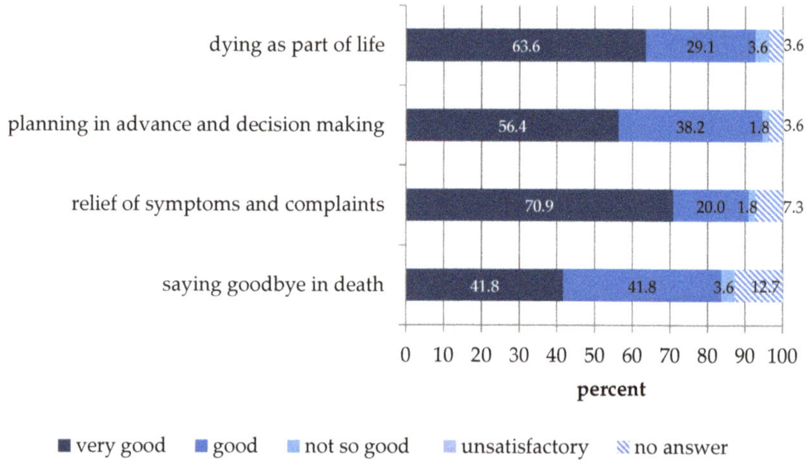

Figure 3. Evaluation of the Last Aid course modules (n = 55).

To evaluate suitability of the Last Aid course curriculum in the hospital setting, we asked the participants about their overall rating of the course: on a 4-point Likert-scale (very good, good, not so good, and unsatisfactory): 45.5% (n = 25) judged the course as "very-good", 30.9% (n = 17) as "good", with 23.6% (n = 13) missing answers. When the participants were asked if they would recommend the course to others, a high percentage answered positively: "applies completely" was 79.2% (n = 42), "rather applies" was 18.9% (n = 10), "does rather not apply" was 1.9% (n = 1), "does not apply" was 0%, and there were two missing answers. Likewise, most participants found that the content of the course was conveyed in an understandable manner: "applies completely" was 85.5% (n = 47), "rather applies" was 10.9% (n = 6), and there were two missing answers. Similarly, participants mostly stated that they had learned something new during the course: "applies completely" was 49.1% (n = 27), "rather applies" was 38.2% (n = 21), "rather does not apply" was 7.3% (n = 4), "does not apply" was 1.8% (n = 1), and there were two missing answers. When we correlated the answers to this question with medical competence, we found that medical staff were more likely to indicate a lower level of learning something new than non-medical staff (Kendall tau r = −0.36; $p = 0.01$).

4. Discussion

The Last Aid courses were well accepted and helped to reduce information deficits on care of the dying in a heterogeneous population of hospital staff, with mostly non-medical staff attending. Participants indicated emotional preparation, the need for information on supportive services, and preparation for medical and nursing aspects of end-of-life care as the most important learning goals.

We encountered gender disparities as attendees were mostly female, which is consistent with gender distribution in hospice and end-of-life care, as well as the care for individuals with dementia [10,11]. The gender disparity was also seen in a multicenter-study from Germany, Austria, and Switzerland, which conducted Last Aid courses in the community setting with more than 5000 participants [12]. This study revealed that 88% of the participants were female and the median age was 56 years, which might indicate that people attending want to prepare for a caregiver role [12]. Despite changing social expectations, females carry most of the caregiving at the end-of-life [10]. Within the context of a compassionate community, widespread Last Aid courses could—just like First-Aid courses—provide a low threshold learning opportunity that might facilitate involvement of men in end-of-life care and contribute to social change on the long run.

Interestingly, 30.9% of the Last Aid course participants had a medical background (physicians, nurses, or midwifes), although the curriculum is aimed at laypeople [12], and the courses were announced for non-medical staff on the hospital's intranet platform. This shows the importance and public interests in the subject of death, dying, and end-of-life care. Additionally, we speculate that the interest of medical staff in Last Aid courses could indicate deficiencies in the teaching of these subjects in the training of medical professionals.

Medical (in contrast to non-medical) staff were less satisfied with the course content. When asked if "they had learned something new", they answered with significantly lower ratings. As the Last Aid course curriculum was not designed for healthcare professionals, this finding is not surprising, but warrants an extended curriculum to meet their specific informational needs. Such a curriculum, comprising one full day with eight teaching units (each 45 min), was developed by Last Aid Germany, and is currently in the pilot-testing phase.

Furthermore, the amount of patient contact correlated with burden by death and dying. Current research gives special interest to frontline healthcare workers engaged in treating patients with COVID-19 who were at great risk of burdening symptoms of depression, anxiety, insomnia, and distress [13]; to our knowledge non-medical staff was not investigated. It is conceivable that also non-medical staff in hospitals feels burdened by death and dying especially during the COVID-19 pandemic. For medical staff, basic knowledge on palliative and hospice care is, nowadays, part of the curriculum (nurses, physicians, etc.), and advanced courses in specialized palliative care are offered in education programs. In contrast, there are no such offers for non-medical professions, even though many of them are confronted with seriously ill and dying patients (e.g., medical technologist, cleaning staff, and administration) [14]. Our results suggest that Last Aid courses are feasible to meet the informational needs in these professions. The Last Aid course curriculum addresses the core competencies recommended by the European Association for Palliative Care [15]. A recent study on online Last Aid courses for the public showed that it was feasible to hold the courses online. The results suggested that the online format enabled more people in a caregiver situation, as well as younger people, to attend [16].

Utilizing open questions, we identified and ranked reasons for participants to sign up for Last Aid courses. The three most important reasons were "preparation for emotional aspects in care of dying", "preparation for medical/care aspects in care of dying", and "knowledge of supportive services and facilities". All three aspects are covered by the Last Aid course curriculum, possibly explaining why the vast majority of participants would recommend the course to others. Future studies should investigate if meeting the informational needs could contribute toward reduce the burden of death and dying in non-medical staff with patient contact. Additionally, more research on the effects of Last Aid courses on a caregiver's willingness and capability to provide end-of-life care at home is needed.

In conclusion, Last-Aid Courses were feasible to meet the informational needs of non-medical hospital staff with high approval ratings while medical staff called for an extended curriculum.

Author Contributions: Conceptualization, E.M. and C.B.; methodology, E.M. and C.B.; formal analysis, E.M., G.B. (Georg Bollig), G.B. (Gerhild Becker), C.B.; writing—original draft preparation, C.B.; writing—review and editing, E.M., G.B. (Georg Bollig), G.B. (Gerhild Becker). All authors have read and agreed to the published version of the manuscript.

Funding: This research received no external funding.

Institutional Review Board Statement: The survey was anonymous; participation was voluntary. Data are anonymous, no personal data were collected, and the data are not considered to be of sensitive or confidential nature. No vulnerable or dependent groups were included. Therefore, ethical approval was waived.

Informed Consent Statement: Informed consent was obtained from all participants involved in the evaluation survey. Participation was voluntary. By completing the survey, the participants consented to participate.

Data Availability Statement: The data presented in this study are available on request from the corresponding author. The data are not publicly available due to privacy restrictions.

Acknowledgments: We thank Bettina Couné for critical appraisal of the manuscript. We thank Michael Mueller, Brigitte Froeschen-Ludwig, Reiner Fritzsche and Ursula Rohrer for conducting the courses.

Conflicts of Interest: GBo receives financial compensation for Last Aid instructor courses.

Appendix A

Table A1. Pre-Survey examples of answers to the question: "What were your goals and concerns before joining the course?" These can be professional or private concerns.

Preparation for emotional aspects in care of dying

- What do the dying want/need? What is positive for them, what is negative?
- Assistance in dealing with the dying.
- I was hoping for a few practical tips and "encouragement" in dealing with the dying.

Preparation for medical/care aspects in care of dying

- Understand the dying process, the possibility of active accompaniment.
- Better handling of the dying (especially patients), respectful handling of the wishes and how can I draw attention to [the needs] of them [the dying].
- Suggestions, ideas for dealing with dying people.

Reduction of own anxiety and insecurity when dealing with the subject of death

- During the previous dying processes, I noticed a helplessness on my part.
- To get rid of the fear of the unexpected. Not to be quite so helpless when loved ones/parents die.
- Reduce shyness from the subject of dying—also with regard to one's own dying.
- Only the private desire to be better prepared for the situation, fear of "dying" and helplessness.

Knowledge of supportive services/facilities

- My goal above all was, how to deal with relatives who are dying and what options one can get for support in care (e.g., palliative care).

Appendix B

Table A2. Questionnaire "Last Aid" Courses 3–5 (translated from German).

1.	**Profession**		2. **Work assignment at the university hospital**		
3.	**Do you have direct contact with patients in your work?**				
	never O	rarely O	sometimes O	often O	always O
4.	**In what way do you come into contact with the topic of death and dying in your professional work?**				
	How much does the topic of death and dying burden you in your professional work?				
	no burden O	low burden O	medium burden O	high burden O	very high burden O
5.	**Are you currently dealing with seriously ill or dying people in your private environment?**				
	O no	O yes			
	How much of a burden is the topic of death and dying in your private life at the moment?				
	no burden O	low burden O	medium burden O	high burden O	very high burden O

Table A2. *Cont.*

6. **Are you directly and regularly involved in the care and/or support of a seriously ill or dying person in your private environment?** O yes O no → if no, continue with question 7 ↓ **If yes, what is your relationship to the person?**				
If yes, do you live in a flat with the person you care for and/or look after?	O no	O yes		
If yes, does the care and support affect your occupation?	O no	O yes		
If yes, in what way does the care/support affect your occupation?				
7. Whether you are currently caring for someone or not: **What support would you like to see from the University Hospital for employees caring for seriously ill relatives at home? How important are the following support options to you?**				
Adaptation of working conditions	**very important**	**rather important**	**rather unimportant**	**unimportant**
Flexible working hours	O	O	O	O
Short-term and flexible time off for end-of-life care	O	O	O	O
More generous time off work in case of death	O	O	O	O
Possibility of home office	O	O	O	O
Support				
Palliative medicine competent contact persons here at the clinic (e.g., hotline)	O	O	O	O
	very important	**rather important**	**rather unimportant**	**unimportant**
Courses on the topic	O	O	O	O
Possibility to exchange experiences (e.g., group meetings for exchange)	O	O	O	O
Possibility of psycho-social support and relief	O	O	O	O
What other suggestions do you have?				
8. **How important were the following goals and issues to you before you came to the course?** These can be professional or private concerns.				
	very important	**rather important**	**rather unimportant**	**unimportant**
Preparation for medical and nursing aspects of end-of-life care	O	O	O	O
Preparation for emotional aspects of end-of-life care	O	O	O	O
Reduce (my) fear and insecurity in dealing with the topic of death.	O	O	O	O
Contributing to the social discussion on the topic of dying	O	O	O	O
Knowledge about possibilities of support through special services and facilities	O	O	O	O
Other				
9. **Evaluation of the course content:** Please rate how you found the teaching of the different course topics. Tick one box for each topic.				
Topic	**very good**	**good**	**not so good**	**unsatisfactory**
1. Dying as normal part of life	O	O	O	O
2. Planning ahead and decision making	O	O	O	O
3. Relieve suffering	O	O	O	O
4. Final goodbyes	O	O	O	O
Assessment of the whole course	O	O	O	O
10. **Please indicate to what extent you agree with the statements.**				
	strongly agree	**agree**	**disagree**	**strongly disagree**
I have learned new things.	O	O	O	O
The topics were taught in a comprehensible way.	O	O	O	O
I will recommend the course to others.	O	O	O	O
11. **Age:**	12. **Gender**	O male	O female	
13. **Comments**				

Not all results of this survey are reported in the publication.

References

1. Scholten, N.; Günther, A.L.; Pfaff, H.; Karbach, U. The size of the population potentially in need of palliative care in Germany-an estimation based on death registration data. *BMC Palliat. Care* **2016**, *15*, 29. [CrossRef] [PubMed]
2. Murtagh, F.E.; Bausewein, C.; Verne, J.; Groeneveld, E.I.; Kaloki, Y.E.; Higginson, I.J. How many people need palliative care? A study developing and comparing methods for population-based estimates. *Palliat. Med.* **2014**, *28*, 49–58. [CrossRef] [PubMed]
3. Etkind, S.N.; Bone, A.E.; Gomes, B.; Lovell, N.; Evans, C.J.; Higginson, I.J.; Murtagh, F.E.M. How many people will need palliative care in 2040? Past trends, future projections and implications for services. *BMC Med.* **2017**, *15*, 102. [CrossRef] [PubMed]
4. Kellehear, A. Compassionate communities: End-of-life care as everyone's responsibility. *Qjm Int. J. Med.* **2013**, *106*, 1071–1075. [CrossRef]
5. Patel, P.; Lyons, L. Examining the Knowledge, Awareness, and Perceptions of Palliative Care in the General Public Over Time: A Scoping Literature Review. *Am. J. Hosp. Palliat. Med.* **2019**, *37*, 481–487. [CrossRef] [PubMed]

6. Bollig, G.; Kuklau, N. Der Letzte Hilfe-Kurs–ein Angebot zur Verbesserung der allgemeinen ambulanten Palliativversorgung durch Information und Befähigung von Bürgerinnen und Bürgern. *Palliativmedizin* **2015**, *16*, 210–216. [CrossRef]
7. Bollig, G.; Brandt, F.; Ciurlionis, M.; Knopf, B. Last Aid Course. An Education for All Citizens and an Ingredient of Compassionate Communities. *Healthcare* **2019**, *7*, 19. [CrossRef] [PubMed]
8. Mills, J.; Rosenberg, J.P.; Bollig, G.; Haberecht, J. Last Aid and Public Health Palliative Care: Towards the development of personal skills and strengthened community action. *Prog. Palliat. Care* **2020**, *28*, 343–345. [CrossRef]
9. Bollig, G.; Pothmann, R.; Mainzer, K.; Fiedler, H. Kinder und Jugendliche möchten über Tod und Sterben reden–Erfahrungen aus Pilotkursen Letzte Hilfe Kids/Teens für 8- bis 16-Jährige. *Palliativmedizin* **2020**, *21*, 253–259. [CrossRef]
10. Washington, K.T.; Pike, K.C.; Demiris, G.; Oliver, D.P.; Albright, D.L.; Lewis, A.M. Gender Differences in Caregiving at End of Life: Implications for Hospice Teams. *J. Palliat. Med.* **2015**, *18*, 1048–1053. [CrossRef] [PubMed]
11. Xiong, C.; Biscardi, M.; Astell, A.; Nalder, E.; Cameron, J.I.; Mihailidis, A.; Colantonio, A. Sex and gender differences in caregiving burden experienced by family caregivers of persons with dementia: A systematic review. *PLoS ONE* **2020**, *15*, e0231848. [CrossRef] [PubMed]
12. Bollig, G.; Kristensen, F.B.; Wolff, D.L. Citizens appreciate talking about death and learning end-of-life care–a mixed-methods study on views and experiences of 5469 Last Aid Course participants. *Prog. Palliat. Care* **2021**, *29*, 140–148. [CrossRef]
13. Lai, J.; Ma, S.; Wang, Y.; Cai, Z.; Hu, J.; Wei, N.; Wu, J.; Du, H.; Chen, T.; Li, R.; et al. Factors Associated With Mental Health Outcomes Among Health Care Workers Exposed to Coronavirus Disease 2019. *JAMA Netw. Open* **2020**, *3*, e203976. [CrossRef]
14. Jors, K.; Tietgen, S.; Xander, C.; Momm, F.; Becker, G. Tidying rooms and tending hearts: An explorative, mixed-methods study of hospital cleaning staff's experiences with seriously ill and dying patients. *Palliat. Med.* **2016**, *31*, 63–71. [CrossRef]
15. Gamondi, C.; Larkin, P.; Payne, S. Core competencies in palliative care: An EAPC White Paper on palliative care education–part 1. *Eur. J. Palliat. Care* **2013**, *20*, 86–91.
16. Bollig, G.; Meyer, S.; Knopf, B.; Schmidt, M.; Bauer, E.H. First Experiences with *Online Last Aid Courses* for Public Palliative Care Education during the COVID-19 Pandemic. *Healthcare* **2021**, *9*, 172. [CrossRef] [PubMed]

healthcare

MDPI

Article

Last Aid Course—The Slovenian Experience

Erika Zelko [1,2,*], Larisa Vrbek [3] and Melita Koletnik [4]

1 Institute for General practice, Johannes Keppler University, 4020 Linz, Austria
2 Department for Family Medicine, Faculty of Medicine University Maribor, Taborska cesta 8, 2000 Maribor, Slovenia
3 Cerebral Paralysis Association of Slovenia, Rožanska ulica 2, 1000 Ljubljana, Slovenia; vrbek.larisa@gmail.com
4 Faculty of Arts, University of Maribor, 2000 Maribor, Slovenia; melitakk@gmail.com
* Correspondence: erikazelko@gmail.com

Abstract: Educating and raising awareness among lay members of the public about palliative care can significantly improve the care for terminally ill patients and their quality of life. This paper reports on the survey aimed at assessing the experience and expectations of participants in the Last Aid course launched in Slovenia in 2019 to train hospice volunteers and promote dialogue on death and dying. The course implementation was supported by materials prepared, translated, and/or adapted from German under the PO-LAST project, which linked Slovenian medical and healthcare professionals, hospice representatives, and university students. The Last Aid course follows an international four-module curriculum that has been successfully applied in 18 countries so far. In Slovenia, the course was delivered 30 times with 21 in-person deliveries and 9 online events attended by 450 participants of different sexes, ages, and professions. The surveyed population included 250 people who returned the evaluation questionnaires by October 2020. The aim of the analysis was to gain insight that can be applied broadly in future work and research on adult education on palliative care and the erasure of death-related taboos.

Keywords: palliative care; education; lay public; Last Aid course

check for updates

Citation: Zelko, E.; Vrbek, L.; Koletnik, M. Last Aid Course—The Slovenian Experience. *Healthcare* **2022**, *10*, 1154. https://doi.org/10.3390/healthcare10071154

Academic Editors: Paolo Cotogni and Ingalill Rahm Hallberg

Received: 4 May 2022
Accepted: 16 June 2022
Published: 21 June 2022

1. Introduction

Globally, life expectancy has been steadily increasing over the past two centuries. Based on the latest United Nations Population Division Estimates [1] the average life expectancy at birth in 2022 amounted to 73.2 for both sexes and was the highest in developed eastern and western countries, e.g., Hong Kong with 85.3 or Switzerland with 84.7 years. Driven by increases in life expectancy and by falling fertility rates, the world population is aging at an accelerated pace. If, a few decades ago, the most common cause of death in the developed world was infectious disease, today, it is noncommunicable illnesses, such as heart disease, stroke, cancer, and diabetes, which according to the WHO data [2], collectively accounted for more than 70% of all deaths worldwide—even during the recent COVID-19 pandemic.

In modern society, death is an important process. However, talking about death is still painful and agonizing for most people [3] and commonly referred to by negative metaphors, e.g., "a foe to be conquered" or the "loss of the battle", frequently resulting from the long "war against disease" [4]. Moreover, in our consumer society, death is often marginalized [5] and placed outside the confines of our everyday existence.

A similar, uneasy status is attributed to palliative care, which is regularly conceptualized as specialized (medical) care that supports the patients diagnosed with life-threatening and terminal illnesses, provides relief from pain and other symptoms, and aims to improve the quality of life for both patients and their families "by means of early identification and impeccable assessment and treatment of pain and other problems" [6]. Palliative care is a holistic approach that actively addresses an individual's total needs—physical, psychological, social, and spiritual suffering of patients and psychological, social, and spiritual suffering of family members—and should be based on good teamwork and collaboration between its providers [7]. Among the general public, there is substantial misunderstanding of and lack of awareness about palliative care [8], and lay people are frequently unaware of its fundamental principles. Consequently, palliative care is underused [9,10]. A terminal or life-threatening illness is an illness or condition which cannot be cured and is likely to lead to someone's death [9]. End-of-life care is defined as support for people who are in the last months or years of their life [11,12]. Last Aid comprises both palliative and end-of-life care, and offers support to patients who need long-term care or palliation to the very end of their lives, in life situations where death is known to be close, and in the dying process.

Greater public awareness, education, and training, on the other hand, support the implementation of palliative care. These elements positively affect people's quality of life and contribute to wider acceptance of death as a natural part of life [13].

The idea of a Last Aid course and a public knowledge approach to palliative care were first described by the future emergency care physician and consultant Georg Bollig in the late 2000s. The original aim was to discontinue the discourse on death and dying as a taboo within many communities and to teach the public about palliative care. Consequently, the course educates participants about palliative and end-of-life care, while at the same time, it provides information on how and where to obtain help from professionals and the local community. The Last Aid course is modelled on the First Aid course because Last Aid should be considered as important as first aid, with which we all have been acquainted at some point in our personal or working lives [14].

On the other hand, we know little about dying and death, although at some time, we all will be faced with the process and the transience of our loved ones or ourselves. End-of-life care, when partnered with community efforts to provide support and care for death, dying, and loss, leads to the establishment of compassionate communities, as described by Kellehear [15], whose members can participate in the provision of palliative care within the limits of their skills and abilities [16].

The recent COVID-19 pandemic exposed the vulnerability of the individual, e.g., to mental health problems [17,18], and of the society, e.g., to highly disrupted rehabilitation services, including the delivery of specialist palliative care [19]. Developing truly compassionate communities which can face illness, death, and bereavement as part of the life cycle and preserve human dignity to the very end helps build resilience on the personal and the societal level, with all members contributing to the best of their ability to the good of all.

2. Barriers to Palliative Care, Compassionate Communities, and the Last Aid Course

The barriers to accessing palliative care are very well-known, and the policy reports describing them keep emerging. Very often, relatives who need to care for a loved one diagnosed with a life-threatening and/or terminal illness face a crisis. Dionne-Odom et al. [10], e.g., reported that more than one-half of unpaid family caregivers in the US caring for relative with a medical, behavioral, disability, or other condition had never heard of palliative care. Even among those who had, most had not distinguished it from hospice care and death. Based on their findings, authors appealed for more awareness of palliative care among the lay public, focusing on the needs of the patient and their family. Further to this, Bollig [16], acknowledged an urgent need to educate nonprofessionals in palliative care and end-of-life care. The involvement of lay people in palliative care is necessary and important for several reasons, which range from demographic changes, increasing numbers of elderly suffering from chronic diseases, and a shortage of care professionals, to changes in family structure and the preservation of human dignity of the dying.

Nevertheless, raising public awareness on such a difficult subject requires a subtle approach. Compassionate communities, pioneered by A. Kellehear in the mid-2000s, are perfectly positioned to achieve this by placing palliative care within everyone's responsibility [15]. Compassionate communities are defined as naturally occurring networks of support in neighborhoods and communities, surrounding those experiencing death, dying, caregiving, loss, and bereavement [20]. They are formed around a group of people who are concerned about the quality of life of the community's members and play a much stronger role in the care of both people at end-of-life and their families. However, compassionate communities represent only one of the four pillars that comprise palliative and end-of-life care. The others are specialist palliative care, i.e., a medical specialty within medical and nursing training programs; generalist palliative care, i.e., care at the end-of-life that is not provided by specialist palliative care teams; and civic end-of-life care offered or rather supported by, e.g., schools, workplaces, or churches. Their effective coordination contributes significantly to access to palliative care and the wellbeing of the terminally ill [20].

In their recent article, reimagining access to palliative care, Abel, Kelleher, Mills, and Patel added that "the community itself must become part of the palliative care offer/provision to help regulate and mediate its own internal differences and services". This should go beyond merely volunteering toward recognizing that every citizen has a role to play in palliative care, thus allowing that community engagement evolves into "community development and self-provision (changing the power dynamics)" of end-of-life care [21].

An important achievement supporting the objective that palliative care become everyone's responsibility is the Last Aid course, a recent course concept for educating the public about palliative care. It is based on the premise that knowledge about palliative care should become part of public education, which is frequently very limited or totally absent in most communities [16], and relies almost exclusively on personal experience as the main source of information [22]. Stemming from the idea presented by Bollig, the course encourages public discourse on taboo topics of death and dying and educates the lay public about them [13,16,23].

The method pursued by the Last Aid courses is a combination of situated learning, which is conditioned by interaction between participants and builds on prior knowledge and experience [24], and of community of practice, where participants with similar interests are brought together to improve their knowledge for practice and future action [25].

The course follows a public knowledge approach and consists of four modules: Care at the End of Life, Advance Care Planning and Decision Making, Symptom Management, and Cultural Aspects of Death and Bereavement. Comparable to the Chain of Survival in emergency medicine, the Chain of Palliative Care is used to visualize the networks of palliative care in a community. The Chain, presenting the cooperation between nonprofessionals and healthcare professionals in palliative care, establishes a link to Kellehear's pillars that make up palliative care, and the public knowledge approach centered on widespread education of the lay public aims to change attitudes and behaviors in the community in the direction of a more positive attitude toward participating in palliative care.

It is important that the course be adapted to the cultural diversity and constraints of the environment. Thus far, localized versions of Last Aid courses have been implemented and well-received in several countries including, e.g., Australia, Ireland, Brazil, Switzerland, Scotland, Germany, and Denmark. Furthermore, 99% of Last Aid course participants say they would recommend them to others [26].According to them, the course contributes to improving the discussion about death and dying in families, at the workplace and elsewhere. The participants' overall response has been thus very positive [27]. A special edition of the Last Aid course was recently developed to address bereaved children and teenagers. A pilot study showed it was met with a positive response and proved that most children and teenagers want to talk about death and dying [28].In total thus far, Last Aid courses have been attended by over 26,000 people, and more than 2000 Last Aid trainers have been educated to implement Last Aid activities in their local communities [16].

3. Organization of Palliative Care in Slovenia, Last Aid Slovenia, and the PO-LAST Project

In Slovenia, the strategy for palliative care is set out in the National Program for Palliative Care [12].The plan requires all hospitals to provide from 10 to 15 beds for palliative patients, depending on the demographic and socio-economic profile of the region where the hospital is located. Consequently, the two main medical centers in Ljubljana and

Maribor have two separate palliative care wards, while smaller hospitals provide individual palliative care beds. Additionally, the hospice house *Hiša Ljubhospica* was built in 2010 in Ljubljana, and six mobile palliative care teams attend to palliative care cases throughout the country. Nevertheless, most patients in need of palliative care are cared for by palliative care nurses and family doctors. Some are placed in nursing homes or have home caregivers. No official data on how many patients receive palliative care in Slovenia are available, but it is estimated that some 20% of those in need of palliative care also receive it [29].

The first edition of the Last Aid course was organized in 2019 by the Institute for Palliative Medicine and Hospice Care at the University of Maribor's Faculty of Medicine Maribor. Since then, it has been delivered, in cooperation with the Slovenian Lions clubs and the Slovenian Hospice Association, twenty-five times over a period of two years, with five deliveries taking place online during the COVID-19 pandemic. A special online course (webinar) was developed for the deaf and hard of hearing using sign language so that an even more diverse population could be reached. To allow for unimpeded interaction and active participation, the number of participants did not exceed 15 per delivery. The professional profiles of the participants included, e.g., medical and healthcare students and practitioners (nurses and physicians), teachers, social workers, business professionals, lawyers, engineers, priests and nuns, homemakers, and people without current employment.

The course implementation was supported by materials prepared, translated, and/or adapted from German under the Slovenian government-financed Assistance for a Better Quality of Life in the Last Phase of Life (PO-LAST) project, which connected Slovenian medical and healthcare professionals, hospice representatives, and university teachers and students. The Slovenian Hospice Association and University of Maribor's Medical Faculty and the Faculty of Arts cooperated with the project, as well as Alma Mater Europaea, an independent higher learning institution.

The main objective of the project was to provide information and/or access to information for people with life-threatening illness and their caregivers, which would also be of use for the implementation of the Last Aid course. The thirteen project members (1) prepared the Slovenian Atlas of Palliative Care [30], dealing with support options and information sources for the terminally ill and their caregivers; (2) translated the manual for Last Aid instructors from German into Slovene and adapted the content for the Slovenian context; (3) prepared a brochure with essential information on palliative care in Slovenia; and (4) organized and implemented dissemination workshops. The four-month project was successfully concluded in June 2020. All materials that were produced during the project support the implementation of Last Aid courses in Slovenia, which have been, thus far, received extremely well by the participants, as is detailed below.

4. Methods

To gain a more in-depth insight into the implementation of the Last Aid course in Slovenia, we decided to analyze the participants' responses in 2021. Our overarching research question was to investigate their experience and to identify suggestions for improvement of the course. For this purpose, we used the pre-prepared international Last Aid questionnaire with open-ended and closed-ended questions. The used tool was a validated questionnaire including both quantitative and qualitative data, which has been previously used in Germany, Switzerland, and Austria [27]. The questionnaire was administered to our participants immediately after the course, irrespective of whether it had been held online or in-person, and it was sent or given to them with documents confirming their participation on the course. In total, 386 questionnaires were distributed personally or sent out by e-mail, of which 250 were returned. The response rate was thus 64.7%. The non-respondents were not analyzed, and we cannot speculate or draw any conclusions about the reasons why the questionnaires were not returned. All participants were informed that participation in this evaluation was voluntary and that they could choose not to complete the questionnaire if they did not want to. Data were collected from June 2019 to December

2021.The questionnaire was divided into three sections. The first section included four closed-ended questions evaluating the total course as well as individual modules on a 5-point rating scale. The second section summarized personal reflections of the participants and consisted of two open-ended questions and four yes or no questions exploring the participants' understanding of the specific topics covered in the course, while an additional open-ended question elicited the "highlights" of the course and suggestions for future work. The third section collected the participants' demographic data. Our sample was limited with the available resources. Thus, we are aware that the participants of the course and of our study do not constitute a representative sample of the entire Slovenian population and cannot be immediately generalizable to the entire population. However, we believe the number of respondents to be large enough to give the data validity and attention. The advertising for the course was interest-based (e.g., to hospice volunteers and healthcare providers), and we used chain referral. Registration and attendance were voluntary, and the size of individual course groups was limited to 15 participants as recommended by Last Aid International.

We used descriptive statistics combined with qualitative analysis of the open-ended questions to investigate the data obtained. Included in the analysis were 250 questionnaires: 243 were fully answered and 7 were missing one answer, but we nevertheless considered these relevant and included the answers in the analysis of the relevant sections. The coding of qualitative answers was carried out by three independent researchers. For quantitative answers, statistical significance was assumed at the $p < 0.05$ level. Descriptive answers to open-ended questions were qualitatively thematically analyzed to identify, analyze, and report themes, i.e., patterns, within the data. A cumulative understanding of the results was created by identifying themes and patterns and organizing them into categories. We believe that the methodological conditions (qualitative and quantitative) guarantee the overall quality of the study in terms of internal validity (risk of bias), external validity (generalizability), and reporting quality. The quantitative and qualitative results are mutually supportive, and it is our belief that they will contribute to the further improvement of the Last Aid course and deliver suggestions for advancement to the Last Aid International group, which is responsible for the international course development and quality.

5. Results

Table 1 below shows basic course participants statistics.

Table 1. Last Aid participants—sociodemographic data.

		Number	Share (%)
Sex	Men	37	15.2
	Women	206	84.8
Average age (standard deviation) (in years)		50.44 (16.122)	
Age bracket	Young (under 35)	48	19.9
	Middle-aged (35–64 years)	139	57.7
	Elderly (65 years and over)	54	22.4
Level of education	Primary	3	1.8
	Secondary	62	37.6
	Tertiary	100	60.6

Table 2 presents participant ratings for the entire course and for the individual modules. In relative terms, most participants rated both the entire course (87.7%) and individual modules (more than 75% for all modules) as "excellent" (5).

Table 2. Participant ratings for the course and individual modules.

Rating	The Entire Course (n = 243)	Module 1 (n = 250)	Module 2 (n = 249)	Module 3 (n = 248)	Module 4 (n = 248)
1 unsatisfactory	1 (0.4%)	1 (0.4%)	1 (0.4%)	1 (0.4%)	1 (0.4%)
2 satisfactory	0 (0.0%)	1 (0.4%)	0 (0.0%)	0 (0.0%)	0 (0.0%)
3 good	2 (0.8%)	4 (1.6%)	4 (1.6%)	5 (2.0%)	3 (1.2%)
4 very good	27 (11.1%)	38 (15.2%)	50 (20.1%)	33 (13.3%)	33 (13.3%)
5 excellent	213 (87.7%)	206 (82.4%)	194 (77.9%)	209 (84.3%)	211 (85.1%)
Average (SD)	4.86 (0.436)	4.79 (0.522)	4.75 (0.518)	4.81 (0.493)	4.83 (0.466)

SD—standard deviation

Based on the age of the participants, we defined three age brackets: young (under 35), middle-aged (35–64), and elderly (65+). We used these to compare the participants' evaluations of the overall course and the individual modules to establish any age-based differences. Table 3 presents the ratings by age bracket. The results showed that satisfaction both with the course as a whole and with individual modules was highest among middle-aged participants, who on average assessed the course better than the young or the elderly.

Table 3. Participant ratings by age bracket.

	Young	Middle-Aged	Elderly	Kruskal-Wallis H Test
	Average (SD)	Average (SD)	Average (SD)	
The entire course	4.78 (0.471)	4.93 (0.264)	4.76 (0.687)	H = 6.360; df = 2; p = 0.042 *
Module 1	4.65 (0.565)	4.87 (0.398)	4.70 (0.735)	H = 9.993; df = 2; p = 0.007 *
Module 2	4.58 (0.613)	4.85 (0.354)	4.66 (0.717)	H = 1.836; df = 2; p = 0.004 *
Module 3	4.79 (0.504)	4.86 (0.387)	4.67 (0.718)	H = 4.071; df = 2; p = 0.131
Module 4	4.73 (0.536)	4.89 (0.314)	4.76 (0.687)	H = 4.437; df = 2; p = 0.109

* Indicates statistically significant values at $p < 0.05$.

On average, female participants rated the entire course better than their male counterparts (4.89 vs. 4.69). The average grades for individual modules also differed by sex and its represented in Table 4.

Given the very limited number of participants with primary education (only three), we subsequently created only two categories to analyze education-based differences in satisfaction with the course: secondary or lower education, and higher education. The average scores showed that better educated participants rated the total course more favorably than those with less education (4.86 vs. 4.83). However, these differences were small and not statistically significant. The results were similar with regard to the individual modules. On average, the more educated participants rated the modules higher than the participants with a high school degree or lower. The most significant differences in participants' average scores by education category were found in relation to Module 2 (Advance Care Planning and Decision Making) (0.12), and the least significant in relation to Module 3 (Symptom Management) (0.03). The difference for Module 1 (Care at the End of Life) amounted to 0.06 and for Module 4 (Cultural Aspects of Death and Bereavement) to 0.07.

Table 4. Participant ratings (the entire course and individual modules) by sex (Mann–Whitney U test).

	Men	Women	Mann–Whitney U Test
	Average (SD)	Average (SD)	
The entire workshop	4.69 (0.796)	4.89 (0.332)	U = 3.093,5; $p = 0.102$
Module 1 Care at the End of Life	4.59 (0.798)	4.82 (0.456)	U = 3.176,0; $p = 0.033$ *
Module 2 Advance Care Planning and Decision-making	4.51(0.804)	4.80 (0.437)	U = 2.967,0; $p - 0.007$ *
Module 3 Symptom Management	4.69 (0.749)	4.82 (0.442)	U = 3.342,5; $p = 0.284$
Module 4 Cultural Aspects of Death and Bereavement	4.69 (0.749)	4.85 (0.398)	U = 3.283,0; $p = 0.173$

* Indicates statistically significant values at $p < 0.05$.

A total of 185 (72.5%) participants answered the open-ended question about which topic particularly spoke to them, what they missed from the course, and their opinion about it. The results are represented in Table 5.

Table 5. Thematic analysis of open-ended questions—results.

Theme	Categories	Code
Time	Period before death Period after death Perceived need Support for the bereaved	48
Suggestions	Ethical and cultural aspects Regular education Spirituality Children	35

After conducting a detailed thematic analysis, the following two themes were identified: time, with participants' comments related to different periods of taking care of patients diagnosed with a life-threatening and/or terminal illness, and suggestions for improvement of the course in Slovenia. The responses were grouped into the following categories: (1) period before death; (2) period after death; and (3) support for the bereaved and perceived needs as the disease progresses. The second theme, suggestions, included the following categories: ethical and cultural aspects, regular education, spirituality, and children. Almost a quarter of participants (23.1%) suggested that such courses should be held more frequently or on a regular basis to raise awareness and educate people. The following two salient statements testify to this: "...the topic should be taught in secondary schools, e.g., in the school of nursing ... " (No. 135) and "A lecture that makes you realize there are more important things in life because too often we don't realize that death is part of life, and we don't learn enough about it at the faculty" (No. 101). Additionally, the participants recognized the benefits, quality, and usefulness of the course, with over 99% of them writing that they would recommend it to their friends. Other interesting ideas and suggestions were advanced by the participants in regard to the future implementation of the course. "There is too little talk about the subject; when my relative was dying in hospital, I didn't know where to turn for information, all [I got] referred to his medical condition. To spread the news about the course in the community" (No. 123). Other participants suggested an "upgrade and expansion of the module" (No. 10) on how to "communicate with aggressive relatives, and more [information] on spiritual care" (No. 54). Finally, combined quantitative and qualitative results showed that the Last Aid course was useful for the participants, with almost 95% of them confirming that they had heard and acquired new information and knowledge.

6. Discussion

Palliative and hospice care education initiatives, such as the Last Aid course, are needed to increase awareness of and reduce misperceptions about palliative and end-of-life care conceptions and services reported by more researcher [8,31–33]. The introduction of the Last Aid course in Slovenia, supported by materials prepared by the PO-LAST project, has aimed to achieve just this.

In terms of general population statistics, statistically significantly more women attended the course (Table 1), which was expected. In Slovenia, women are more likely to be employed as health and midwifery care professionals and health and midwifery care assistants. According to the data of the Statistical Office of the Republic of Slovenia, at the end of 2019, "87.5% of nursing and midwifery professionals were women and only 12.5% were men, while 82.5% of associate professionals were women and 17.5% were men" [34]. In average all participants rated the course and the modules very positive (Table 2). Statistically significantly more higher-educated participants and those aged between 35 and 64 were more satisfied with the course (Tables 3 and 4). According to Slovenian statistic agency, 24.5% of Slovenians are higher educated. Adapting the course in an easy language may help to reach less educated people. In particular, the modules Care at the End of Life and Advance Care Planning and Decision-making showed a slight positive deviation from satisfaction with other course modules as reported by participants. Further research is needed to account for this difference. The structure of the participants and their responses are not surprising in relation to international research, which shows that also informal caregivers are most often middle-aged women [35–37].

As presented above, the evaluation of the course by the participants showed a high level of satisfaction with both the content and the delivery of the course. The average rating of the total course was "excellent" (5) as evidenced by 87.7% of the returned questionnaires. Moreover, 75% of the questionnaires also rated individual modules as "excellent" (Table 2). Socializing and sharing of personal experience on the course were seen as a major benefit of the course by our participants. They also gave interesting suggestions and orientations for future work. Similar results have been reported by researchers in other countries, e.g., Germany, Denmark, and Switzerland, as described by [26]. Furthermore, in line with results from other countries, the Slovenian participants advised expanding some of the currently addressed topics and organizing courses in schools [28]. Based on this, we can assume that in Slovenia, there is growing recognition of the need to "normalize" death and to provide opportunities for individuals and communities to recognize death and dying as a social process, in line with observations made by Abel and Kellehear [38]. The need to educate the public about palliative and hospice care and to increase public awareness of and reduce misconceptions about the topic were also reflected in our participants' qualitative answers, which included, e.g., the appeal to "spread the news about the course in the community". Their opinion corresponds to the recent findings by Zelko and her colleagues in the Slovenian context that, in order to widely implement palliative care in Slovenia, the awareness of and education about palliative care need to be improved [39]. Consequently, if we want to successfully raise awareness of this topic, which is still too frequently taboo, we need to find ways to reach out to the lay public and involve them in the process of exchanging views and information. "Cultural interventions" such as Death Cafés [40], and intensified promotion of palliative care by healthcare providers and education about death and dying, as well as the creation of truly compassionate communities [41], are all examples of strategies that aim to jointly encourage individuals and communities to reflect on death and respond to end-of-life issues. Another promising example of good practice is the Japanese educational program using stories as a primary learning tool, which showed that it is possible to deepen understanding among the lay public of the concept of end-of-life care through a narrative [9]. It is important that palliative care education initiatives be adapted to the cultural context of the environment where they are delivered, as highlighted by, e.g., Shen et al. [42], Isaacson [43], Hayes et al. [11], or in the Australian context by McGrath and Holewa [44]. The particulars for such adaptation, also in the Slovenian context, include the institutional and legal framework(s), organization of palliative care, and the level of public awareness of palliative care, as discussed above. In terms of palliative care organization, McGrath and Holewa [44], highlight the following important factors: equity (equal access); autonomy and empowerment (respect for the patient's choice); trust (recognition of and respect for the historical context, and empathy during the provision of care); humane approach (non-judgmental care with an emphasis on quality of life and choice for patients and their families); high quality of care (involvement of a multidisciplinary team of healthcare professionals and community-based organizations working together throughout the care pathway); emphasis on living (rather than dying); and honoring of cultural identity (respect for cultural practices, beliefs, and lifestyle). Thus, even though some steps have been undertaken in this direction, including through the Last Aid course and the PO-LAST project, much still needs to be done in Slovenia. Therefore, a key future challenge for the implementation of the Last Aid course in Slovenia is to take greater account of the country's socio-cultural diversity, which stems from the fact that the course has been developed in an international environment. Consequently, an important objective is to pay more attention to the needs of individual local communities. In the past, the importance of responding to local needs was highlighted by both international [43,43]. and Slovenian researchers [45]. The need for greater socio-cultural diversity in the delivery of the Last Aid course in Slovenia is also reflected in the fact that we were unsuccessful in attracting course participants with lower levels of education and representatives of minority ethnic groups (e.g., the Roma ethnic community).

Limitations of the Study

Selection bias could be one limitation of the study since all informants chose to participate in our course voluntarily. The fact that informants were asked about their opinion directly after the course limits the recall bias, but it does not provide any information about the impact of the course on the provision of palliative care. We also did not reach people with lower education, possibly partly due to the pandemic, which led to altered formats and delivery modes of the course, and partly due to rather limited advertising opportunities in local communities. However, the data we were able to analyze are interesting not only because of the extremely positive evaluations of the course but also because of the suggestions for organizing future discussions and training on this topic.

7. Conclusions

The Slovenian Last Aid experience is comparable to that reported by countries where the course had been previously organized. In all those countries, the course has raised awareness among the lay public about death, dying, and palliative and end-of-life care. In Slovenia, the courses were extremely well-received and favorably rated, with participants lauding both content and delivery. However, the pandemic has impacted the in-person experience and encouraged new, web-based formats. We are aware that, in the future, it may be necessary to develop standards for online delivery of the course and to ensure that this is promoted in different communities and considers the socio-cultural diversity of the local environment. Socio-cultural diversity is a part of the Slovenian reality, and this has to be taken into account when preparing community education programs [46].

Nevertheless, the adaptation to Slovenian cultural requirements with information from the local communities was supported by materials prepared by the PO-LAST project, which entailed cooperation among Slovenian medical and healthcare professional, hospice volunteers, and university students. We are convinced that this work has also contributed to the excellent acceptance of the Last Aid course by the Slovenian community, but we are aware there is still a substantial amount of work to be done.

Author Contributions: Conception and design: E.Z. and M.K.; collection and assembly of data: L.V. and E.Z.; data analysis and interpretation: E.Z., M.K. and L.V.; manuscript writing: E.Z., L.V. and M.K. All authors have read and agreed to the published version of the manuscript.

Funding: PO-LAST Project (part of the study), was founded and supported with EU Grands and Ministry for Education, Research and Sport Republic Slovenia.

Institutional Review Board Statement: For this study we did not need the approval of Institutional Ethic board. On 2 September 2021 we receive that written statement.

Informed Consent Statement: Informed consent was obtained from all subjects involved in the study.

Data Availability Statement: The data presented in this study are available on request from the corresponding author. The data are not publicly available due to (language of it).

Conflicts of Interest: The authors declare no conflict of interest.

References

1. Life Expectancy of the World Population. Available online: https://www.worldometers.info/demographics/life-expectancy (accessed on 20 March 2022).
2. Noncommunicable Diseases. Available online: https://www.who.int/health-topics/noncommunicable-diseases#tab=tab_1 (accessed on 12 April 2022).
3. Payne, S.; Seymour, J.; Ingleton, C. Palliative care nursing: Principles and evidence for practice: Principles and evidence for practice. *Nurs. Stand. Off. Newsp. R. Coll. Nurs.* **2009**, *23*, 30.
4. Gellie, A.; Amber, M.; Michele, L.; Gemma Steephensonand, E.F. Death: A foe to be conquered? Questioning the paradigm. *Age Ageing* **2015**, *44*, 7–10. [CrossRef] [PubMed]
5. Kang, J. Striving for a Good Death: End-of-Life Care in a South Korean Tertiary Hospital System. Unpublished. Ph.D. Thesis, University of Virginia, Charlottesville, VA, USA, 2020. Available online: https://libraetd.lib.virginia.edu/public_view/47429966t (accessed on 10 March 2022).
6. Palliative care—WHO. Available online: https://www.who.int/news-room/fact-sheets/detail/palliative-care (accessed on 15 March 2022).
7. World Health Organization. Palliative Care—1990 and 2002 WHO Definitions. IAHPC Pallipedia. Available online: https://pallipedia.org/palliative-care-1990-and-2002-who-definitions/ (accessed on 1 June 2022).
8. Lane, T.; Ramadurai, D.; Simonetti, J. Public awareness and perceptions of palliative and comfort care. *Am. J. Med.* **2019**, *132*, 129–131. [CrossRef] [PubMed]
9. Haruta, J.; Oishi, A.; Den, N. How and what do laypeople learn about end-of-life care using narrative? A case study in educational research. *TAPS 2020* **2021**, *5*, 16–24. [CrossRef]
10. Dionne-Odom, N.; Ornstein, K.; Kent, E. What do family caregivers know about palliative care? Results from a national survey. *Palliat. Support Care* **2019**, *17*, 1–7. [CrossRef]
11. Hayes, B.; Fabri, A.M.; Coperchini, M.; Parkar, R.; Austin-Crowe, Z. Health and death literacy and cultural diversity: Insights from hospital-employed interpreters. *BMJ Support Palliat. Care* **2020**, *10*, 8. [CrossRef]
12. Državni Načrt Paliativne Oskrbe. [National Plan for Palliative Care]. Ministrstvo za Zdravje, Ljubljana. 2010. Available online: https://www.gov.si/assets/Ministrstva/MZ/DOKUMENTI/pomembni-dokumenti/47cbef2cb3/Drzavni-program-paliativne-oskrbe.pdf (accessed on 1 June 2022).
13. Bollig, G. The last aid course—A simple and effective concept to teach the public about palliative care and enhance the public discussion about death and dying. *Austin Palliat. Care* **2016**, *2*, 1010.
14. Mills, J.; Rosenberg, J.; Bollig, G.; Haberecht, J. Last aid and public health palliative care: Towards the development of personal skills and strengthened community action. *Prog. Palliat. Care* **2020**, *28*, 343–345. [CrossRef]
15. Kellehear, A. Compassionate communities: End-of-life care as everyone's responsibility. *QJM Int. J. Med.* **2013**, *106*, 1071–1075. [CrossRef]
16. Bollig, G.; Frans, B.; Marius, C.; Boris, K. Lat aid course. an education for all citizens and an ingredient of compassionate communities. *Healthcare* **2019**, *7*, 19. [CrossRef]
17. Blix, I.; Birkeland, M.; Thoresen, S. Worry and mental health in the Covid-19 pandemic: Vulnerability factors in the general Norwegian population. *BMC Public Health* **2021**, *21*, 928. [CrossRef] [PubMed]
18. Nam, S.-H.; Nam, J.-H.; Kwon, C.-Y. Comparison of the mental health impact of COVID-19 on vulnerable and non-vulnerable groups: A systematic review and meta-analysis of observational studies. *Int. J. Environ. Res. Public Health* **2021**, *18*, 10830. [CrossRef] [PubMed]

19. Bayly, J.; Bradshaw, A.; Fettes, L.; Omarjee, M.; Talbot-Rice, H.A.; Walshe, C.; Sleeman, K.; Bajwah, S.; Dunleavy, L.; Hocaoglu, M.; et al. Understanding the impact of the Covid-19 pandemic on delivery of rehabilitation in specialist palliative care services: An analysis of the CovPall-Rehab survey data. *Palliat. Med.* **2022**, *36*, 319–331. [CrossRef] [PubMed]
20. Abel, J.; Kellehear, A.; Karapliagou, A. Palliative care—The new essentials. *Ann. Palliat. Med.* **2018**, *7*, S3–S14. [CrossRef]
21. Abel, J.; Kellehear, A.; Mills, J.; Patel, M. Access to palliative care reimagined. *Future Healthc. J.* **2021**, *8*, 699–702. [CrossRef]
22. McIlfatrick, S.; Helen, N.; Mc Corry, N.K.; Roulston, A.; Hasson, F.; Mc Laughlin, D.; Johnston, G.; Rutherford, L.; Payne, P.; Kernohan, G.; et al. Exploring public awareness and perceptions of palliative care: A qualitative study. *Palliat. Med.* **2014**, *28*, 273–280. [CrossRef]
23. Bollig, G. Palliative Care für alte und Demente Menschen Lernen und Lehren. LIT-Verlag. 2010. Available online: http://www.lit-verlag.de/isbn/3-643-90058-6 (accessed on 5 November 2021).
24. Stein, D. Situated Learning in Adult Education. In ERIC Clearinghouse on Adult, Career, and Vocational Education, Center on Education and Training for Employment, College of Education, the Ohio State University. 1998. Available online: https://www.ericdigests.org/1998-3/adult-education.html (accessed on 20 April 2022).
25. Wenger-Trayner, E.; Wenger-Trayner, B. Introducing Community of Practice. 2015. Available online: https://wenger-trayner.com/introduction-to-communities-of-practice/ (accessed on 4 June 2021).
26. Bollig, G.; Frans, B.K.; Wolff, D.L. Citizens appreciate talking about death and learning end-of-life care—A mixed-methods study on views and experiences of 5469 Last Aid Course participants. *Prog. Palliat. Care* **2021**, *29*, 140–148. [CrossRef]
27. Bollig, G.; Kuklau, N. Der Letzte Hilfe Kurs—Ein Angebot zur Verbesserung der Allgemeinen Ambulanten Palliativversorgung durch Information und Befähigung von Bürgerinnen und Bürgern. *Z. Für Palliativmed.* **2015**, *16*, 210–216. [CrossRef]
28. Bollig, G.; Mainzer, K.; Fiedler, H.; Pothmann, R. The last aid course for kids and teens from 8-14 years—Preliminary results from the first pilot test. *Hosp. Palliat. Med. Int. J.* **2021**, *4*, 1–3. [CrossRef]
29. Krčevski Škvarč, N. *Personal kommunikation with the Author*; Univerza v Mariboru: Maribor, Slovenia; p. 2022.
30. Slovenian Atlas of Palliative Care. Available online: http://paliativa.si/last-aid-paliativna-oskrba-kam-po-pomoc-v-sloveniji-informacijski-atlas-sipk-2020/ (accessed on 15 May 2022).
31. Shalev, A.; Phongtankue, V.; Kozlov, E.; Johnson, S.; Megan, A.; Ronald, R. Awareness and misperceptions of hospice and palliative care: A population-based survey study. *Am. J. Hosp. Palliat. Care* **2018**, *35*, 431–439. [CrossRef] [PubMed]
32. Ramasamy, V.; Sirala, J.; Elavally, S.; Pappas, Y.; Mhlanga, F.; Pallipalayam, V. Public, patient and carers' views on palliative and end-of-life care in India. *Int. Nurs. Rev.* **2018**, *65*, 292–301. [CrossRef] [PubMed]
33. Patel, P.; Lyons, L. Examining the knowledge, awareness, and perceptions of palliative care in the general public over time: A scoping literature review. *Am. J. Hosp. Palliat. Care* **2020**, *37*, 481–487. [CrossRef] [PubMed]
34. Statistical Office of the Republic of Slovenia. How are Persons in Employment in the Exposed Occupational Groups Distributed by Municipalities? Available online: https://www.stat.si/StatWeb/en/News/Index/8781. (accessed on 1 June 2020).
35. Miyawaki, A.; Tomio, J.; Kobayashi, Y.; Takahashi, H.; Noguchi, H.; Tamiya, N. Impact of long-hours family caregiving on non-fatal coronary heart disease risk in middle-aged people: Results from a longitudinal nationwide survey in Japan. *Geriatr. Gerontol. Int.* **2017**, *17*, 2109–2115. [CrossRef]
36. AARP Public Policy Institute in National Alliance for Caregiving. *Caregiving in the U.S.: 2015 Report*; NAC: Chicago, IL, USA; AARP: Chicago, IL, USA, 2015.
37. Yee, J.L.; Schulz, R. Gender differences in psychiatric morbidity among family caregivers: A review and analysis. *Gerontol.* **2000**, *40*, 147–164. [CrossRef]
38. Abel, J.; Kellehear, A. Palliative care reimagined: A needed shift. *BMJ Support Palliat. Care* **2016**, *6*, 21–26. [CrossRef]
39. Zelko, E.; Dorotea, G.; Estera, G.; Nevenka, K.Š. Awareness and expectations of visitors to family medicine practices about palliative care in Slovenia. *Acta Med. Biotech.* **2021**, *14*, 34–43.
40. Richards, N.; Koksvik, G.; Gerson, M.; Clark, D. The global spread of death café: A cultural intervention relevant to policy? *Soc. Policy Soc.* **2020**, *19*, 553–572. [CrossRef]
41. Kellehear, A. Commentary: Public health approaches to palliative care—The progress so far. *Prog. Palliat. Care* **2016**, *24*, 36–38. [CrossRef]
42. Shen, J.; Dingley, C.l.; Yoo, J.W.; Rathi, S.; Kim, S.K.; Kang, H.-T.; Frost, K. Sociocultural factors associated with awareness of palliative care and advanced care planning among Asian populations. *Ethn. Dis.* **2020**, *30*, 459–468. [CrossRef]
43. Isaacson, M. Addressing palliative and end-of-life care needs with Native American elders. *Int. J. Palliat. Nurs.* **2018**, *24*, 160–168. [CrossRef] [PubMed]
44. Mc Grath, P.D.; Holewa, H. Seven principles for Indigenous palliative care service delivery: Research findings from Australia. *Austral-Asian J. Cancer* **2006**, *5*, 179–186.
45. Zelko, E.; Švab, I. Overcoming cultural cleavages: Results from a health promotion intervention among Roma. *Acta Med. Bioteh.* **2016**, *9*, 33–41.
46. Lipovec Čebron, U. Jezikovne in Kulturne Ovire v Zdravstvenih Ustanovah. In *Neenakosti in Ranljivosti v Zdravju v Sloveniji: Kvalitativna Raziskava v 25 Okoljih*; Huber, I., Lipovec, U., Pistotnik, S., Pistotnik, Č., Eds.; NIJZ: Ljubljana, Slovenia, 2020; pp. 120–140.

healthcare

MDPI

Article

Last Aid Training Online: Participants' and Facilitators' Perceptions from a Mixed-Methods Study in Rural Scotland

Leah Macaden [1], Kirsten Broadfoot [2,3], Clare Carolan [1,*], Kevin Muirhead [1], Siobhan Neylon [4] and Jeremy Keen [4]

[1] Department of Nursing & Midwifery, University of the Highlands & Islands, Inverness IV3 5SQ, UK; leah.macaden@uhi.ac.uk (L.M.); kevinmuirhead106@gmail.com (K.M.)
[2] Sterena Consultancy, Cromarty IV11 8XA, UK; sterenaconsultancy@gmail.com or Kirsten.broadfoot@cuanschutz.edu
[3] Anschutz Medical Campus, University of Colorado, Aurora, CO 80045, USA
[4] Highland Hospice, Inverness IV19 1AF, UK; s.neylon@highlandhospice.org.uk (S.N.); j.keen@highlandhospice.org.uk (J.K.)
* Correspondence: clare.carolan@uhi.ac.uk

Abstract: (1) Background: Palliative and end-of-life care services are increasingly gaining centre stage in health and social care contexts in the UK and globally. Death and dying need are relational processes. Building personal and community capacity along with resilience is vital to support families and communities to normalise death and dying. Last Aid Training (LAT) is one such innovative educational initiative which teaches the general public about the fundamentals of palliative care and promotes public discussion about death and dying. The Highland Hospice [HH] in Scotland has pioneered delivery of LAT in face-to-face settings since March 2019 and online since March 2020 to accommodate pandemic restrictions. (2) Methods: This study used a mixed-methods approach, combining an online survey with LAT participants followed by individual semi-structured qualitative interviews with both LAT participants and facilitators. The primary aim of this study was to investigate the impacts of LAT for participants at the individual, family, and community levels, as well as explore participant and facilitator experiences and perspectives of LAT in an online environment. (3) Results: Overall, this evaluation demonstrates that provision of foundational death literacy education in social contexts enhances the personal knowledge, skills, and confidence of individual community members and supports the notion that this personal growth could lead to strengthened community action. (4) Conclusions: Findings from this study concluded that there is potential to include LAT as the foundational core training to promote death literacy in communities with further exploration to integrate/align LAT with other national/global end-of-life care frameworks.

Keywords: public health; Last Aid; online; death literacy; perceptions; participants; facilitators; mixed methods; Scotland

check for updates

Citation: Macaden, L.; Broadfoot, K.; Carolan, C.; Muirhead, K.; Neylon, S.; Keen, J. Last Aid Training Online: Participants' and Facilitators' Perceptions from a Mixed-Methods Study in Rural Scotland. *Healthcare* **2022**, *10*, 918. https://doi.org/10.3390/healthcare10050918

Academic Editors: Georg Bollig, John Rosenberg and Paolo Cotogni

Received: 11 April 2022
Accepted: 6 May 2022
Published: 16 May 2022

1. Introduction

By 2040, the number of people with increasingly complex palliative care needs in Scotland is projected to rise by 20% [1]. A recent Scottish expert consultation identifies the need to build community capacity and resilience to support informal palliative caregiving so people can remain at home if they so wish [2]. One mechanism to build community capacity is to adopt a public health approach to palliative care as informed by the Ottawa Charter for Health Promotion [3,4]. 'Compassionate Communities' uses a community development framework to enhance personal capacity and community empowerment, and is promoted as a public health-promoting palliative care initiative [5]. Recognising palliative and end-of-life care as key issues of major public interest, Scotland's national framework for palliative and end-of-life care for 2016–2021 is committed to driving a new culture of openness about death, dying, and bereavement [6].

Death literacy has been defined "as a set of knowledge and skills that make it possible to gain access to understand and act upon end-of-life and death care options" and considered an outcome of peoples' experience of death and dying as well as formal and informal learning [7]. Death education initiatives aimed at the general public to raise citizens' awareness and knowledge of palliative care to enhance death literacy align well with the theoretical underpinnings of health-promoting palliative care and public health approaches to death and dying [8]. The Kerala model has successfully changed the narratives around death and dying, redefined care at the end of life, influenced national policy, and challenged global models of end-of-life care through community participation and empowerment [9].

Last Aid is an innovative instructor-led educational initiative developed by George Bollig which teaches the general public about the fundamentals of palliative care and promotes public discussion about death and dying [10]. It endorses a simple concept paralleling the universal promotion of First Aid training to enhance citizens' everyday capacity to deal with minor injury or illness, in that Last Aid can similarly enhance citizens' everyday capacity to support death and dying in their communities [11]. Since its inception, Last Aid has grown globally and has been supported by the European Association of Palliative Care's Taskforce on Last Aid and Public Palliative Care Education [7].

Last Aid Training (LAT) is delivered as four short modules over three hours focused on care at the end of life; advanced care planning and decision making; symptom management; and cultural aspects of death and bereavement. The course materials were developed by an international working group [10] and aim to (i) create an awareness of, and discussion on, topics related to death and dying, (ii) build capacity for a more formal palliative care befriending and facilitator role, and (iii) develop a range of Last Aid international age-specific courses particularly for young people [7]. In addition to didactic learning using the course material, informal sharing of experiential learning by course participants is supported by Last Aid facilitators.

Through its development of personal skills and capabilities, Last Aid is a key means of enhancing death literacy and furthering the aims of building community capacity to develop Compassionate Communities, including workplaces. Hospices, in particular, are well-positioned to support such public health care approaches within the communities they serve [12]. In Scotland, the Highland Hospice has pioneered delivery of LAT in face-to-face settings since March 2019 and online since March 2020 via Zoom to accommodate pandemic restrictions. LAT is delivered by a pair of facilitators, drawn from a larger cadre of eight trained facilitators. Facilitators are everyday citizens trained via HH. The shift to online delivery means that participants living outside the region can attend; however, LAT enrolment data confirm that the majority of LAT participants are drawn from the Highland locality (Highland Hospice 2021). A total of thirteen online sessions have been delivered since the beginning of the COVID pandemic.

Whilst recent evidence supports the feasibility and acceptability of LAT both in face-to-face and online environments, the need to evaluate the impact of public health interventions beyond course evaluation has been argued [13,14].

The primary aim of this study was to investigate the impacts of LAT for participants at the individual, family, and community levels, as well as explore participant and facilitator experiences and perspectives of LAT in an online environment. Specific research aims explored participants' perceptions of their knowledge and confidence on end-of-life care before and after LAT; participants' experiences on providing end-of-life care before and after LAT; participants' perspectives on the online delivery of LAT, and facilitators' experiences of delivering LAT both in online and offline settings.

2. Materials and Methods

This study used a mixed-methods approach, combining an online survey with LAT participants followed by individual semi-structured qualitative interviews with both LAT participants and facilitators. Data were collected between October 2020 and April 2021.

2.1. Participants

Both LAT participants and facilitators were recruited through HH.

2.1.1. LAT Participants

The publicly available LAT registration form on the HH website was amended to include an option for participants to opt in to participate in this evaluation. In the absence of the registrant's preference, the Last Aid coordinator from HH sent a follow-up email to clarify participation in the evaluation. If the registrant had opted out of the evaluation, no further contact was made.

LAT participants who indicated their interest in participating received a follow-up email with the Participant Information Leaflet (PIS) and a short electronic flyer on the project with the contact details of the research team. Participants were sent a secure link to the survey, with informed consent obtained electronically prior to survey access. Participants were also able to indicate their preference to take part in a one-to-one interview within the survey.

To recruit interview participants, the Research Associate on the project team worked in collaboration with the Last Aid coordinator from HH. All participants were required to sign the consent form and send the Research Associate a scanned copy via email to then arrange a convenient date and time for the virtual interview via WebEx. The Research Associate established identity and verbal consent prior to proceeding with the virtual interview that was video-recorded.

Alongside written communication, Last Aid facilitators also shared information on the ongoing evaluation at the close of each online training session and invited participants to take part. The Hospice Communications team also posted two general invites via the Hospice's Facebook and Twitter to aid recruitment of participants to this study.

A total of 105 people opted in to participate in the evaluation at the time of registration. Subsequently, 68 people attended training sessions, with 26 participants completing the survey, giving a response rate of 38%. Participants were predominantly female (n = 22) and aged between 35 and 64 years (n = 19). Most participants were employed (n = 21), with around 40% (n = 11) working in health or social care. More than half of the participants were educated to graduate level or above. Reasons for attending LAT were most frequently related to employment or attributed to personal interest. Most participants did not have previous experience of working with people at end of life, but had professional experience with grief and loss and had attended similar training previously. Six participants (two male and four female) completed interviews online for the study.

Demographic information for participants is shown in Table 1. Information on participants' backgrounds and experience is shown in Table 2.

2.1.2. LAT Facilitators

LAT facilitators were contacted by the Last Aid coordinator at HH via email to inform them about the study. The email included a participant information sheet and a consent form. A follow-up email was sent two months later to remind facilitators about the ongoing study. Participants with interest to participate in the study contacted the Research Associate to then arrange a convenient date and time for the virtual interview via WebEx. The Research Associate established identity and verbal consent prior to proceeding with the virtual interview that was video recorded. Five LAT facilitators (one male and four female) were interviewed in this study.

2.2. Data Collection

This study used two forms of data collection. An online survey contained both quantitative and qualitative items and was distributed solely to LAT participants. The semi-structured interviews were conducted using interview topic guides with both LAT facilitators (Supplementary File S1) and participants (Supplementary File S2).

Table 1. Demographic Information.

Age	N	%	Gender	N	%
18–24 years	1	3.8	Male	3	11.5
25–34 years	2	7.7	Female	22	84.6
35–44 years	4	15.4	Rather not say	1	3.8
45–54 years	9	34.6			
55–64 years	6	23.1			
65–79 years	4	15.4			
Education	N	%	**Employment**	N	%
National 5 or equivalent	1	3.8	Employed—full-time	10	38.5
Highers or equivalent	2	7.7	Employed—part-time	9	34.6
Certificate or Diploma	5	19.2	Self-employed	2	7.7
Undergraduate degree	8	30.8	Retired	4	15.4
Postgraduate degree	7	26.9	Student	1	3.8
Rather not say	3	11.5			
Employer	N	%	**Residence**	N	%
NHS	6	23.1	Urban area	10	38.5
Social Care	1	3.8	Semi-Urban area	4	15.4
Third Sector	4	15.4	Rural area	5	19.2
Education	7	26.9	Remote area	2	7.7
Other	8	30.8	Semi-Rural area	5	19.2
Relationship Status	N	%	**Networks**	N	%
Married	15	57.7	Family	22	84.6
Never married	2	7.7	Neighbours	9	34.6
Widowed	2	7.7	Community Groups	7	26.9
Divorced	1	3.8	Religious Groups	5	19.2
Separated (not divorced)	1	3.8	Friends	22	84.6
Partnered (not living together)	1	3.8			
Single	2	7.7			
Other	2	7.7			
Reason for Attendance	N	%	**Source of Access**	N	%
Personal interest	21	80.8	Family	1	3.8
COVID-19	1	3.8	Colleague	10	38.5
Long-term condition	1	3.8	Email	3	11.5
Terminal illness	1	3.8	Social Media	4	15.4
Related to work	16	61.5	Hospice Newsletter/Website	11	42.3

Table 2. Background and Experience.

Background and Experience		N	%
Religious/Spiritual Background	Yes	13	50.0
	No	12	46.2
	Rather not say	1	3.8
Religious/Spiritual Practice	Yes	10	38.5
	No	15	57.7
	Rather not say	1	3.8
Experience with people at end of life—Paid	Yes	10	38.5
	No	16	61.5
Experience with people at end of life—Volunteer	Yes	10	38.5
	No	16	61.5
Work experience with grief and loss	Yes	13	50.0
	No	13	50.0
Volunteer experience with grief and loss	Yes	12	46.2
	No	14	53.8
Previous training on dying, grief, or bereavement	Yes	15	57.7
	No	11	42.3

2.2.1. Online Survey

The survey was designed to gather (i) participant knowledge and experiences of Talking about Death and Dying, (ii) Knowledge and Confidence around Death and Dying, and (iii) Decision making and intentions to support end-of-life care needs. In the following section, we present both quantitative and qualitative survey data addressing these topics.

The online survey aimed to evaluate the impact of LAT on participants' knowledge, understanding, awareness, and confidence related to palliative and end-of-life care issues and decision making and their perceptions of the LAT. The questionnaire (Supplementary File S3) was informed by the Death Literacy Index Questionnaire [15], enabling evaluation of key features of death literacy, i.e., knowledge, skills, experiential learning, and social action as an intended outcome of LAT. The survey also included evaluation of the content and delivery of LAT.

The survey questionnaire was administered using the Jisc Online Survey (JOS) platform. JOS is designed for education and research and the University of the Highlands and Islands holds a license for its use [16].

2.2.2. Interviews

One-to-one semi-structured virtual video interviews were conducted through WebEx. Participant interviews ranged from 28 to 42 min long, with a mean interview time of 35 min. Facilitator interviews ranged from 17 to 40 min long, with a mean interview time of 29 min. All interviews were conducted by the Research Associate and audio from the interviews was extracted to ensure participant anonymity. Data were transcribed verbatim by a professional transcription service.

2.3. *Data Analysis*

Quantitative survey data were analysed using descriptive statistics. The sample size was small (n = 26) and not suitable for analysis using inferential statistics/significance testing. Survey data were downloaded from JOS and analysed in Microsoft Excel Version 2013. Participant responses on questionnaire items were captured using a one-time survey from two time periods—pre- and post-LAT. They were asked to provide data for items on the questionnaire pre- and then post-LAT training, where they were reflecting back on their perceptions/experiences before attending LAT rather than having completed the survey at different time points.

Either percentage values of Likert-scale responses or median responses were reported for questionnaire items. Textual survey data were analysed thematically and reported with representative participant quotes.

Qualitative interview data were analysed thematically [17]. For both facilitator and participant samples, one transcript was independently coded by each member of the research team (Kirsten Broadfoot, Leah Macaden, and Clare Carolan). The research team then met to compare and assess emergent coding and the preliminary set of codes and themes derived by the Research Associate. From this, a coherent set of codes and themes was derived and applied to the remaining transcripts.

3. Results

This study originally had four specific research aims involving the exploration of participants' perceptions of their knowledge and confidence on end-of-life care before and after LAT; participants' experiences on providing end-of-life care before and after LAT; participant perspectives on the online delivery of LAT, and facilitator experiences of delivering LAT both in online and offline settings. Given the mixed-methods study design and presence of quantitative and qualitative data for LAT participants, and solely qualitative data for facilitators, findings are presented to align with combined objectives as follows:

1. Participant perceptions of their knowledge, confidence, and experiences providing end-of-life care

2. Participant perspectives on the online delivery of LAT and facilitator experiences of delivering LAT in online and offline settings.

3.1. Participant Perceptions of Their Knowledge, Confidence, and Experiences Providing End-of-Life Care

The main findings for this combined objective were gathered through the quantitative and qualitative items from the online survey. However, participant interviews also provided rich insights into their experiences of LAT.

3.1.1. Knowledge and Experiences Talking about Death and Dying

Participants indicated high levels of comfort talking about death and dying before attending LAT, with only 15% of participants responding that they would avoid the topic of death and dying, and 4% indicating they would avoid people who were grieving. After LAT, participant discomfort with these activities fell to zero. Prior to LAT, when asked why they might avoid conversations on death and dying, 27% of participants indicated they might avoid conversations due to fear of upsetting others, and 19% due to personal discomfort. After LAT, none of the participants indicated they would avoid conversations due to personal discomfort and only 4% indicated they would avoid conversations due to fear of upsetting others (Figure 1).

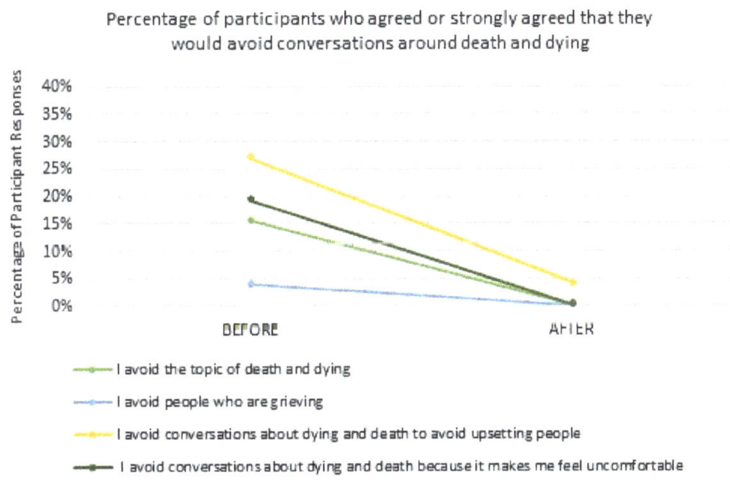

Figure 1. Talking about Death and Dying.

When asked where and when they discussed death and dying, participants reported a 20% increase in discussing death and dying with family members, a 19% increase within their community, and 11% in the workplace after LAT. No increase in discussions within church or religious settings was reported. Notably, the religious setting was not applicable to 65% of respondents (Table 3).

Participants also reported relatively high levels of confident conversations on death and dying prior to participating in LAT, with 85% of participants indicating they were at least somewhat confident discussing death and dying with a close friend, 62% with a child, 65% with a recently bereaved person, 54% with a GP about support for a dying person, and 54% were confident when talking to someone who is dying. After LAT, these percentages increased to 100%, 88%, 96%, 100%, and 96%, respectively, as seen in Figure 2.

Table 3. Talking about death and dying with others.

Talking about Death & Dying	Time Point	Agree (%)	Disagree (%)	Unsure (%)	NA (%)
We discuss death and dying in my family	1	57.8	38.4	0.0	3.8
	2	77.0	15.4	3.8	3.8
We discuss death and dying in my community	1	30.8	53.8	15.4	0.0
	2	50.0	38.5	11.5	0.0
We discuss death and dying in my workplace	1	46.2	34.6	3.8	15.4
	2	57.7	26.9	3.8	11.5
We discuss death and dying in my church/ religious gathering	1	34.6	0.0	0.0	65.4
	2	34.6	0.0	0.0	65.4

Timepoint 1 is before LAT and timepoint 2 is after LAT. Agree is the total percentage of participants who either agreed or strongly agreed with the question. Disagree is the total percentage of participants who either disagreed or strongly disagreed with the question. N (Number of Participants); NA (Not applicable).

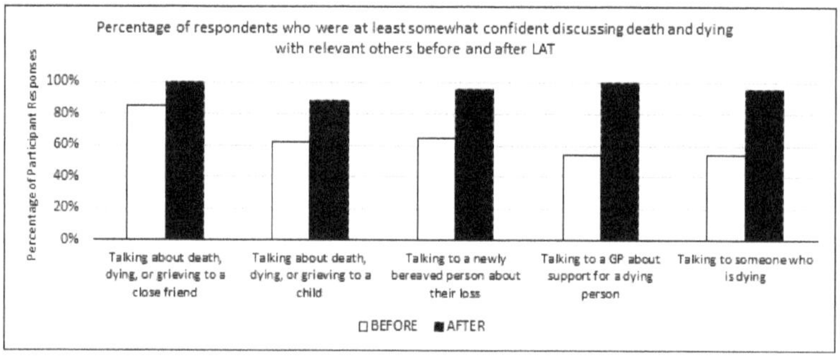

Figure 2. Confident Conversations on Death and Dying.

3.1.2. Knowledge and Confidence around Death and Dying

Beyond participant comfort and confidence in holding conversations on death and dying, participants were also asked to rate their knowledge of end-of-life care and community support available. Figure 3 presents median response values demonstrating an increased value for the majority of items following LAT.

Participants were then asked to rate their confidence in providing care and support to people who are dying. As seen in Figure 4, confidence levels increased in all domains (administering medication, moving and handling, bathing, assisting with eating and drinking, using non-pharmacological intervention to increase comfort, and symptom recognition) following LAT.

3.2. Decisions and Intentions to Support End-of-Life Care Needs

In the final section of the survey, participants were asked to indicate whether they had undertaken or intended to undertake various measures relating to end of life pre- and post-LAT. There was an increase in the number of participants who indicated they had undertaken or intended to undertake all the measures after the training. The greatest increases (>30%) were observed in practical measures involving future planning (e.g., making a will, advance care planning, and financial planning) and practical aspects of providing palliative care, as seen in Figure 5.

EXPERIENTIAL KNOWLEDGE	BEFORE	AFTER
Individual		
Initiating end-of-life care decisions about myself	3	4
Participating in advance care planning for myself	3	4
Prioritising what is important and not important in life	4	4
Being compassionate or kind towards myself	4	4
Accessing skills and strategies to cope myself emotionally	4	4
Family		
Initiating end-of-life care conversations with a family member	3	4
Participating in advance care planning for a family member	3	4
Participating in advance care planning for a friend	3	4
Community		
Supporting others with death and dying processes	3	4
Empathising with others	4	4
Using my skills to support others facing similar challenges	4	4
FACTUAL KNOWLEDGE	**BEFORE**	**AFTER**
What a DNACPR form is and how it is used	4	4
What a treatment escalation plan is and how it is used	2	4
What documents you need to complete in planning for death	2.5	4
How to navigate the health care system to support a dying person	2	4
How to access palliative care in my area	2.5	4
What constitutes quality at end of life	3	4
The law regarding what to do after a death in Scotland	3	4
How to navigate funeral services and options	3	4
The contribution the funeral director can make	3	4
COMMUNITY SUPPORT	**BEFORE**	**AFTER**
Accessing community support available	3	4
Providing day-to-day care for the dying person	3	4
Accessing equipment required for care	3	4
Accessing culturally appropriate support	3	4
Support groups for people with life threatening illnesses	3	4
Support groups for people who are dying	2	4
Support groups for carers of people who are dying	2	4
Support groups for people who are grieving	3	4

Figure 3. Experiential Knowledge, Factual Knowledge, and Knowledge of Community Support. Experiential knowledge (1 = Not at all comfortable; 2 = Not very comfortable; 3 = Somewhat comfortable; 4 = comfortable; 5 = Very comfortable). Factual knowledge and Knowledge on Community Resources (1 = None; 2 = Weak; 3 = Fair; 4 = Good; 5 = Very Good).

In summary, data from the survey clearly indicate that LAT had an impact on participant preparedness, comfort, and confidence in discussing death and dying, as well as their decisions and intentions to support end-of-life care needs. Open-ended survey items and participant interviews were also used to gather more in-depth insights of participant experiences of LAT. Themes and data from these qualitative sources are presented in the next section.

3.3. *Overall Impact of LAT on Participants*

Thematic analysis of both participants' free-text survey responses and interview data produced three main themes: (i) demystifying palliative care and enhancing understanding, (ii) creating normalised conversations around death and dying, and (iii) thinking ahead and advocating for self and others.

3.3.1. Demystifying Palliative Care and Enhancing Understanding

As indicated in the survey data, participants' existing understandings of palliative or end-of-life care were split along personal experience and professional expertise. Participants who were professionally expert in the area described little change in their knowledge from attending LAT. However, participants with no prior understanding described changed sensemaking of personal experiences of dying and changed understandings of palliative care. The latter included differentiation between palliative and end-of-life care, care beyond professionally delivered care, and alleviation of suffering as a primary goal.

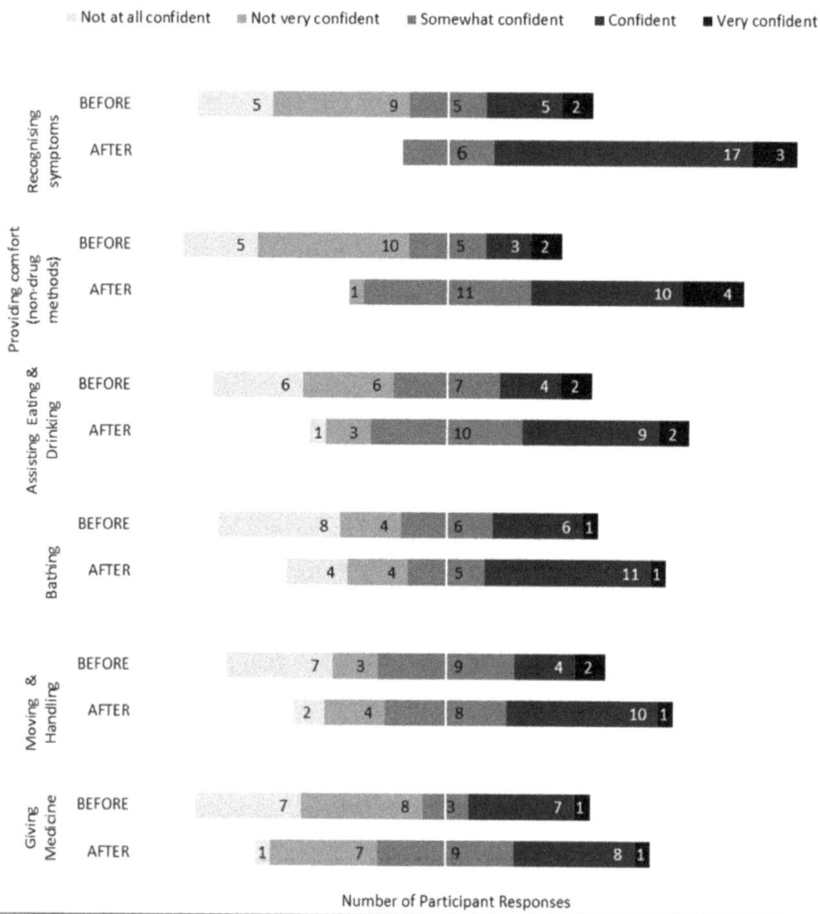

Figure 4. Confidence in supporting care of people dying.

> *"I don't know about not understanding about it but from a personal, life . . . somebody who was ill in my own family and obviously I didn't know what to expect then, but by the end of this training I learnt much more about it and it made me understand what I went through . . . and if this ever happened again, I'd have a greater understanding, it helped me deal with it".*
>
> (Interview Participant 3)

Participants also described enhanced knowledge about access to a larger support network and voiced a better understanding of stages and structured actions related to death and dying (reduced death anxiety, clarity of legal aspects of death and dying, anticipatory care planning, and grief and grieving) and individualised responses to death and dying within society.

"Well, the main thing was that I learnt more (. . .) various stages, how you should not be frightened of it. And it's . . . just a good (. . .) thing for you to learn, you know more about what may happen and also afterwards, like the grieving bit, there's no right or wrong way that people grieve".

(Interview Participant 3)

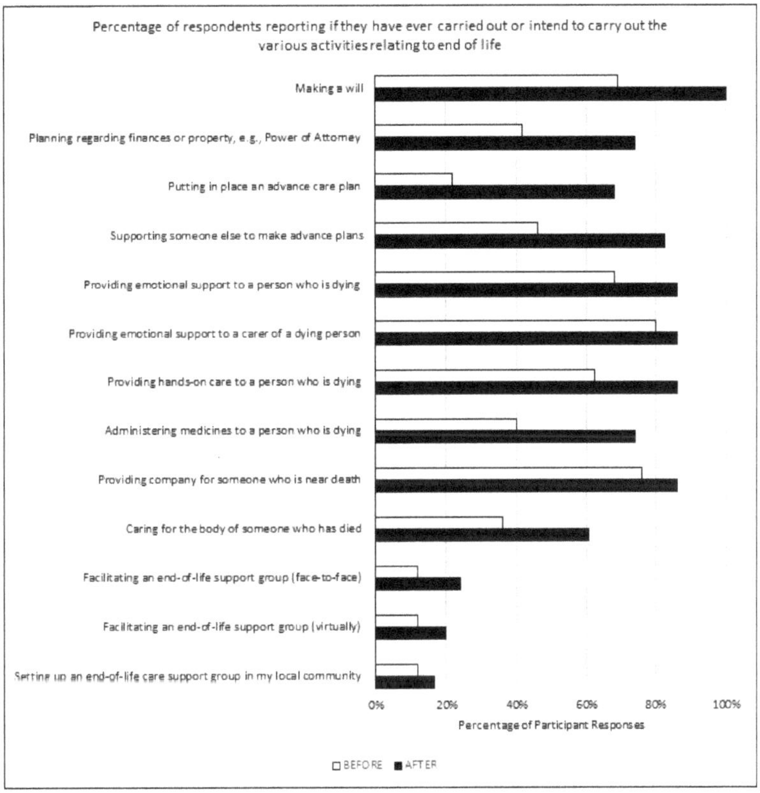

Figure 5. Decisions and Intentions to Support End-of-Life Care Needs.

3.3.2. Creating Normalised Conversations around Death and Dying

When asked about applying LAT to everyday life, participants reported a need to find conversational openings to normalise death and to tailor conversations across difference, highlighting the amount of awareness and confidence raised through their own clearer understanding of death and dying processes and how to serve those who are dying. Overwhelmingly, participants reported the need to talk more about death and dying as a normal part of life.

"How positive it is for society to have accepted that it's a good, kind, loving thing to be able to talk about death".

[Survey respondent 4]

All participants shared that LAT had boosted their confidence in being able to have constructive conversations, especially difficult family conversations around death due to gendered emotional expressions and fears of negatively impacting interpersonal family dynamics.

"I already know and already talk about these things but as I say, I think the course did make me think 'yeah, we need to talk about them more frequently and not when it's about

> *to happen', you know, you need to talk about them just over Sunday dinner when nobody is dying. That's probably the key thing; let's not wait until it's needed, let's talk about it all the time."*
>
> (Interview Participant 11)

However, the impact of COVID restrictions on meeting people outside their friends and families had placed limits on opportunities for such conversations.

> *"I would say because of the current situation again I have not really had much opportunity to. Not a matter or bias to the course, I mean, it's only been a matter of weeks and we've not had the opportunity to put any of these choices into practice"*
>
> (Interview Participant 10)

3.3.3. Thinking Ahead and Advocating for Self and Others

Finally, pro-actively planning for one's own future and encountering death was a significant outcome of LAT. Participants described getting their own 'house in order' including conversations to be had, and practical planning such as legal and funeral arrangements.

> *"I don't have power of attorney and that's the thing that we talked about quite a lot. So yes, it's made me think very seriously about that and in fact my husband and I have been speaking about that. I teach it but I don't do what I preach."*
>
> (Interview Participant 5)

Moreover, 'thinking ahead' impacts described above extended beyond their own individual perspective to encompass those within their family networks. With increased confidence in conversations around death and dying, participants felt a need to advocate for such conversations within their families and wider social networks.

> *"I am a great advocate of conversations and I know that they don't happen, people don't want to talk about death or dying, I am quite an advocate that people need to do that. So, it almost gave me permission to carry on doing that."*
>
> (Interview Participant 5)

Participants also reported feeling better equipped to guide close or intimate others as they had a better understanding now of their own experiences and could be of better support to those in need. LAT enabled increased awareness and confidence in participant preparations and planning for the future including seeking permission to advocate and discussions around legal processes, wills, future wishes, preferred place of care, etc.

> *"There were certain things that we talked about that were more vague ideas that are now relatively clear as far as knowing what would need to be done. And in terms of my own life, it's put into focus that my wife and I should start looking at things like getting wills and things like that, regardless of the fact that we're only in our mid-thirties, it's never too early."*
>
> (Interview Participant 9)

In summary, participants experienced not only increased knowledge and understanding of palliative and end-of-life care, but also felt more confident to initiate and hold conversations as well as prepare, plan, and advocate for self and others at end of life.

3.4. Participants' and Facilitators' Perceptions and Experiences of LAT within the Virtual Online Environment

As shown in the findings from the first combined objective, there is no doubt that LAT had a significant impact on participants. However, there was some uncertainty as to the effect a move to online delivery might have on the experiences of both participants and facilitators. Objectives 3 and 4, combined here to represent the perceptions and experiences of participants and facilitators, sought out such data through semi-structured interviews predominantly, with some additional insights gleaned from the online survey.

It should be noted that, unlike participants surveyed and interviewed for the study, LAT facilitators had experience of both online and in-person session delivery. To address this difference, while both participant populations were asked a series of questions on course design, content and delivery, facilitators were also asked to compare experiences. Thematic analysis of all interviews revealed four analytical themes: (i) accessibility, (ii) desired diversification, (iii) connectedness, and (iv) discomfort and difficulties.

3.4.1. Accessibility

The convenience and flexibility of virtual online delivery was a widely reported strength of LAT, enhancing access to LAT and mitigating geographical constraints of delivering LAT in remote and rural contexts.

> *"We can't physically manage to take presenters and take facilitators out to small rural communities in the Highlands. Highlands geographically—it's so difficult. And there is a lot to learn, I suspect, from doing it on Zoom—doing it online—in terms of taking it out to people in little remote rural communities, where they don't have access to anything. I do think that online sessions in all sorts of areas have a huge potential."*
>
> (Interview Participant 7)

While participant survey data indicated that no modality of course delivery was preferred over another, online LAT was reported as offering flexibility in scheduling and accessibility to those with diverse abilities and circumstances. Some participants reported online delivery facilitated easier access to LAT material, which was perceived as beneficial.

> *It was a good mix of being interactive with trainers and other participants and engaging solo through listening or reading. The trainers were very approachable and relatable.*
>
> [Survey respondent 5]
>
> *Ability to attend! I probably wouldn't have found the time otherwise. Home comfort. Being able to take notes without feeling rude or not present.*
>
> [Survey respondent 6]

Although most participants did not report limitations with online delivery of LAT, there was a general consensus from participants and facilitators about potential threats to access including digital connectivity and the need for technical support, as well as a call for LAT to be able to accommodate diverse levels of digital literacy.

> *"We've got to learn how to use them and to learn how to get the best out of them—and it's a steep learning curve and an uphill struggle."*
>
> (Interview Participant 7)

3.4.2. Desired Diversification

When asked about course content, participants enjoyed the content and spoke clearly to its flow, format, and modular design. However, one in five survey participants indicated that they would welcome additional content, such as integrating philosophical perspectives and examples from real human experience and non-traditional relationships.

> *Content could do more to recognise secular philosophical aspects of death/dying & life/living, as well as addressing issues surrounding death/dying and caring for someone who is dying in circumstances where partnership is non-traditional, i.e., LGBTQIA+ relationships.*
>
> [Survey respondent 7]

Similarly, in interviews, some participants voiced a need for topic diversity and illustrative examples, including discussions of different types of death and how to prepare for them, alternative arrangements, or contingencies to be aware of and how to manage unexpected death.

> *"something I think could be improved, in the way they want to take it out to general communities and things, was it was very, very heavily about—the context of the death that they were talking about was very much a predicted, expected planned death and I guess there's room for that course to be much wider, to include people having at least some thoughts and discussions about what if somebody doesn't die in a predicted or expected way."*
>
> (Interview Participant 11)

Likewise, LAT facilitators expressed the desire to have some flexibility and the ability to use one's own notes or scripts to deliver the course rather than deliver from the prescriptive guidance notes made available to them.

> *"I think a script. Although now, it's funny ... the more I think about that now, actually I wouldn't like that because I've tried using other people's notes and I just re-write them because they are not my words, they are not how I would say it. So there was a handbook and it was being translated but actually I would still want my own notes because that's not how I would say it, it's not me, so it doesn't sit comfortably for me to say it that way."*
>
> (Interview Participant 6)

3.4.3. Connectedness

While participants described LAT as informative, person-centred, meaningful learning delivered in a sensitive and collaborative way, connectedness or a sense of connection between participants and facilitators was critical to facilitating learning and enhancing the experience.

> *"If I were speaking to somebody who was about to take the training and didn't know what to expect I'd say, 'don't worry, you are not going to leave curled up in a ball in fear of the unknown', it's ... you know, obviously it's a topic that's difficult for a lot of people to discuss but I feel that it was done in such a way it was as sensitive to that as it could have been and it was, the information that was provided it helped to disarm the topic a bit. It made the subject a little bit less scary, I guess."*
>
> (Interview Participant 9)

Facilitators described the willingness of people to share their stories and were glad to be able to provide help and connect to others who were enduring loss. However, the fragile and temporally constrained nature of connectedness in online delivery was also evident.

> *"Just so people are willing to share this very private part of their lives and to open up the conversation about dying ... it's part of a bigger, national movement to talk about death and dying as a normal part of life. And sometimes I'd like to be just a little fly on the wall in the corner of the room just looking down on that conversation because you just don't appreciate sometimes how profound that is, I think we take it for granted that these people are opening up their lives in the little TV screen in their living room for that short time. And then they are gone, they click a button, and they are gone, and you have no more connection with that person ever again, but you just had that little opportunity to just drop something positive into their experience and hopefully help them along the way."*
>
> (Interview Participant 1)

As such, connectedness was often challenged by a lack of physical proximity, group composition, and tailored connections.

(a) Physical proximity

Online delivery of LAT was perceived to limit formal and informal opportunities to interact with other participants and inhibited opportunities for group discussion and spontaneous and natural conversations. Participants missed physical human connection and the ability to pick up on the body language of others and provide emotional support if necessary.

> *"Subject is difficult and emotional—delivering the course online removes the element of human contact and support that some may find helpful in dealing with these matters, even in an educational setting".*
>
> [Survey respondent 7]

Similarly, LAT facilitators compared their experiences of online delivery to face-to-face/in-person delivery and stated that online delivery was more impersonal, describing difficulties with identifying and discussing emotions. Facilitators felt that there was greater ability to hold emotive discussions, use more anecdotes, and hold more informal conversations during face-to-face delivery, allowing for more intuitive connections and a better participant experience.

> *" ... you can have these really honest conversations when you are face-to-face and you can say to them, if you need a minute you can go out and you can read people's emotions".*
>
> (Interview Participant 2)
>
> *"In a room, you can go round afterwards and say, 'Do you want to look at the pieces of paper?' and chat to people. Or pick out someone who's been uncomfortable, or the quiet one in the corner who's said very little. You've got that ability to relate to people that you just don't have on screen."*
>
> (Interview Participant 7)

Some participants who had only completed LAT online imagined that being face-to-face would allow the sessions to be more interactive, provide more support for emotional conversations in small groups, and potentially enhance spaces for discussion. One participant commented on the need to increase spaces for practice in LAT overall so participants could have small role play or practice conversations in small groups or pairs to put the content into application.

> *"an improvement to the course, I think, would be to actually get people to have that conversation perhaps in pairs, we did go into little break-out rooms, as can often be the case, people talked about other things and kind of avoided talking about the thing that wanted to be talked about ... make it longer and enable people to really have more interaction and more discussion between each other and between themselves and kind of test out having some of these conversations"*
>
> (Interview Participant 11)

(b) Group composition

Group composition also had a significant impact on connectedness. Some participants stated that when there was symmetry between facilitators, the course had a natural flow and interaction. However, for participants, diverse or mixed group participants (e.g., not all clinical or professional participants) was seen to promote interaction and connection. Importantly, participants stated that facilitators must not assume homogeneity within groups and needed to appreciate potential audience diversity when discussing issues of faith and cultural practices.

> *"it would have been quite nice to have been with other people that were not clinical. That's the only ... I know you just can't control that and, as I say, I know a few people couldn't link in that day so there may have been people within that but personally, for me, that would have been good to hear from their viewpoint as well"*
>
> (Interview Participant 5)

(c) Tailoring connections

Relatedly, participants shared that gathering information on learners prior to attending the session would enable content to be tailored more to their needs. Such tailoring would ensure course content would be more contextually appropriate. Participants also desired LAT handouts ahead of time so they could be more prepared, enabling them to balance attending to interaction and didactic delivery within the sessions. This preparation would create common ground and allow sessions to be more interactive.

> *"And again it kind of begs that question to me, that I've obviously got a bit stuck on, is that because they are copyrighted in some way, I mean why on earth would you not give people the slides if they are on a course? It just seems completely wrong to me."*
>
> (Interview Participant 11)

Overall, then, the dimension of connectedness, so central to the LAT experiences of both participants and facilitators, was dependent on several factors for its accomplishment, some of which could be easily strengthened to improve delivery in an online setting. The final theme in this online experience highlights the dialectical tension between emotionally charged content and human experiences and course delivery modalities.

3.4.4. Discomfort and Difficulties

Whilst participants and facilitators described their experience of LAT as a meaningful learning experience, and online delivery as enabling greater access and flexibility, it was not without participant discomfort or difficulty.

Given the emotional nature of the content, online delivery afforded participants the comfort of learning in their own home environment and enabled them to process emotion privately by turning off sound and camera if so desired. Some participants also stated that online LAT enabled them to learn at their own pace. One participant went further, suggesting that the training could take place over a few days so that the content did not overwhelm the lay audience. Other participants highlighted the physical discomfort of sitting for prolonged periods during virtual training and recommended more breaks.

While participants spoke to the discomfort associated with session design and the volume/nature of the content, LAT facilitators voiced considerable difficulties and discomfort delivering Last Aid due to (a) knowledge base, (b) role autonomy, and (c) online facilitation skills.

(a) Knowledge base

Some facilitators expressed concern initially about their perceived lack of knowledge; however, facilitators also shared that being prepared and being honest when you do not know something were important skills. Accessing other resources such as books and papers to reference or address knowledge gaps was perceived to be more challenging in the online environment. Overall, however, facilitators shared that such knowledge gaps were also learning opportunities and made their facilitation experiences meaningful in their own daily lives.

> *"I feel that it's given me a bit more confidence and knowledge behind it and it's certainly facilitated conversations in my own life".*
>
> (Interview Participant 2)

One of the ways suggested by facilitators to address variability in knowledge was for there to be a foundational script or slide set to be used in their facilitator training and/or the creation of a facilitation guide or booklet to which they could refer. This was seen as increasingly important when there were considerable gaps in time between their training and facilitation as well as session facilitations to mitigate concerns.

> *"I think my expectations were that we would probably get a script that we were going to use when we were actually facilitating the sessions. Especially when I don't have a clinical background and I don't have a knowledge of end-of-life care in the same way: I see it as a bystander. So I did think we would get a training manual ... Definitely a script that would help".*
>
> (Interview Participant 6)

(b) Role Autonomy

Beyond knowledge base, some facilitators described differing degrees of comfort and agreement with course content, experiencing challenges to their autonomy and authenticity as facilitators. Some facilitators struggled with their role and content control as facilitator versus that of the creator. Some experienced this struggle as feeling like an imposter as it was not their content and also being unsure about how individual changes or additions would either augment or distract from the original message and vision of LAT.

(c) Online facilitation skills

Finally, technology and the online learning environment itself posed some difficulties for facilitators, as they often felt 'powerless', 'abandoned to the technology', and the experience as 'nerve wracking'. Struggles around managing technology including breakout rooms and technological mishaps, navigating time constraints, varying degrees of comfort in clarifying the group's composition, individual needs, and agendas as well as challenges around public speaking were all shared by LAT facilitators. Some stated they felt more self-conscious within the online environment, feeling a loss of authenticity and professionalism.

> *"I feel self-conscious with the technology, I feel it takes away a little bit of my personality, my ability to be my real self because I'm self-conscious. So I think probably in-person but I do see the need for the technology".*
>
> (Interview Participant 1)

As a result, facilitators wanted more face-to-face discussions, chances to practice co-facilitation before a session, more regular session delivery, and the provision of a manual or booklet for facilitation guidance. They also suggested increased discussion of content and delivery as a group so they could learn from each other and also how to make the most of the online experience.

> *"I just need to keep delivering the material regularly so I can keep up my skills. One of my worries is if they take on board too many new facilitators then we all end up just doing one course a year or something. That will just be pointless to me, I think to keep your skills up and your . . . you tuned in to it, I think you have to keep doing it regularly".*
>
> (Interview Participant 1)

In summary, delivering LAT online posed many of the challenges experienced in online education in general around technological familiarity, connectivity, and the constant negotiations of time and space for authentic interaction. Participants and facilitators expressed that this modality held great promise in terms of granting access and awareness to a wider audience, and the expansion of public understanding of death, dying, and end-of-life care at a foundational level. With some adjustments, participants and facilitators believed that LAT could capitalise on its many strengths and overcome barriers to the construction of a vibrant socio-emotional space for LAT content.

4. Discussion

The first aim of this study was to evaluate the impact of the LAT program delivered online by HH. Findings from this evaluation support the utility of Last Aid as an educational initiative to enhance death literacy. Survey and interview data report increased personal comfort in talking about death and dying and engagement with family and wider community networks following LAT. Importantly, LAT encourages citizens to plan for death and to adopt a socially inclusive approach, i.e., encompassing positive practical considerations for their own death but, importantly, advocacy for others within their own social networks. These findings endorse the view that anticipatory care planning should adopt a wide upstream health-promoting approach driven by community awareness raising [18], rather than current approaches embedded in the last few months of clinical care focussing on harm reduction from unwanted treatment. High levels of understanding of Do Not Attempt Cardiopulmonary Resuscitation DNACPR before undertaking Last Aid supports findings from other studies [18]. The latter likely strengthened by increased public debate about DNACPR consequent on the COVID-19 pandemic [19]. Public health approaches such as LAT as tools and vehicles to promote death literacy warrant wider implementation and evaluation across death systems to rebalance death and dying [9] involving families and communities.

Beyond care planning, care-related knowledge and intent to support care (including administration of medicines) had increased following LAT. While survey data post-LAT demonstrated an overall positive trend in confidence in providing care and support at the end of life, only 50% of participants rated themselves as either confident or very confident in doing so. Notably, the proportion of respondents suggesting modification of the 'relieving suffering' module was broadly similar to the other three modules, with no new additional content specifically requested. However, data from the interviews emphasised that participants had limited time or opportunity because of restrictions imposed by the pandemic to apply their learning in real-life contexts. This suggests that the theoretical framework of a carers' ability 'to know', 'to be', and 'to do' [20] had only been partially addressed, in that activation of carer 'to do,' in terms of preparedness for task-related care, had not been achieved. Unpicking whether this is simply due to lack of opportunity or whether LAT is sufficient in developing confidence and preparedness in task-related care is unknown and merits further evaluation. Moreover, while findings support increased understanding of how to support others and knowledge of support available within their local communities, limited new interest in facilitating and/or setting up an end-of-life care group within their local communities was expressed.

Overall, this evaluation demonstrates that provision of foundational death literacy education in social contexts enhances the personal knowledge, skills, and confidence of individual community members, and supports the notion that this personal growth could lead to strengthened community action. Strengthened community action was evidenced by normalisation of death and dying together with promotion of anticipatory care planning. Thus, Last Aid has demonstrable outcomes similar to other public health interventions in palliative care in terms of community engagement [21]. Community engagement is different to community development. Whilst community engagement involves processes by which communities and services work together to enhance death literacy, community development is operationalised [22] in delineated changes and outcomes for individuals and collective communities to build capacity for practical support and social care [7]. Within this study, evidence of development of community capacity to accomplish elements of practical care and support at end-of-life was less clear. Moreover, self-sustaining community development of compassionate communities was nascent, with little expressed appetite to support community-derived support networks. Hence, whilst Last Aid achieves demonstrable impact in terms of community engagement, promotion of community development is less certain, with the COVID-19 pandemic identified as a possible barrier to strengthening community capacity at the time of writing.

The second aim of the study was to explore participant and facilitator perceptions and experiences of the online delivery of LAT. The shift to online learning necessitated by the pandemic paradoxically presented both threats and opportunities to participants and facilitators alike. Online delivery offered an accessible and convenient mode of delivery, enabling greater reach for a variety of populations; this includes those with carer responsibilities or those living in remote and rural populations in Highland. However, barriers to digital inclusion were evident, with concerns about connectivity and digital literacy portrayed. Given that evaluation only pertained to participants who had accessed LAT online, the influence of digital poverty did not feature. Finally, duality in the emotional qualities of learning environments was evident; some believed that face-to-face learning promoted greater emotional engagement with others, whereas online learning enabled a safe space to privately process one's own emotions. Taken together, these findings underscore the salience of social and emotional context of learning beyond the physical and technological context and acknowledge a wide range of learner preference, implying that, beyond the pandemic, delivery of Last Aid should accommodate participant learning preferences and support.

High rates of satisfaction with LAT were expressed both by participants and facilitators. While the content of the four modules was deemed appropriate by most participants, inclusion of culturally competent learning materials to reflect audience diversity, diverse and person-centred perspectives on death and dying such as sudden death, social interaction, experiential learning with equity of learning experience, and access to materials ahead of sessions to ensure participants share common ground at the outset to enable interactive learning, were recommended. Finally, appreciating learners' backgrounds prior to attendance to enable tailoring or purposefully diversifying groups of learners were proposed as possible mechanisms to enhance inclusive learning.

Facilitation of LAT was highly rated by participants, with LAT facilitators perceived as professional and relatable. Facilitators themselves expressed a need for further facilitator training and support to address unmet learning needs, such as facilitation skills training, and the development of tangible resources such as a facilitation guide. Digital skills development and provision of additional technical support for online delivery was also desired. The need for active regular facilitation practice was perceived as vital for skills development and that development of a community of practice for regular debrief and discussion would further enhance confidence and competence in facilitation skills whilst providing welcome peer support. Support was also conceived as securing 'permission' to tailor materials to embed cultural sensitivities and learner inclusivity.

There were several limitations to this study. The sample size for the survey was relatively small. Whilst recruitment issues in palliative care research are recognised [23], additional issues could have impacted on recruitment strategies. First, survey participants might have been overwhelmed with having to complete the short evaluation as part of the LAT which is mandated through licence of the course. Second, survey participants were perhaps unaware of the distinction and purpose between the two evaluations. Finally, the possibility of 'digital fatigue' from having to engage with virtual environments on a day-to-day basis during a pandemic might have influenced decision making to participate in the study.

The study was also conducted with one course provider serving an area with a predominately white ethnic population, with the majority of survey participants highly educated, married, middle-aged women with previous experience of grief and bereavement training, suggesting possible risks of selection bias. The evaluation also measured impacts at one time point only post-course completion, meaning that translation of learning in terms of intended impacts versus actual impacts cannot be inferred. Thus, longitudinal evaluation is merited and would provide additional insight into knowledge and skills decay over time.

5. Conclusions

To our knowledge, this is the first UK evaluation of Last Aid that provides insights into the outcomes of LAT, thus addressing limitations of earlier evaluations [13,14]. Moreover, this is the first evaluation to include information-rich thick data both with participants and facilitators of LAT delivered online.

Findings from this study concluded that there is potential to include LAT as the foundational core training to promote death literacy in communities, with further exploration to integrate/align LAT with other national/global end-of-life care frameworks.

Supplementary Materials: The following supporting information can be downloaded at: https://www.mdpi.com/article/10.3390/healthcare10050918/s1, File S1: Last Aid Facilitator Participant Interview Topic Guide; File S2: Last Aid Training Participant Interview Topic Guide; File S3: Last Aid Training Participant Survey Questionnaire.

Author Contributions: Conceptualization, L.M.; Data curation, K.B.; Formal analysis, K.B., L.M., C.C. and K.M.; Funding acquisition, L.M., S.N. and J.K.; Investigation, K.B.; Methodology, L.M., K.B., C.C. and J.K.; Project administration, L.M. and S.N.; Resources, C.C. and J.K.; Supervision, L.M.; Writing—original draft, L.M. and C.C.; Writing—review and editing, K.B., C.C., K.M. and S.N. All authors have read and agreed to the published version of the manuscript.

Funding: This research was funded by The Highland Hospice, Scotland—Grant Number 1741LM. The APC was funded by the same grant.

Institutional Review Board Statement: The project had ethics approval from the Research Ethics Committee of the University of the Highlands & Islands: ETH2021-0078 [24 September 2020].

Informed Consent Statement: Informed consent was obtained from all subjects involved in the study.

Data Availability Statement: Data for this research are stored on the University's secure SharePoint provided through its Microsoft 365 tenancy. Access to the tenancy, any areas within it, and to the UHI SharePoint implementation is regulated by Active Directory and by specific allocation of users to permissions groups for restricted access areas. Access to anyone not employed by the University is only permitted after a request to create an external account for access to specific areas is approved. These accounts have restricted access and duration regulated by the account requester as well as centrally by the University Archivist and Records Manager and designated staff in the IT department. On conclusion of the research, the University Archivist and Records Manager must be consulted for instructions on how and when to dispose of data in line with the University Partnership Retention and Disposal policy.

Conflicts of Interest: The authors declare no conflict of interest.

References

1. Finucane, A.M.; Bone, A.E.; Etkind, S.; Carr, D.; Meade, R.; Munoz-Arroyo, R.; Moine, S.; Iyayi-Igbinovia, A.; Evans, C.J.; Higginson, I.J.; et al. How many people will need palliative care in Scotland by 2040? A mixed-method study of projected palliative care need and recommendations for service delivery. *BMJ Open* **2021**, *11*, e041317. [CrossRef] [PubMed]
2. Finucane, A.M.; Bone, A.E.; Evans, C.J.; Gomes, B.; Meade, R.; Higginson, I.J.; Murray, S.A. The impact of population ageing on end-of-life care in Scotland: Projections of place of death and recommendations for future service provision. *BMC Palliat. Care* **2019**, *18*, 112. [CrossRef] [PubMed]
3. Kellehear, A.; O'Connor, D. Health-promoting palliative care: A practice example. *Crit. Public Health* **2008**, *18*, 111–115. [CrossRef]
4. World Health Organization. *Ottawa Charter for Health Promotion*; WHO/EURO: 1986-4044-43803-61677; WHO: Copenhagen, Denmark, 1986.
5. Wegleitner, K.; Heimerl, K.; Kellehear, A. *Compassionate Communities*; Routledge key themes in health and society; Routledge: London, UK, 2015.
6. *Strategic Framework for Action on Palliative and End of Life Care 2016–2021*; Scottish Government Health and Community Care: Edinburgh, UK, 2015.
7. Noonan, K.; Horsfall, D.; Leonard, R.; Rosenberg, J. Developing death literacy. *Prog. Palliat. Care* **2016**, *24*, 31–35. [CrossRef]
8. Mills, J.; Rosenberg, J.P.; Bollig, G.; Haberecht, J. Last Aid and Public Health Palliative Care: Towards the development of personal skills and strengthened community action. *Prog. Palliat. Care* **2020**, *28*, 343–345. [CrossRef]
9. Sallnow, L.; Smith, R.; Ahmedzai, S.H.; Bhadelia, A.; Chamberlain, C.; Cong, Y.; Doble, B.; Dullie, L.; Durie, R.; Finkelstein, E.A.; et al. Report of the Lancet Commission on the Value of Death: Bringing death back into life. *Lancet* **2022**, *399*, 837–884. [CrossRef]
10. Bollig, G.; Heller, A. The last aid course-a simple and effective concept to teach the public about palliative care and to enhance the public discussion about death and dying. *Austin Palliat. Care* **2016**, *1*, 1010.
11. Bollig, G.; Brandt, F.; Ciurlionis, M.; Knopf, B. Last Aid Course. An education for all citizens and an ingredient of compassionate communities. *Healthcare* **2019**, *7*, 19. [CrossRef] [PubMed]
12. Paul, S.; Sallnow, L. Public health approaches to end-of-life care in the UK: An online survey of palliative care services. *BMJ Support. Palliat. Care* **2013**, *3*, 196–199. [CrossRef] [PubMed]
13. Bollig, G.; Brandt Kristensen, F.; Wolff, D.L. Citizens appreciate talking about death and learning end-of-life care–A mixed-methods study on views and experiences of 5469 Last Aid Course participants. *Prog. Palliat. Care* **2021**, *29*, 140–148. [CrossRef]
14. Bollig, G.; Meyer, S.; Knopf, B.; Schmidt, M.; Hayes Bauer, E. First Experiences with Online Last Aid Courses for Public Palliative Care Education during the COVID-19 Pandemic. *Healthcare* **2021**, *9*, 172. [CrossRef] [PubMed]
15. Leonard, R.; Noonan, K.; Horsfall, D.; Psychogios, H.; Kelly, M.; Rosenberg, J.P.; Rumbold, B.; Grindrod, A.; Read, N.; Rahn, A. *Death Literacy Index: A Report on Its Development and Implementation*; Western Sydney University: Penrith, UK, 2020.
16. JISC. JISC Online Surveys. 2021. Available online: https://www.jisc.ac.uk/online-surveys/ (accessed on 22 April 2021).
17. Glaser, B.G.; Strauss, A.L. *The Discovery of Grounded Theory: Strategies for Qualitative Research*; Routledge: New York, NY, USA, 2017.
18. Abel, J.; Kellehear, A.; Millington Sanders, C.; Taubert, M.; Kingston, H. Advance care planning re-imagined: A needed shift for COVID times and beyond. *Palliat. Care Soc. Pract.* **2020**, *14*, 2632352420934491. [CrossRef] [PubMed]
19. Oliver, D. David Oliver: Detoxifying DNACPR decisions. *BMJ* **2020**, *371*, m4069. [CrossRef] [PubMed]
20. Andershed, B.; Ternestedt, B. Development of a theoretical framework describing relatives' involvement in palliative care. *J. Adv. Nurs.* **2001**, *34*, 554–562. [CrossRef] [PubMed]
21. Sallnow, L.; Richardson, H.; Murray, S.A.; Kellehear, A. The impact of a new public health approach to end-of-life care: A systematic review. *Palliat. Med.* **2016**, *30*, 200–211. [CrossRef] [PubMed]
22. Sallnow, L.; Paul, S. Understanding community engagement in end-of-life care: Developing conceptual clarity. *Crit. Public Health* **2015**, *25*, 231–238. [CrossRef]
23. Kars, M.C.; van Thiel, G.J.; van der Graaf, R.; Moors, M.; de Graeff, A.; van Delden, J.J. A systematic review of reasons for gatekeeping in palliative care research. *Palliat. Med.* **2016**, *30*, 533–548. [CrossRef] [PubMed]

healthcare MDPI

Article

Is There a Need for Cultural Adaptation of the Last Aid Course?—A Mixed-Methods Study across the Danish-German Border

Georg Bollig [1,2,3,4,*], Mariam Safi [2], Marina Schmidt [4] and Hermann Ewald [5]

1 Department of Anesthesiology, Intensive Care, Palliative Medicine and Pain Therapy, HELIOS Klinikum, 24837 Schleswig, Germany
2 Internal Medicine Research Unit, Department of Regional Health Research University of Southern Denmark, University Hospital of Southern Denmark, 6400 Sønderborg, Denmark; mariam.safi2@rsyd.dk
3 Last Aid International, 24837 Schleswig, Germany
4 Letzte Hilfe Deutschland gGmbH, 24837 Schleswig, Germany; marina.schmidt@letztehilfe.info
5 Katharinen Hospiz am Park, 24937 Flensburg, Germany; hermann.ewald@katharinen-hospiz.de
* Correspondence: georg.bollig@helios-gesundheit.de

Abstract: Last Aid courses (LAC) have been established in 20 countries in Europe, Australia, and America to improve the public discourse about death and dying and to empower people to contribute to end-of-life care in the community. A mixed-methods approach was used to investigate the views of LAC participants about the course and cultural differences in relation to care and nursing at the end of life in the border region of Germany and Denmark. One-day workshops were held, including Last Aid courses in German and Danish, focus group interviews, and open discussions by the participants. The results show that almost all participants appreciate the LAC as an option to talk and learn about death and end-of-life care. The informants find individual differences more important than cultural differences in end-of-life care but describe differences connected to regulations and organization of services across the border. Suggestions for adaptation and improvement of the LAC include the topics of organization and support across the border, religions, and cultures, and supporting people in grief. The findings of the study will inform a revision of the Last Aid curriculum and future projects across the border and will help to include the views of minorities.

Keywords: Last Aid course; palliative care; public palliative care education; citizens; qualitative interview; mixed methods

check for updates

Citation: Bollig, G.; Safi, M.; Schmidt, M.; Ewald, H. Is There a Need for Cultural Adaptation of the Last Aid Course?—A Mixed-Methods Study across the Danish-German Border. *Healthcare* **2022**, *10*, 658. https://doi.org/10.3390/healthcare10040658

Academic Editors: Paolo Cotogni and Robbert Gobbens

Received: 1 February 2022
Accepted: 29 March 2022
Published: 31 March 2022

1. Introduction

Since 2015, Last Aid courses have been introduced in 20 different countries in Europe, Brazil, Australia, and Canada [1], and Last Aid International includes, at present, 20 countries worldwide. The Last Aid course (LAC) aims to educate people about palliative care and end-of-life care, seeks to enhance the public discourse about death and dying in general, and to improve people's participation in end-of-life care provision at home [2–6]. A recent review summarized that Last Aid courses are both feasible and well accepted by people in different countries and with different cultural backgrounds and nationalities [1]. The courses can contribute to a public debate on death and dying and may contribute to empowering people to engage in end-of-life care [1]. Participation of the public in palliative care provision and end-of-life care and the formation of compassionate communities are important in order to secure appropriate support for the increasing numbers of people in need of palliative care at home in the future [6–10]. Previous studies have shown that most people wish to die in their own home and that over 60% of these require general palliative care [7,8,11]. General palliative care provision should be a cooperation of the healthcare services in the community (general practitioners and district nurses) and citizens. Public palliative care education and LAC may contribute to improving palliative care in the communities by providing knowledge and opportunities for discussing the subject of death and dying openly and can contribute to motivating and empowering citizens to engage in end-of-life care [1,3,4]. As LAC is currently implemented in different countries and regions of the world with people from different nationalities, ethnic and cultural backgrounds, the question arises if the LAC should be adapted in order to respect the needs of different cultures and ethnic groups, including minorities and indigenous people.

Therefore, the aim of the present study was to investigate the opinions and views of Last Aid course participants about the course and cultural differences in relation to care and compassion at the end of life in the border region of Germany and Denmark with minorities living on both sides of the border.

In order to reach this aim, people with a variety of cultural backgrounds living in the Danish-German border region were invited to participate in workshops and to be included as informants in the study. The results from the study are intended to inform a revision of the international Last Aid course curriculum and materials in order to make it suitable for people from different cultures and nationalities.

2. Materials and Methods

2.1. The Last Aid Course Concept

The international Last Aid course concept is based on a standardized curriculum grounded in a consensus of a multi-professional working group of international experts from the field of palliative care [1–4]. The idea of LAC was first described in 2008 by Bollig, and the courses have spread around the world after first experiences in Norway, Germany, and Denmark during the years 2014–2016 [1–4]. The LAC consists of four modules of 45 min each and is usually taught during one afternoon or evening in a classroom setting with 6 to 20 participants attending. The main themes of the four modules are: (1) dying as a normal part of life; (2) planning ahead; (3) relieving suffering; and (4) final goodbyes. The LAC consists of educational lectures, practical demonstrations, and practical training (e.g., measures to relieve pain, breathlessness, nausea, and information about locally available palliative care services and support) plus reflection on and discussion about death and dying in general [1–4]. The course includes, for example, themes such as end-of-life care, advance care planning and decision making, symptom management, burial, and cultural aspects of death and bereavement. Table 1 provides an overview of the Last Aid course modules and contents. All certified LAC instructors have experience in the field of palliative care and include nurses, physicians, social workers, priests, hospice volunteers, and others. The LAC must be held by a team of two certified instructors, one of whom must be either a nurse or a doctor working in palliative care [1–4].

Table 1. The Last Aid course contents.

Module No.	Topic	Course Content
Module 1	Dying as a normal part of life	• Welcome and introductions • First aid and Last Aid • What you can do to care • The process of dying
Module 2	Planning ahead	• Networks of support • Making decisions • Medical and ethical aspects • Advance care planning • Advance directive • Medical power of attorney
Module 3	Relieving suffering	• Typical problems and symptoms • Caring/relieving suffering • Nutrition at the end of life • How to comfort
Module 4	Final goodbyes	• Saying goodbye/final farewell rituals • Funeral and various forms of burials • Grieving is normal • Grief and ways of grieving • Questions, comments

2.2. Setting and Participants

The first plans for the current project were made before the start of the worldwide COVID-19 pandemic. Before the COVID-19 pandemic started, three one-day workshops were planned to be held in the German-Danish border region. These workshops aimed to combine two groups, one in Danish and one in German. Both groups were planned to attend a normal LAC in the language of their choice (Danish or German). Afterward, the participants would be invited to join a focus group interview about their views on the Last Aid course and cultural aspects of end-of-life care. Thereafter, a joint meeting with open discussions among the two groups was planned. However, following the start of the pandemic, meetings with many people and classroom teaching were either very restricted or impossible to perform as planned. Therefore, Last Aid courses in the present study were held in a classroom setting or online due to varying restrictions connected to the COVID-19 pandemic. Material for practical training was sent to the participants of the online LAC prior to the online course. Participants were recruited via a network of cooperating and supporting organizations in Denmark and Germany. Invitations to participate were published in the media using different information channels such as newspapers, radio, and social media channels, including Instagram, Facebook, and podcasts. All interested people were invited to participate and comprised of laypersons without experience in palliative care, experts from the field of palliative care, and representatives from different organizations. The workshops usually lasted one day, including a normal LAC in the morning and a focus group interview in the afternoon, followed by the opportunity to participate in a joint open discussion between the German and Danish participants. Figure 1 provides an overview of the one-day Last Aid workshops.

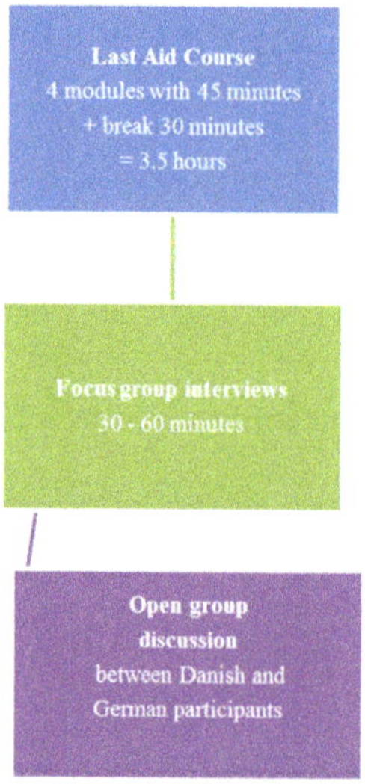

Figure 1. Overview of the one-day Last Aid workshops.

Purposive sampling was used for data collection. All participants of the workshops and Last Aid courses were asked to provide their feedback using a standardized questionnaire. All people who had participated in the one-day workshops and Last Aid courses were invited as informants for our study without any other selection criteria. This approach was chosen to ensure a high number of informants with different nationalities, private, religious, social, and professional backgrounds to provide a broad picture of different views and opinions on end-of-life care and the Last Aid course.

2.3. Professional Background of the Authors

The professional background of the authors was as follows: GB was working both as a senior consultant in palliative medicine at the University Hospital of Southern Jutland in Sønderborg, Denmark, and as a clinical associate professor in palliative care at the University of Southern Denmark; since march 2022 he is a senior consultant in palliative medicine and pain therapy and the head of palliative medicine at the HELIOS Klinikum Schleswig, Germany; MSA is a PhD student at the University of Southern Denmark; MSC is a nurse specialized in palliative care and CEO of the non-governmental organization Letzte Hilfe Deutschland gGmbH in Schleswig, Germany; HE is is a medical doctor (MD) specialized in palliative medicine, and the medical director of the Katharinen Hospiz am Park gGmbH, Flensburg, Germany, an ecumenical center for hospice and palliative care, providing a palliative care unit as well as specialized palliative care for outpatients among other things.

2.4. Data Collection and Analysis

The study was based on a mixed-methods approach [12] with a combination of quantitative and qualitative data from a questionnaire and focus group interviews. The reason for using a mixed-methods approach was to provide a bigger picture and to be able to explore the informants' views more in-depth via interviews. All participants were asked to provide their feedback using a questionnaire (in Danish or German). The questionnaire was an adapted version of a questionnaire that was used in a previous multicenter study with more than 5000 participants on the Last Aid course [13] and included questions on the participants' views on the different modules and the course, a rating of the course modules on a four-point scale, four questions on the informants' views on the course that could be answered with yes or no plus the possibility to provide comments in own words of the informants and information about the informant's age, sex and profession. The questionnaire is available in Danish and German from the first author on request. Descriptive statistics were used for the presentation of the quantitative data from the questionnaires. After having participated in the Last Aid course, all participants were invited to participate in focus group interviews. Two researchers with experience in qualitative research facilitated the focus group interviews. A semi-structured guide for the focus group interviews used the following introductory questions:

- What are your views on the Last Aid course in general?
- What is important for you in care at the end of life?
- What is important in your culture in end-of-life care?
- Do you have suggestions for cultural adaptation of the Last Aid course?
- Do you have suggestions for improvement of the Last Aid course?

The interviews were held in either a classroom setting or online as a video meeting, digitally recorded and transcribed verbatim by experienced researchers and trained secretaries. Qualitative content analysis and qualitative description were used to analyze the qualitative data from the interviews and the qualitative data from the questionnaire [14–16]. Qualitative description aims to provide a comprehensive description and a summary of experiences in everyday language and is the method of choice for a straightforward description of phenomena [14]. Qualitative description is a useful method in mixed-methods research [17] and was used here to provide rich and straightforward descriptions of the participants' views in everyday terms. It is a qualitative method that is close to the data and less interpretive than other methods such as interpretive description or grounded theory.

Quantitative data included the variables described above. Descriptive statistics were used to describe the quantitative data from the questionnaires. Analysis of the qualitative data was based on the qualitative description and qualitative content analysis with an inductive approach and collection of data-derived themes [12,14–17]. GB, MSA, and HE analyzed the qualitative data by repeated reading of the transcripts and establishing preliminary codes from the material. Codes were thereafter discussed between all the authors and revised in three discussion rounds. As the last step of the analysis, GB, MSA, and HE checked the data again and questioned the findings using meta-positions. Finally, all authors agreed on the codes and themes found in the qualitative data material and the interpretation of the data. Data collection, analysis, and presentation of the qualitative data are based on the Consolidated criteria for reporting qualitative research guidelines (COREQ) [18]. Supplementary File S1 provides a detailed report in accordance with the COREQ guidelines and a complete checklist with all 32 items for reporting qualitative research.

2.5. Ethical Considerations and Ethics Approval

Informants in the study were asked to complete a questionnaire after participation in the Last Aid course. They were also invited to participate in a focus group interview. The present study is a part of an ongoing larger research project that aims to evaluate the effects of Last Aid courses and has been reported to the Regional Ethical Committee of Southern Denmark. The Regional Ethical Committee concluded that no formal application was required (The Regional Committees on Health Research Ethics for Southern Denmark; nr. 20182000-33). Informed consent was obtained from all participants who received information about the purpose of the study prior to participation. In order to protect privacy, no personal data other than age, sex, and professional education were collected. The informants could choose whether they wished to provide this information or not.

3. Results

Due to the COVID-19 pandemic, classroom teaching was restricted and partly impossible in some periods during the project period from January 1st to 31st of December 2021. Therefore, a number of courses and workshops were held online. In total, eight Last Aid courses were held on five different dates. 79 people participated in Last Aid courses and workshops between 20th May and 7th December 2021. A total of 38 participants attended a course/workshop in Danish and 41 in the German language. Participants could choose the language themselves and were not divided into groups according to nationality or citizenship. Some Danish participants preferred to participate in a German-speaking course and workshop.

3.1. Results from the Quantitative Data from the Questionnaire

A total of 53 of the 79 participants returned a questionnaire resulting in a return rate of 67%. Information on age was provided by 46 of 53 participants (87%). The informants' age ranged from 34 to 81 years, with a median of 63 and a mean of 60 years of age. A total of 41% of the informants who provided information about their age were 65 years or older, whereas only three participants (7%) were under 40 years old. A total of 90% of the participants were female. A total of 30% of the informants who provided information about their profession had a medical background. Descriptive statistics were used for the presentation of the quantitative data from the questionnaires and the description of the used variables.

Table 2 shows the data from the participants and participants' ranking of the Last Aid course content. Almost all participants rated the course contents as very good or good. A total of 96% of the participants would recommend the course to others.

Table 2. Data from the participants and participants' ranking of the Last Aid course content from the questionnaire (n = 53).

Number of Returned Questionnaires		n = 53
Age group	18–64	27
	65+	19
	No information provided	7
Sex	Female	43
	Male	5
	No information provided	5
Profession	Medical	13
	Non-medical	30
	No information provided	10
Rating—Module 1: Dying as a normal part of life	Very good	42
	Good	10
	Satisfactory	1
	Inadequate	0
Rating—Module 2: Planning ahead	Very good	39
	Good	13
	Satisfactory	1
	Inadequate	0
Rating—Module 3: Relieving suffering	Very good	40
	Good	12
	Satisfactory	1
	Inadequate	0
Rating—Module 4: Final goodbyes	Very good	40
	Good	11
	Satisfactory	2
	Inadequate	0

Table 2. *Cont.*

Number of Returned Questionnaires		$n = 53$
Overall ranking of the course as a whole	Very good	41
	Good	11
	Satisfactory	1
	Inadequate	0
Beneficial for everyone	Yes	51
	No	0
	No information provided	2
Learned a lot of new things	Yes	43
	No	8
	No information provided	2
The contents were easy to understand	Yes	51
	No	0
	No information provided	2
I will recommend the course to others	Yes	51
	No	0
	No information provided	2

3.2. Results from the Qualitative Data from the Focus Group Interviews and Questionnaire

A total of 49 of the 79 participants (62%) joined one of seven focus group interviews in Danish (three focus groups) or German (four focus groups). The analysis of the focus group interviews during the workshops led to four main themes and eight subthemes that will be described in more detail below (Figure 2). No predefined codes were used in the process of analyzing the qualitative data. The four main themes that are shown in the result section are connected to the research questions and the subthemes that emerged from the data material during the analysis of the interview transcripts. Data saturation [19] was reached for the qualitative data from the focus group interviews, including both data saturation for the data collection and inductive thematic saturation during the analysis of the qualitative data.

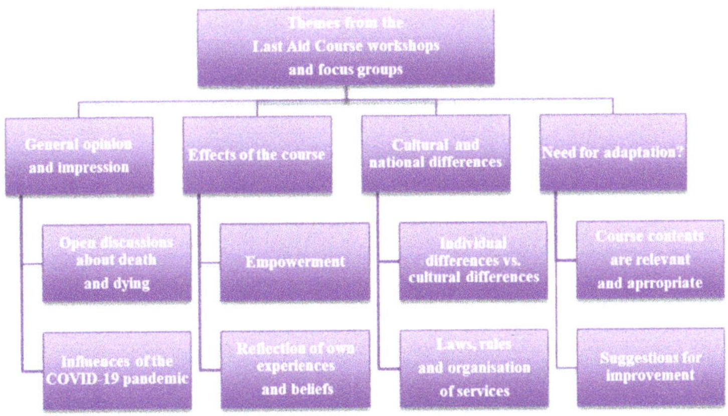

Figure 2. Themes from the Last Aid course workshops and focus groups.

Quotations from the focus group interviews are provided to support each theme and are associated with anonymized codes for the informants. The codes for the informants provide the following information: date of the focus group interview, language (G for German or D for Danish), and participant number.

3.2.1. General Opinion and Impression

Most participants appreciate the Last Aid course and its contents. Many informants find participation in the course meaningful and helpful. Many want to engage in future conversations about death and dying with other people and wish that these topics should receive more space in the public discourse.

> My wish is that it (the topic of death and dying) had more space in the public . . . This has to be integrated into the society . . . (11 September 2021, G1)

Open Discussions about Death and Dying

Participants' experiences during the course are that it is both possible and meaningful to talk openly about death, dying, and care at the end of life. Many participants feel encouraged to talk about these issues with others after the course.

> I think, what is important is, when you come back now and you have your circle of friends, that you simply talk about it (death and dying). (18 August 2021, G6)

One important lesson learned for many participants is the recognition and acceptance that death is a normal part of life and not a catastrophic or avoidable event. A public debate about death and dying can also have an impact on the reflection of one's own life and daily life, including the meaning of life and individual aims people would like to achieve during their lifetime.

> When does the rest of your life start? It is also a question to discuss how you will spend the rest of your life? . . . and probably also to make decisions about my end of life . . . both things (life and death) belong together. (18 August 2021, G1)

Some participants confirm that they gained new knowledge about death and dying in general by attending the Last Aid course.

> I think it (the course) has given me more knowledge about everything that has to do with: what happens to those who are dying?; what happens with the relatives? And which natural mechanisms—both physical and mental- are happening in humans? (11 September 2021, D2)

Influences of the COVID-19 Pandemic

The COVID-19 pandemic has led to major changes in public life, including many restrictions on meeting, working, and traveling. Many people died from COVID-19, and death may have been experienced much closer in their everyday life. The pandemic has also changed communication throughout society and has obviously had a great impact on the traditional Last Aid courses held in a classroom setting. Our informants stated that COVID-19 has made it much more complicated to accompany people. The pandemic has also led to a lack of the possibility to say farewell as needed.

> . . . I have experienced funeral services within the corona year and have seen what is lacking if people are not able to say farewell (5 June 2021, G6)

In order to respond to the need to talk about death and dying and to provide information about palliative care despite the pandemic, online Last Aid courses were established shortly after the start of lockdowns of public life. Although many participants stated that they would prefer classroom teaching, they appreciated online courses as an option in pandemic times.

> The online format . . . I am astonished again and again at what is possible to communicate online . . . I would not have thought that this is possible . . . (5 June 2021, G5)

Some participants think that online teaching is the best option for them as living in rural areas makes it complicated to attend classroom teaching.

> For me, it (the online course) is the first choice. If I imagine travelling from the edge of Eastern Holstein to Flensburg, this is a long journey . . . I have recognized

> throughout the last months that I have attended more online training than I could participate in, in a classroom setting. (5 June 2021, G3)

For others, online courses are experienced as strenuous and only acceptable as an emergency measure or a second-best option for teaching during a pandemic. A much-appreciated option to sustain practical training as a part of the online Last Aid course was sending material for practical training to the participants prior to the online course. This can support practical training despite teaching online.

> The supplement by mail was good . . . the mouth care package . . . that has added something to this online course and has established other possibilities . . . that we could practice mouth care. That was good. (5 June 2021, G6)

3.2.2. Effects of the Course

Many participants stated that they feel encouraged to talk about death and dying, and many feel more prepared to encounter death and to participate in end-of-life care provision at home.

Empowerment

People feel strengthened to talk openly about death.

> I am definitely strengthened to deal more openly with it (death and dying) . . . I often experience that older people interrupt me, because you do not talk about that, and change the topic . . . We just have been talking about children. To allow for their naturalness and assimilate it. Their curiosity, being allowed to ask questions. Yes, I think that is important. (11 September 2021, G1)

Participants learn that there are many things they can do and that simple measures can have great importance in the care of the dying. Some people are motivated to start their own advance care planning and to talk to their family and friends about wishes for their end of life.

> . . . I met my son outside, he was working in the garden, and I have told him that he shall be my representative in the future. That is what I have learned today, how important a representative is . . . who is able to take care of different issues . . . and I will contact a funeral bureau to find out how much that will cost, this interests me. (20 May 2021, G2)

> I have been inspired to try to write a letter to my two girls who are really close to me. They cannot stand to hear about my wishes (for the end of life and burial) because they do not want to face it. (18 August 2021, D5)

Many participants recognized the need for public engagement and volunteering within palliative care and end-of-life care and that doing shopping for others can be a simple thing to do.

Reflection on Own Experiences and Beliefs

Many participants reflected on their own attitudes and beliefs connected to death and dying, and many experienced reflection on the meaning of life, spirituality, religious beliefs, and other philosophical questions as an effect of participating in the LAC.

> The course was good because it encouraged me to reflect, in addition to providing information. It leads to reflection on how we handle things in our family and where we are coming from . . . if you have not experienced it (death) before you do not know how the process works. (20 May 2021, D10)

One participant shared the story of her sister, who was able to talk about the death of her child for the first time after she had participated in the Last Aid course. This example indicates that the course may support the bereavement process for some people.

> I have experienced how important this course was for my sister. She has participated in the (Last Aid) course two or three years ago in Hamburg. She had lost her four month old baby in 1979. After the course, she has talked about that for the very first time with me. Before she had repressed it. She ran towards the emergency doctor with her dead child ... that was an awful experience. But after the course, she talked about it. (18 August 2021, G10)

Many informants stated that they have changed their view on the importance of individuality and think that individual decisions should be more respected at the end of life. Respecting wishes is paramount in the dying phase, where respecting wishes can inform carers of what to do and how to care.

> That one respects the wishes of the dying. These may be totally different. Some want contact and touch; others just want to be left in peace. That it is possible to find out what the person wants and what one should avoid doing although they (the Dying) are not able to talk anymore. (18 August 2021, G4)

Interestingly, some participants attended the course after they had been involved in end-of-life care for others. Some participants stated that if they had participated in the course before they had to care for a dying person, they would have done things differently. Others describe it as a relief to hear that they did it right—as a sort of confirmation and relief that they did what they could to care for a dying person.

> ... to receive a confirmation that things that I have done were right. That one does not need to have a guilty conscience to have done something wrong. In my view, this is a conclusion from this event. (18 August 2021, G7)

One participant described a very moving story about how they stayed with a dying person until the end and the very last breath.

> We knew that my dad was going to die. And he was struggling to breathe ... And then we told him: You are going to die. You do not need to breathe anymore. Then he became more relaxed and died an hour after. But he was really calm ... We sang for him and everyone said farewell ... Just say: You do not need to breathe anymore. (18 August 2021, G7)

Other participants who had contributed to end-of-life care for someone stated that they wished that they had taken the course before they had to care for a dying person.

> I must say that if I had taken the course a year ago ... the situation when I had to care for my dying wife would have been different. Then I would have had other tools to use. I had to find out everything on my own ... Our family doctor was not helpful at all ... Yes, it was a good course ... But it would have been good to know all these things a year ago. (11 September 2021, D3)

3.2.3. Cultural and National Differences

Individual Differences vs. Cultural Differences

Most informants state that they do not experience important cultural differences between Denmark and Germany. Many stated that there are important individual differences between different persons or families that need attention. The Danish participants had not experienced any cultural differences. They thought that most often, rituals related to death were very individual. Some participants described differences in organization and service within palliative care and levels of bureaucracy.

> We are always confronted with questions that are not easy to answer. Fortunately, we do have a regional representative here in Padborg ... I have his number and can ask questions about citizenship (rules and regulations). (20 May 2021, G2)

> What I have heard today is that there are some cultural differences but that I may ask the affected person or his relatives if I do not know ... but I am able to be

> there as a human being and can look at what I might be able to contribute actively with. (11 September 2021, G8)

Different rituals and customs are not only determined by nationality and religion but have many regional and individual aspects. Thus, it seems that they are more individually than culturally influenced.

> I too think it is very much the same in Southern Jutland where we come from ... If one dies at home, the neighbors set flowers on the road the hearse uses. If one dies in the hospital, the hearse will pass by one's house to say farewell, if you may say so. But, I have never heard about that up in Northern Jutland, no, they do not know that (custom). (11 September 2021, D4)

> We sing and we accompany them (the deceased) on the way out. The more people participate the better it is. When the undertaker leaves the room (with the coffin) we stand in line. (18 August 2021, G9)

One informant stated that it should not be too religious.

> In my culture, for me, it is very important for me that it should not be religious. (11 September 2021, G12)

Some participants mentioned the importance of mother tongue at the end of life and appreciated that many people are able to speak both Danish and German in the border region.

> The German-Danish ... the experience shows that many German-born speak in their mother tongue when they need care (at the end of life) (20 May 2021, G2)

Laws, Rules, and Organization of Services

The organization of services for home care and palliative care shows vast and important differences between Denmark and Germany, for example, how often the home care service offers home visits per day. Often people have questions about different rules and services on both sides of the border.

> My girlfriend is often here with me in Denmark but lives in Flensburg (Germany). That is a relationship across the border. We are always confronted with questions that are not easy to answer. Fortunately, we have a regional representative here in Padborg ... I have his number and can ask questions about citizenship (rules and regulations). (20 May 2021, G2)

3.2.4. Need for Adaptation?

Most informants from both the Danish and German groups view the current Last Aid course as complete without the need for other themes, extensions of the contents, or timeframe. They prefer the course to stay as it is.

> From my point of view, the Last Aid Course is very well balanced ... when I imagine that it is made for normal citizens I think it covers everything needed without using technical language. (5 June 2021, G3)

Course Contents Are Relevant and Appropriate

Most participants appreciate the course format with lectures, discussions, and practical training. Most of them view the course contents as informative, complete and do not have suggestions for additional content.

> More could be too much. One is saturated with one day. Probably something comes up on the way home. But you can then read or ask about it, or talk to others. (18 August 2021, G9)

Other suggestions from the participants were that LAC should be offered in the whole country and should become as normal as first aid courses.

> We need Last Aid Courses. They should be as integrated as first aid courses. (11 September 2021, G2)

Suggestions for Improvement

The informants have some suggestions for improvement and want more information and/or discussion on the following three topics: (1) Organization and support across the border; (2) Religions and cultures and (3) Supporting people in grief. One participant suggested that information about Last Aid could be spread through an application running on a smartphone. Some participants think that the course contents are appropriate but would also like to receive written information about the course contents.

> I have no suggestions (to improve the course content) but I would like to get a handout, something that I could take home. (11 September 2021, G1)

Information about organization and support across the border

In general, there is a need to inform the public about options for palliative care provision and support in the local community.

> What I experience is that many relatives are not aware of where to get help, what is available and how to contact someone to support them ... and that they do not need to do it alone, that one can do it as a team and not alone. (11 September 2021, G3)

Some participants would like to receive more information about the option for support and palliative care services on both sides of the border. Both the Danish and German participants mentioned this. Information about the health services and available support is of great importance because many families have close relations across the border.

> There are families that live on both sides of the border where there can be different laws and rules. Especially about things like "plejeorlov" (financiall supportted leave from work for caring relatives in Denmark) for example. (18 September 2021, D8)

Information about Religions and Cultures

Some participants suggested including basic information about the most common religions.

> I would appreciate information about the different religions, short and including basic information about other religions ... It does not need to fill so much; just a short introduction. (20 May 2021, D11)

Other participants highlight that there is a need for respect for individuality and different religions and that individuality might be more important than religion in general. This suggested that one should attend to the individual's beliefs and wishes rather than assuming that a member of a particular religion follows a certain way of dying provided by his/her religion.

> I think that dying is very individual and I believe that it is not possible to cover all religions, then you could take the whole day ... but what I have to say is that one should be open-minded ... to look, to hear because people can tell us something ... although someone might be Muslim it is not clear if he practices his religion ... we may ask the relatives ... I think individuality not just present in religion but also in other areas there are individual differences (that need to be addressed) (5 June 2021, G4)

Information about Supporting People in Grief

Fear and grief are themes that are mentioned by some participants as important. Some of them would like to provide these themes more space in the course. The informants would like to receive suggestions on how to behave in contact with grieving people.

The one who is grieving should not have to walk around in the streets begging for company or care. There should be presence of others. They should take initiative. (18 August 2021, G6)

4. Discussion

The results from the qualitative data show that most participants appreciate the Last Aid course, its contents, and the opportunity to talk openly about death and dying. After participating in the course, many feel encouraged to talk about death and dying with others and feel strengthened to participate in end-of-life care provision in the community. For some informants, participation leads to reflection on their own experiences and attitudes connected to dying and palliative care. In some cases, the course led to an ability to talk about experiences with death that had occurred years ago. Most participants find the contents of the Last Aid course appropriate and fitting to their needs and expectations. Although most informants did not see important cultural differences, some had suggestions for improvement and adaptation of the Last Aid course to the national and regional particularities. These suggestions included more information on and/or discussion of the following three topics: (1) organization and support across the border; (2) religions and cultures; and (3) supporting people in grief. The informants from our study find individual differences more important than cultural or religious differences in end-of-life care. Some participants would like to receive more information about different religions and cultures. As the time for these topics is limited during the Last Aid course, other sources for information from brochures and educational material on the Internet, including written materials and videos, could be used as supplements and additional information [20,21]. In addition, several differences are connected to regulations and the organization of services across the border. Information about these differences should be taken into account for a revision and eventually regional adaptation of the Last Aid course contents.

The COVID-19 pandemic has influenced awareness of death and dying in the public and led to more video communication and online learning. Some informants rated online courses as their preferred option for participation in Last Aid courses. During the COVID-19 pandemic, online Last Aid courses were established in different countries such as Germany, Scotland, and Slovenia. The online courses have led to the participation of new groups, such as younger people who prefer Internet-based learning and meeting option and people caring for seriously ill relatives at home who can not leave their homes to participate in classroom education [1,22]. Most informants would prefer personal meetings, but some informants from the present study would prefer online learning. These findings may indicate that online courses should continue to be offered after the pandemic to provide Last Aid courses for the public for specific groups. Previous research has shown that there are two groups that especially appreciate online LAC: namely young people who are frequent Internet users and people who are in a situation caring for others at home [22]. This encourages organizations to continue to offer online LAC also after the pandemic ends.

The quantitative data from the current study show that the majority of the participants appreciate both the course and its contents and rate the course modules and content as very good or good (see Table 2). The high acceptance and appreciation of the Last Aid course are similar in all studies that have been undertaken. Both adults and children want to talk and learn about death and dying, and more than 92% would recommend the course to others [2,3,6,13,22]. In the current study, the informants had a median age of 63 years, 90% (43 of 48) were women, and 30% (13 of 43) had a medical profession. The high percentage of female participants is similar to a large multicenter study from Germany, Austria, and Switzerland with a percentage of 88% [13]. Currently, the caregiving role in families is still often associated with women, and the results indicate that many women who are caregivers want to be informed and prepared for end-of-life care. This sex disparity is similar to care in dementia and hospices [23,24]. Interestingly first experiences from Sweden have shown a higher percentage of male LAC participants [25]. This indicates that efforts should be made to interest more men in participating in Last Aid courses. This can, for example, be done by introducing Last Aid courses in professional education for police officers, a predominantly male profession, as already is ongoing in Scotland and Germany. Compared to previous research, a higher percentage of medical professionals participated in our study. That medical professionals participate in Last Aid courses has been described in different studies, with a percentage of medical professionals ranging from 27% in the first pilot study [3] to 9% in a multicenter study with 5469 participants from Germany, Switzerland, and Austria [13] whereas the number in present data is 30% of the participants. This shows that nurses and doctors also want to talk about death and dying. The reason for the participation of medical professionals could be both the lack of these topics in professional education or the wish to discuss death from a broader perspective. A recent pilot study has shown that many doctors and nurses are interested in an extended Last Aid course [26]. The results of the current study indicate that there is a need to respect and talk about cultural differences and individual wishes. The current results indicate that these can be addressed within the normal international Last Aid course curriculum without major changes needed. The most important method to address these challenges is to talk about the topic in the group of participants and to include the different perspectives within the group. Therefore, the Last Aid course instructors/facilitators should address these issues related to local situation, surroundings, and the participants' needs and experiences. In order to enable the instructors/facilitators to do that, additional training, reflection, and materials may be used [20,21].

Further research on the experiences, wishes, and needs of Last Aid course participants is needed to provide a richer picture of the need for cultural adaptation of Last Aid courses in other regions of the world. The Last Aid Research Group Europe (LARGE) will focus on this topic, which also will be addressed during the third International Last Aid Conference in October 2022 [27]. Another important topic for further research on Last Aid courses and end-of-life care is the sex discrepancy in attending LAC and the provision of layperson end-of-life care in the community. A pilot study on the experiences of caregivers of palliative patients who have participated in LAC is ongoing and will be completed soon.

5. Limitations

The most obvious limitation of the current study is its focus on just one region, the German-Danish border region, and the minorities living there. Furthermore, people from both sides of the border are mixed by working or shopping in the neighboring country or by family bonds. It might therefore be possible that former cultural specialties might have been mixed too and seemingly disappeared. Nevertheless, as the first study on end-of-life care and Last Aid courses across a border addressing different cultures and languages, this is a contribution to knowledge and a first step in studying this topic in different regions of the world. Therefore, similar studies should be undertaken in other regions and with the participation of people from different ethnic, national, and cultural backgrounds.

6. Conclusions

The results of the current study indicate that the Last Aid course curriculum and contents are suitable for a wide range of participants and can be used for people with diverse ethnic backgrounds. Individual values and wishes seem to be of greater importance than the cultural or national background. More studies on Last Aid courses connected to individual and cultural differences are needed from different bordering regions in the world.

Supplementary Materials: The following supporting information can be downloaded at: https://www.mdpi.com/article/10.3390/healthcare10040658/s1, Supplementary File S1: Report on accordance with the COREQ guidelines—checklist for reporting qualitative research.

Author Contributions: Conceptualization, G.B.; Data curation, G.B.; Formal analysis, G.B., M.S. (Mariam Safi), M.S. (Marina Schmidt) and H.E.; Funding acquisition, G.B.; Investigation, G.B. and H.E.; Methodology, G.B. and M.S. (Mariam Safi); Project administration, G.B., M.S. (Mariam Safi), M.S. (Marina Schmidt) and H.E.; Validation, G.B.; Writing—original draft, G.B.; Writing—review and editing, G.B., M.S. (Mariam Safi), M.S. (Marina Schmidt) and H.E. All authors have read and agreed to the published version of the manuscript.

Funding: This project received funding from INTERREG 5a (Interreg-application Nr. 129-4.1-20 The Last Aid course and minorities need for cultural adaptation—a pilot project for German and Danish minorities across the border).

Institutional Review Board Statement: The study was conducted in accordance with the Declaration of Helsinki and was reported to the regional ethics committee of Southern Denmark, which concluded that no formal application was required (The Regional Committees on Health Research Ethics for Southern Denmark; Nr. 20182000-33).

Informed Consent Statement: Informed consent was obtained from all participants involved in the study. Participation was voluntary, and the informants had the opportunity to end participation at any time without consequences for them.

Data Availability Statement: The data presented in this study are available in part on request from the corresponding author. The data are not publicly available due to privacy restrictions.

Acknowledgments: We thank Eithne Hayes Bauer for the critical appraisal of the manuscript. We thank all participants of the Last Aid courses and workshops, all Last Aid instructors, all our network partners, supporters, and others who have contributed to or supported the project.

Conflicts of Interest: G.B. is the leader of Last Aid International, holds a trademark for Last Aid, and receives financial compensation for Last Aid instructor courses. M.S.C. is the CEO of Letzte Hilfe Deutschland gGmbH.

References

1. Bollig, G. Influences of the COVID-19 Pandemic on the Development of Last Aid International and Last Aid Courses for the Public. Lecture EAPC Online Leadership Pre-Conference Session—Sustaining Palliative Care Services in the COVID-19 Pandemic 5 October 2021. Available online: https://www.eapc-2021.org/eupca-workshop/ (accessed on 31 January 2022).
2. Bollig, G.; Hayes Bauer, E. Last Aid Courses as measure for public palliative care education—A narrative review. *Ann. Palliat. Med.* **2021**, *10*, 8242–8253. [CrossRef] [PubMed]
3. Bollig, G.; Kuklau, N. Der Letzte Hilfe-Kurs–ein Angebot zur Verbesserung der allgemeinen ambulanten Palliativversorgung durch Information und Befähigung von Burgerinnen und Burgern. *Z. Palliativmed.* **2015**, *16*, 210–216. [CrossRef]
4. Bollig, G.; Brandt, F.; Ciurlionis, M.; Knopf, B. Last Aid Course. An Education for All Citizens and an Ingredient of Compassionate Communities. *Healthcare* **2019**, *7*, 19. [CrossRef] [PubMed]
5. Mills, J.; Rosenberg, J.P.; Bollig, G.; Haberecht, J. Last Aid and Public Health Palliative Care: Towards the development of personal skills and strengthened community action. *Prog. Palliat. Care* **2020**, *28*, 343–345. [CrossRef]
6. Bollig, G.; Pothmann, R.; Mainzer, K.; Fiedler, H. Kinder und Jugendliche möchten uber Tod und Sterben reden–Erfahrungen aus Pilotkursen Letzte Hilfe Kids/Teens fur 8- bis 16-Jährige. *Z. Palliativmed.* **2020**, *21*, 253–259. [CrossRef]
7. Murtagh, F.E.; Bausewein, C.; Verne, J.; Groeneveld, E.I.; Kaloki, Y.E.; Higginson, I.J. How many people need palliative care? A study developing and comparing methods for population-based estimates. *Palliat. Med.* **2014**, *28*, 49–58. [CrossRef]
8. Scholten, N.; Gunther, A.L.; Pfaff, H.; Karbach, U. The size of the population potentially in need of palliative care in Germany-an estimation based on death registration data. *BMC Palliat. Care* **2016**, *15*, 29. [CrossRef] [PubMed]
9. Etkind, S.N.; Bone, A.E.; Gomes, B.; Lovell, N.; Evans, C.J.; Higginson, I.J.; Murtagh, F.E.M. How many people will need palliative care in 2040? Past trends, future projections and implications for services. *BMC Med.* **2017**, *15*, 102. [CrossRef]
10. Kellehear, A. Compassionate communities: End-of-life care as everyone's responsibility. *QJM Int. J. Med.* **2013**, *106*, 1071–1075. [CrossRef]
11. Gomes, B.; Higginson, I.J.; Calanzani, N.; Cohen, J.; Deliens, L.; Daveson, B.; Bechinger-English, D.; Bausewein, C.; Ferreira, P.; Toscani, F.; et al. Preferences for place of death if faced with advanced cancer: A population survey in England, Flanders, Germany, Italy, The Netherlands, Portugal and Spain. *Ann. Oncol.* **2012**, *23*, 2006–2015. [CrossRef] [PubMed]
12. O'Cathain, A.; Thomas, K. Combining qualitative and quantitative methods. In *Qualitative Research in Health Care*, 3rd ed.; Pope, C., Mays, N., Eds.; Blackwell Publishing: Oxford, UK, 2006; pp. 102–111.
13. Bollig, G.; Brandt Kristensen, F.; Wolff, D.L. Citizens appreciate talking about death and learning end-of-life care—A mixed-methods study on views and experiences of 5469 Last aid Course participants. *Prog. Palliat. Care* **2021**, *293*, 140–148. [CrossRef]
14. Sandelowski, M. Whatever happened to qualitative description? *Res. Nurs. Health* **2000**, *23*, 334–340. [CrossRef]
15. Neergaard, M.A.; Olesen, F.; Andersen, R.S.; Sondergaard, J. Qualitative description—The poor cousin of health research? *BMC Med. Res. Methodol.* **2009**, *9*, 52. [CrossRef] [PubMed]
16. Sandelowski, M. What's in a name? Qualitative description revisited. *Res. Nurs. Health* **2010**, *33*, 77–84. [CrossRef] [PubMed]

17. Malterud, K. *Kvalitative Metoder i Medisinsk Forskning*, 3rd ed.; Qualitative Methods in Medical Research, Universitetsforlaget: Oslo, Norway, 2011.
18. Tong, A.; Sainsbury, P.; Craig, J. Consolidated criteria for reporting qualitative research (COREQ): A 32-item checklist for interviews and focus groups. *Int. J. Qual. Health* **2007**, *19*, 349–357. [CrossRef] [PubMed]
19. Saunders, B.; Sim, J.; Kingstone, T.; Baker, S.; Waterfield, J.; Bartlam, B.; Burroughs, H.; Jinks, C. Saturation in qualitative research: Exploring its conceptualization and operationalization. *Qual. Quant.* **2018**, *52*, 1893–1907. [CrossRef]
20. Nalaych, H. Addressing the cultural, spiritual and religious perspectives of palliative care. *Ann. Palliat. Med.* **2018**, *7* (Suppl. 1), AB016. [CrossRef]
21. Evangelische Kirche im Rheinland. 2017 Die Wichtigsten Religionen und Weltanschauungen. Available online: https://suche.ekir.de/?query=die+wichtigsten+religionen+und+weltanschauung&referrerPageUrl=https%3A%2F%2Fwww2.ekir.de%2F (accessed on 10 March 2022).
22. Bollig, G.; Meyer, S.; Knopf, B.; Schmidt, S.; Bauer, E.H. First Experiences with Online Last Aid Courses for Public Palliative Care Education during the COVID-19 Pandemic. *Healthcare* **2021**, *9*, 172. [CrossRef]
23. Washington, K.T.; Pike, K.C.; Demiris, G.; Parker Oliver, D.; Albright, D.L.; Lewis, A.M. Gender Differences in Caregiving at End of Life: Implications for Hospice Teams. *J. Palliat. Med.* **2015**, *18*, 1048–1053. [CrossRef] [PubMed]
24. Xiong, C.; Biscardi, M.; Astell, A.; Nalder, E.; Cameron, J.I.; Mihailidis, A.; Colantonio, A. Sex and gender differences in caregiving burden experienced by family caregivers of persons with dementia: A systematic review. *PLoS ONE* **2020**, *15*, e0231848. [CrossRef] [PubMed]
25. Woodworth, J. Strengthening the Social Sustainability of Care-Work at the End-of-Life through Last Aid Public Palliative Care Education. EAPC Webinar January 13th 2022. Available online: https://www.eapcnet.eu/eapc-groups/task-forces/last-aid/ (accessed on 10 March 2022).
26. Mueller, E.; Bollig, G.; Becker, G.; Boehlke, C. Lessons learned from introducing Last Aid Courses at a University Hospital in Germany. *Healthcare* **2021**, *9*, 906. [CrossRef] [PubMed]
27. The 3rd International Last Aid Conference, 28–29 October 2022 in Maribor, Slovenia. Available online: https://last-aid.si (accessed on 28 March 2022).

healthcare

MDPI

Article

"I Needed to Know, No Matter What I Do, I Won't Make It Worse"—Expectations and Experiences of Last Aid Course Participants in Germany—A Qualitative Pilot Study

Chantal Giehl [1,*], Nino Chikhradze [1], Georg Bollig [2,3], Horst Christian Vollmar [1] and Ina Otte [1]

[1] Institute of General Practice and Family Medicine (AM RUB), Medical Faculty, Ruhr University Bochum, 44801 Bochum, Germany

[2] Department of Anesthesiology, Intensive Care, Palliative Medicine and Pain Therapy, HELIOS Klinikum, 24837 Schleswig, Germany

[3] Last Aid Research Group International (LARGI), 24837 Schleswig, Germany

* Correspondence: chantal.giehl@rub.de

Abstract: Background: The need to care for a loved one in a palliative state can lead to severe physical as well as psychological stress. In this context, Last Aid courses have been developed to support caring for relatives and to stimulate the public discussion on death and dying. The purpose of our pilot study is to gain an understanding of the attitudes, values, and difficulties of relatives caring for a terminally ill person. Methods: A qualitative approach was used in form of five semi-structured guided pilot interviews with lay persons who recently attended a Last Aid course. The transcripts of the interviews were analyzed following Kuckartz's content analysis. Results: Overall, the interviewed participants have a positive attitude toward Last Aid courses. They perceive the courses as helpful as they provide knowledge, guidance, and recommendations of action for concrete palliative situations. Eight main topics emerged during analysis: expectations regarding the course, transfer of knowledge, reducing fear, the Last Aid course as a safe space, support from others, empowerment and strengthening of own skills, and the improvement needs of the course. Conclusions: In addition to the expectations before participation and the knowledge transfer during the course, the resulting implications for its application are also of great interest. The pilot interviews show initial indications that the impact, as well as supportive and challenging factors regarding the ability to care for relatives to cope, should be explored in further research.

Keywords: Last Aid course; palliative care; caring relatives; qualitative research; interview; Germany

Citation: Giehl, C.; Chikhradze, N.; Bollig, G.; Vollmar, H.C.; Otte, I. "I Needed to Know, No Matter What I Do, I Won't Make It Worse"—Expectations and Experiences of Last Aid Course Participants in Germany—A Qualitative Pilot Study. *Healthcare* **2023**, *11*, 592. https://doi.org/10.3390/healthcare11040592

Academic Editor: Carmelle Peisah

Received: 22 December 2022
Revised: 6 February 2023
Accepted: 14 February 2023
Published: 16 February 2023

1. Introduction

Dying and death are part of life and determine it in many ways. Most people want to be cared for in their familiar surroundings for as long as possible and ultimately die there [1]. In 2019, 70% of the people in Germany expressed the wish to die at home [2]. Good outpatient palliative care can meet this wish of patients and avoid hospitalization and cost-intensive therapies; at the same time, it can lead to a higher quality of life and better symptom control at the end of life [3]. Simultaneously, a shortage of qualified professionals poses a major challenge to the German healthcare system to ensure adequate and high-quality outpatient palliative care [4]. Palliative care is covered by a nursing care insurance which is called "Pflegeversicherung". It was introduced in Germany in 1995 and is mandatory for members of state and private health insurance schemes. The costs are borne jointly by employees and employers. The "Pflegeversicherung" covers the costs of long-term nursing care for the old or disabled. It also pays a certain amount to those who care for relatives at home and reimburses their contributions to social security.

Family caregivers provide the majority of all care services in palliative care and are significantly involved in the outpatient care of palliative patients [5,6]. Kellehear's 95% rule underlines this point. It states that palliative patients spend most of their time with their families and only 5% of their time with healthcare professionals [7]. In this context, family carers in outpatient palliative care in Germany are often exposed to a large number of critical health events when caring for their terminally ill family members. These can cause both physical and psychological stress, such that they require support needs [4,8–12]. This distress is associated with levels of anxiety and helplessness, as well as deterioration in their overall health [9]. For this reason, many of these people do not feel competent enough to care for dying relatives at home. In addition, they often lack the necessary basic knowledge of palliative care and end-of-life care [13]. Good outpatient palliative care includes family education [14] and especially early training in caring for relatives. In this context, it is crucial to support family caregivers in their knowledge and skill development [4,11,15].

In 2014, Last Aid courses were developed in response to this outlined need. Last Aid courses aim to provide the general population with knowledge about death, dying, and palliative care. They are intended to equip family carers and all interested citizens with the necessary basic knowledge about caring for the seriously ill and dying, and thus to alleviate the fears of the course participants through low-threshold access to information. An improvement of the situation for caring for relatives, but above all for the terminally ill and dying, is to be achieved. The courses are offered at various locations by course instructors who have previously been trained by Letzte Hilfe Deutschland [16]. Last Aid courses are usually held by two certified instructors with experience in the field of palliative care (e.g., physicians, nurses, hospice volunteers, priests, and social workers). The courses are offered in different community settings, such as hospitals, churches, schools, and other public places. They are also offered as part of the education of healthcare workers, policemen, or the military. The course (four modules of 45 min each, a total duration of 3.5 to 4 h, including breaks) offers participants not only the opportunity to acquire knowledge but also to reflect on their own experiences with the topic of dying and death and to obtain a palliative attitude [13].

By 2019, more than 26,000 people in German-speaking countries had already attended a Last Aid course [17]. The number of participants has continued to increase since then. At present, more than 50,000 people have participated in Last Aid courses in Germany, Austria, and Switzerland. Participants are recruited via posters and information in the workplace, newspapers, radio, television, and the internet. The course is offered by different organizations such as the Red Cross, hospices, hospitals, churches, and schools, among others. Therefore, it is indispensable to evaluate the course curricula and to further research participants' experiences. To date, there is limited scientific data on the participants and the effects of the courses offered, as no comprehensive scientific evaluation has yet been conducted. This is exactly the starting point for the article presented here, which proposes the first results of the pilot interviews with course participants as a feasibility study for our main research project. So, it is the aim of this study to optimize and complement the interview topic guide for the main research project.

2. Materials and Methods

A qualitative design has been chosen for the pilot study presented here. It consists of five qualitative, semi-structured interviews, which are particularly suited to understanding lay people's attitudes, values, and difficulties in caring for a terminally ill person. After a successful pilot, a larger main study will be focusing on barriers and benefits for laypersons when participating in a Last Aid course.

2.1. Sampling and Data Collection

The purposive sampling consisted of five course participants who indicated an interest in the pilot study. After the study, information had been sent to the course instructors, and they forwarded it to the course participants. The course participants reached out to the course instructors on their own and expressed their interest in participating in the study. In response, the course instructors contacted GB. Chosen course participants were contacted via e-mail or telephone outlining the research. Semi-structured telephone interviews (one via video call using Zoom per request), approximately 25 min in length, were conducted by C.G. The participants were interviewed individually. The participants are all female and lived in Germany and Denmark. Due to the small sample size, we are not able to disclose further characteristics, as their anonymity would be affected. The interviews took place between November 2021 and February 2022. A preliminary semi-structured interview topic guide was used for all interviews, which evolved as new insights were gained during the data-gathering process. The original pilot interview topic guide is in German, as the interviews were conducted in German. For comprehensibility of the methodology, the English translation can be found in the Supplementary Materials File S1. The existing interview topic guide can be revised and adapted for the larger project. The revision and adaptation of the interview topic guide led to a more in-depth exploration of the topics addressed in the aim of the study in preparation for the main project. Question sets included the most important challenges when administering palliative care, participants' takeaways from Last Aid courses, and reasons for participating in Last Aid courses, as well as suggestions for improvement. All participants provided verbal and written informed consent.

2.2. Analysis

The interviews were transcribed verbatim. The transcripts were reviewed independently by IO and CG. Both IO (sociologist and medical ethicist) and CG (health services researcher) are specialized in qualitative research methods and interviewing techniques. CG carried out an independent analysis of all transcripts using MAXQDA software while following Kuckartz's steps of content analysis [18]. In the first step, the data was coded separately, moving from concrete passages to more abstract levels of coding, including emerging themes. C.G. and I.O. then discussed the codes and C.G. re-coded potentially unclear passages again. Critical reviews and plausibility checks of each analysis of each interview were performed in order to help us to become aware of our own backgrounds and potential bias (reflexivity) [19]. The codings were then reviewed by a third independent researcher to ensure inter-rater reliability. After two interviews, a preliminary coding guide was developed which was adapted continuously throughout the analysis, adding new codes emerging from the material, if necessary. In research group meetings, all findings were critically tested and discussed. In this way, any discrepancies could be resolved.

For this paper, C.G. translated the quotes and back-translated them to eliminate any confusion of meaning [20].

3. Results

The presented results consist of the eight major topics that emerged during the analysis of the interviews. They focus on the expectations and experiences of the course participants and give an initial overview of and insight into these topics.

In general, the interviewed course participants have a positive attitude toward Last Aid courses. They perceive the courses as helpful as they provide knowledge and methods of application for concrete palliative situations. In addition to expectations prior to participation and knowledge transfer during the course, the resulting implications regarding the application are of great interest as well.

Therefore, the results are clustered and presented as follows: expectations regarding the course, transfer of knowledge, reducing fear, Last Aid courses as a safe space, support from others, empowerment and strengthening of own skills, and improvement needs of the course. For a better overview of the topics, see the following figure (Figure 1).

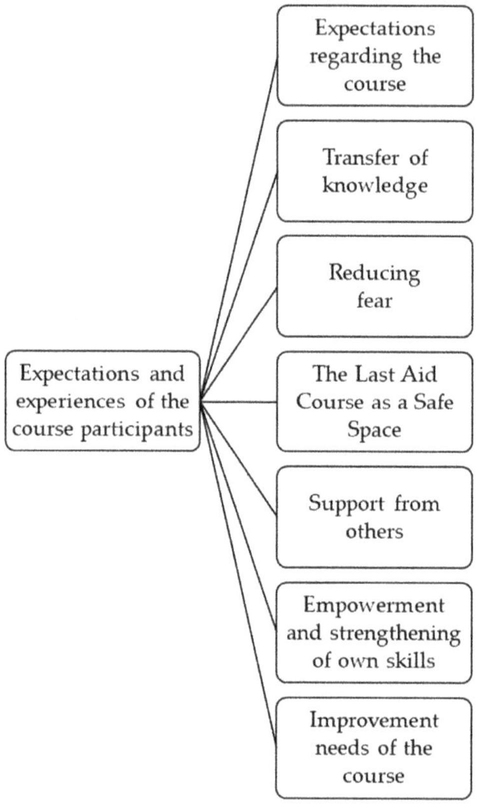

Figure 1. Main topics emerged from the analysis.

3.1. Expectations Regarding the Course

Attending a Last Aid course is based on an underlying motivation, which is tied to certain expectations of the course. The motivation arises from either interest in the topic or a concrete palliative situation, for example at home or with a close circle of friends and family. However, people might also go into the course with no expectations, as they do not know exactly what to expect in terms of content:

> *"Actually, I didn't have any great expectations. I just thought, "Well, it can't hurt!". And somehow I find the topic interesting anyway."* [Interview Participant 4]

> *"I didn't really have any expectations. I went into the course completely free. I let myself be surprised, I couldn't imagine [...] how it would work or what I would actually have to face. I said: I'm interested, but I don't know what to expect."* [Interview Participant 1]

Other people might have a concrete idea of what they want to take away from the course due to a concrete palliative situation and their resulting need for support and assistance:

> *"Because it was already clear that my friend was already in the hospice and I had the feeling that I still needed some kind of support,* i.e., *guidelines on how to interact with her. [...] Well, I somehow lacked the know-how, I'll say. And that was the first time that I accompanied someone so closely."* [Interview Participant 3]

> *"Actually, the expectation was that you would actually receive assistance. In other words, concrete assistance. No? Because when you care for someone at home, it's something different than when they're in a nursing home, so to speak."* [Interview Participant 5]

3.2. Transfer of Knowledge

Participants hoped for said assistance mainly through the transfer of knowledge. One main component was information about physical changes in the process of dying. These were particularly essential for one interview participant:

> *"Especially helped [was to know] how to make it a little easier for the sick person and what's going on physically in a dying person. Because you actually have no idea what happens in the body when it dies. And, yes, she explained that very, yes, more or less vividly and, yes, I actually took away quite a lot."* [Interview Participant 1]

While knowledge transfer is an essential point of Last Aid courses, the implementation of it and how the newly gained knowledge equips the course participants for future palliative care situations were as equally important. Through the knowledge gained, course participants were strengthened in their daily practices. After attending the course, they report approaching palliative situations in a more calm manner, as they now have a more profound background knowledge which gives them security and reduces their helplessness:

> *"Yes, that you simply approach the situation in a calmer and more relaxed way."* [Interview Participant 2]

> *"However, I would actually recommend such a course to anyone who has parents or parents-in-law in the house and who wants to and can take over care [...] because you simply [...] have a slightly different approach than if you have no idea at all [...] what you're facing. You know that everyone dies one day, but, yes, when the time comes, you are not so helpless. And that's a little bit of security, that there's someone there when you don't know what to do, at least just to ask questions, or who comes by once in a while and maybe comforts you."* [Interview Participant 1]

3.3. Reducing Fear

Through the transfer of knowledge and the open discussion in the courses, the fears of participants were reduced and safety in everyday life was promoted. Since the topics of dying, death, and grief are rarely reflected upon in society, there is a lack of knowledge about the last phase of life. This is why the fears of informal caregivers in dealing with palliative situations are present:

> *"What has actually remained is an overall impression and a feeling that this is a topic you don't have to be afraid of, where you should simply deal with it in a lighthearted manner. [...] I think the most important thing is that the fear of dealing with it at all was taken away. [...] In any case, I'm no longer afraid of it. And I think that is also one of the most important things, yes, that you simply lose this fear."* [Interview Participant 4]

3.4. The Last Aid Course as a Safe Space

Not only the content but also the environment in which a Last Aid course takes place is essential. Only in a safe environment can participants fully open up to talk and learn about often very emotional topics that are otherwise rarely addressed in daily life. Therefore, it is important to fulfill certain conditions, such as building and offering a safe space in which the participants can trust each other and the course instructor and also be emotionally supported:

> *"First of all, it was incredibly relieving to sit between people who had the same reason, so to speak, and the same topic and questions and also to be able to allow such a sadness. [...] Well, it was such a protected space, it was built in a way that you could just cry there. Because I was always strong, strong, strong, with the family, with friends, and somehow*

pushed it far away. And there was room for it. I actually found that really moving." [Interview Participant 3]

"There were also very personal things told and you also had the feeling that you can tell everything there and that it stays within the group." [Interview Participant 4]

3.5. Support from Others

Support from others includes, on the one hand, professional support from care providers, such as nursing services. On the other hand, the exchange with the other course participants can also offer support, as they are in similar situations with similar challenges and often similar emotions.

3.5.1. Support from Care Providers

Although the Last Aid course provides basic palliative care knowledge for the general population, it cannot and is not intended to replace palliative care provided by professional caregivers. The interviewed course participants experienced that through their participation they got to know care providers they could contact afterward. This gives them a certain security because they know who they can turn to when the limits of their own knowledge or their own possibilities for action have been reached:

"Well, so what helped me most was actually the security of knowing that I wasn't completely on my own in the situation and that I knew where to get help." [Interview Participant 2]

The same participant reported calling the course instructor, who is also a palliative care nurse, at night for reassurance about medication:

"Then I was able to call [a palliative care nurse] and she told me, yes, do that, do that, do that and then you also have a good feeling that you're not doing anything wrong." [Interview Participant 2]

3.5.2. Support from Other Course Participants

The support from other course participants is expressed mainly through their similar situations with similar challenges. Meeting other people affected by the condition and exchanging experiences with them can have a supportive effect. In addition, participants can give each other tips and support:

"So I do believe that it helps at that moment. So, when you sit with others who are also in that position. And say, man, no, with us we do it like this or like this. Right? And it's difficult anyway to put everyone who dies into one category, so to speak." [Interview Participant 5]

3.6. Empowerment and Strengthening of Own Skills

The aspects described above directly and indirectly lead to empowerment and strengthening of the skills of the participants of a Last Aid course. Through the knowledge gained and the resulting confidence, course participants feel empowered and are encouraged to address challenges in a context that they would not have dared to address before:

"The day she died, I was so strengthened by the course to tell the truth that I managed to pick them all up. I absolutely organized it and ran it so it didn't turn into chaos. [...] I was pretty proud of myself. So the only time I allowed myself to do that was when I was at home with my husband at night, really crying and saying, today she died."

"But I just had the [person] in the back of my mind and everything you heard in the Last Aid course, and then we said: Let's at least try it." [Interview Participant 2]

Strengthening self-confidence is another effect that can result indirectly from participation. Through the exchange with course instructors and other course participants, the participants reported acting more self-confidently and, above all, that listening to one's intuition is often a good way to go:

> *"For me, the course was actually, if I have to draw a conclusion, a confirmation that no matter how you do it, you do it right. So that you shouldn't blame yourself afterwards for not having done this or that. Everyone does it as well as they can. And I found that very comforting for myself."* [Interview Participant 4]

3.7. Improvement Needs of the Course

Although many positive aspects were mentioned regarding the impact of the courses, participants also suggested some room for improvement. Above all, the participants would like more information about local structures and professional networks. Even if you do not need it at that moment, it is helpful to come back to it later if needed. Furthermore, more advertising should be conducted to spread the courses further among the general audience. Various media channels should be used for this purpose:

> *"Maybe just more advertising, like that. Even more publicity. [...] I think it would be very good if the same happens even more in the media."* [Interview Participant 3]

4. Discussion

Although identified through a small number of respondents, the results of the pilot interviews show that the Last Aid course seems to be an appropriate means to prepare relatives for outpatient palliative care, as it increases people's confidence and empowerment. Sample determination was not used based on data saturation. This is a limitation of the results presented here. Further research would be needed to confirm our findings.

However, it was very challenging for the interview participants to talk about their concrete expectations of the Last Aid course. It is known from the literature that people are not prepared for the different challenges that arise within the family due to a terminal illness. Therefore, relatives tend to feel overwhelmed and often do not know how to act in different demanding situations [4,10–12]. This results from the uncertainty about the course of the disease or how an incurable disease manifests itself and how to appropriately deal with the symptoms. Understandably, this can result in confusion and anxiety. Relatives, therefore, often know their need for information but cannot specify exactly what that information should be.

A study by Dillen et al. aimed to identify the components that contribute to an increase in the feeling of safety within the context of palliative care. A total of 197 patients and 10 caregivers (relatives) were interviewed [14]. The feeling of safety was primarily related to the availability and provision of information and education, professional competence, patient empowerment, and trust. These phenomena coincide with the pilot interviews presented here. Through the contents learned, course participants were able to experience security, reduce fears, and strengthen their skills in dealing with seriously ill patients. Gaining security in everyday life and reducing fears are important factors in palliative care because it allows informal caregivers to feel safe providing home care during the last phase of a loved one's life [6,12] and thus reduces their worries in everyday life and about the ill person [5,11]. This could also reduce their tendency to physical as well as psychological stress [5,10] through increased self-confidence [21,22].

According to a study by Hacker, Slobodenka, and Titzer, a closed and safe space ensures the well-being of course participants [23]. It allows people to talk to each other about their challenges and to benefit from each other's experiences as well as from the theoretical course content. These results were also confirmed in the pilot interviews, as the participants perceived the Last Aid course as such a space and were, therefore, able to speak openly about their everyday family situations and the challenges they face. One example of the open exchange is the encouragement that rather unconventional approaches can be just right for the person. These include, for example, taking another vacation or moving to a nicer hospice room.

Support from others in similar situations was perceived by the interviewees to be especially helpful and accommodating. During a terminal illness, carers' daily routines are reduced. The demands of everyday life and illness are manifold. In this situation, many family members often overlook the stresses within the family, be it their stresses or the stresses of others. Concerns about the well-being of the seriously ill person and maintaining daily routines overshadow all other needs. Therefore, it is important to create a different, external perspective on the different dynamics of the disease, to recognize resulting demands within a family system, and to support the caregiver or relative in the process of coping [8,10,11,24].

Nevertheless, the interviewed course participants also need theoretical content and practical support in everyday life that is structured according to general and individual needs, which is in line with the results of the literature. In the last phase of life of a close person with a terminal illness, people have to deal with the changing complex situations in everyday life [11]. These are characterized by the fact that family members are often overwhelmed due to their multiple roles as a child, (spousal) partner, carer, and friend, as well as an unclear picture of how to care for their family member. This makes it difficult for them to deal with their relatives in the last phase of life and to take over care at home [12]. Relatives also have to deal with the unpredictable course of the disease and need close support from health professionals in everyday life [11]. In this context, the negotiation of practical actions between health professionals and informal caregivers serves to support them [24]. Thus, health literacy and empowerment of relatives can be promoted as early as possible, and the specific consideration of relatives' needs can ensure home-based care in the long term [25–27]. This would allow the family to accommodate the wishes of the dying person: to care for them in their familiar surroundings for as long as possible and ultimately to die there [1,28–30]. Similar results were confirmed in the pilot interviews, as the participants wish to have concrete contact persons whom they can get in touch with in cases of emergency or if they have further questions about their specific situation. These contact persons may include general practitioners, nurses from a home care service, specialized palliative care teams, and others. Information about the local structures would be helpful, as would a handout with contact details of the relevant institutions and contacts of support.

5. Conclusions

Overall, by conducting pilot interviews, initial indications of categories were obtained that provide valuable guidance for adapting the interview topic guide and serve as the basis for the main study. The findings of this pilot study indicate impacts beyond just knowledge transfer, i.e., empowerment, creating a safe space for learning, strengthening skills, and managing anxiety. Thus, the interviewed course participants showed a positive attitude toward Last Aid courses. They found the courses helpful because they gained knowledge and methods to use in concrete emergencies and were able to practice them afterward. In addition to the expectations before participation and the knowledge transfer during the course, the resulting implications are also of great interest. Since the number of initial interviews is manageable, further research is needed to answer the questions discovered through this pilot research and to achieve data saturation. Parallel to the interviews with the course participants, another perspective, namely that of the Last Aid course instructors, should also be explored to evaluate Last Aid courses and their effects in more depth in order to provide a richer picture. The inhibiting, as well as facilitating, factors for the participants and lecturers should also be investigated—especially since new web-based formats (online or hybrid) for the courses were established due to the COVID-19 pandemic [31] and could be used more frequently in the future. To explore the new course formats and the other phenomena mentioned above, the initiation of a more extensive academic project is essential.

Supplementary Materials: The following supporting information can be downloaded at: https://www.mdpi.com/article/10.3390/healthcare11040592/s1, File S1: Pilot interview topic guide.

Author Contributions: Conceptualization: C.G., G.B. and I.O.; recruitment and interview conduction: C.G. and G.B.; data analysis: C.G., I.O. and N.C.; data interpretation: C.G., I.O. and N.C.; manuscript writing: C.G., I.O., H.C.V. and N.C.; manuscript reviewing: C.G., G.B., H.C.V., I.O. and N.C. All authors have read and agreed to the published version of the manuscript.

Funding: This research received no external funding.

Institutional Review Board Statement: The presented study follows the principles of the Declaration of Helsinki. The described pilot study is part of a bigger research project on the effects of the Last Aid courses that was reported to the regional ethics committee of Southern Denmark, which concluded that no formal application was required (The Regional Committees on Health Research Ethics for Southern Denmark, No. 20182000-33). For a further larger study, an ethics approval will be obtained.

Informed Consent Statement: All participants attended voluntarily and agreed to the publication of the results. All participants provided both verbal and written informed consent to participate in the pilot study and to process the interviews. All quotes listed here were pseudonymized so that only the research team can attribute them to a specific person.

Data Availability Statement: The data presented in this pilot study are available upon request from the corresponding author. The data are not publicly available.

Conflicts of Interest: G.B. is the leader of Last Aid International, holds a trademark for Last Aid, and receives financial compensation for Last Aid instructor courses. The other authors declare no conflicts of interest.

References

1. Hochheim, E.; Otto, U. Das Erstrebenswerteste ist, dass man sich so lange wie möglich selbst versorgt: Altersübergänge im Lebensbereich Wohnen. *Z. Fur Gerontol. Und Geriatr.* **2011**, *44*, 306–312. [CrossRef] [PubMed]
2. Statistisches Bundesamt. Bevölkerung nach Altersgruppen 2011 bis 2021 in Prozent. Available online: https://www.destatis.de/DE/Themen/Gesellschaft-Umwelt/Bevoelkerung/Bevoelkerungsstand/Tabellen/bevoelkerung-altersgruppen-deutschland.html (accessed on 2 September 2022).
3. Stiel, S.; van Baal, K.; Ülgüt, R.; Stahmeyer, J.T.; Schneider, N. Analysing the administration of an intermediate level of outpatient palliative care in Germany and developing recommendations for improvement (Polite): A study protocol for a mixed-methods study. *PLoS ONE* **2021**, *16*, e0256467. [CrossRef] [PubMed]
4. Deutsche Gesellschaft für Palliativmedizin e.V.; Deutscher Hospiz- und PalliativVerband e.V.; Bundesärztekammer. (Eds.). Charta zur Betreuung Schwerstkranker und Sterbender Menschen in Deutschland. 8. Auflage. 2015. Available online: https://www.dgpalliativmedizin.de/images/stories/Charta-08-09-2010%20Erste%20Auflage.pdf (accessed on 20 December 2022).
5. Becka, D.; Riese, A.; Rychlik, R.P.T.; Huenges, B.; Rusche, H. Stand der hausärztlichen Palliativversorgung in Deutschland. Ein systematischer Literaturreview. *Dtsch. Med. Wochenschr.* **2014**, *139*, 2254–2258. [CrossRef] [PubMed]
6. Deutsche Gesellschaft für Allgemeinmedizin und Familienmedizin e.V. (Ed.). S3-Leitlinie Pflegende Angehörige von Erwachsenen: AWMF-Register-Nr.053-006, DEGAM-Leitlinie Nr. 6. 2018. Available online: https://www.degam.de/files/Inhalte/Leitlinien-Inhalte/Dokumente/DEGAM-S3-Leitlinien/053-006_Pflegende%20Angehoerige/053-006l_DEGAM%20LL%20Pflegende%20Angeho%CC%88rige_4-3-2019.pdf (accessed on 20 December 2022).
7. Kellehear, A. The social nature of dying and the social model of health. In *Oxford Textbook of Public Health Palliative Care*; Abel, J., Kellehear, A., Eds.; Oxford University Press Incorporated: Oxford, UK, 2022.
8. Krug, K.; Bölter, R.; Ballhausen, R.A.; Engeser, P.; Peters-Klimm, F. Burden Experienced by Family Caregivers of Patients at the End of Life: What do General Practice Teams Offer? *Gesundheitswesen* **2016**, *78*, e128–e134. [CrossRef] [PubMed]
9. Galatsch, M.; Prigerson, H.G.; Schnepp, W.; zu Sayn-Wittgenstein, F.; Li, J. Caregiver exposure to critical events and distress in home-based palliative care in Germany a cross-sectional study using the Stressful Caregiving Adult Reactions to Experiences of Dying (SCARED) scale. *BMC Palliat. Care* **2019**, *18*, 9. [CrossRef] [PubMed]
10. Schmid-Büchi, S.; Halfens, R.; Dassen, T.; van den Borne, B. Die psychosozialen Bedürfnisse von Frauen mit Brustkrebs und ihren Angehörigen. *Pflege* **2012**, *25*, 149–150. [CrossRef]
11. Chikhradze, N.; große Schlarmann, J.; Büscher, A.; Schnepp, W. Auswirkung einer fortgeschrittenen Brustkrebserkrankung auf die Familie. *Pflegewissenschaft* **2015**, *17*, 28–35. [CrossRef]
12. Stajduhar, K.I.; Nickel, D.D.; Martin, W.L.; Funk, L. Situated/being situated: Client and co-worker roles of family caregivers in hospice palliative care. *Soc. Sci. Med.* **2008**, *67*, 1789–1797. [CrossRef]
13. Bollig, G.; Kuklau, N. Der Letzte Hilfe-Kurs—Ein Angebot zur Verbesserung der allgemeinen ambulanten Palliativversorgung durch Information und Befähigung von Bürgerinnen und Bürgern. *Palliativmedizin* **2015**, *16*, 210–216. [CrossRef]
14. Dillen, K.; Joshi, M.; Krumm, N.; Hesse, M.; Brunsch, H.; Schmidt, H.; Strupp, J.; Radbruch, L.; Rolke, R.; Voltz, R. Availability as key determinant in the palliative home care setting from the patients' and family caregivers' perspectives: A quantitative-qualitative-content analysis approach. *Palliat. Support. Care* **2021**, *19*, 570–579. [CrossRef]

15. Bollig, G.; Brandt, F.; Ciurlionis, M.; Knopf, B. Last Aid Course. An Education For All Citizens and an Ingredient of Compassionate Communities. *Healthcare* **2019**, *7*, 19. [CrossRef] [PubMed]
16. Letzte Hilfe Deutschland gemeinnützige GmbH. Projekt—Letzte Hilfe. Available online: https://www.letztehilfe.info/ (accessed on 23 January 2023).
17. Bollig, G.; Pothmann, R.; Mainzer, K.; Fiedler, H. Kinder und Jugendliche möchten über Tod und Sterben reden—Erfahrungen aus Pilotkursen Letzte Hilfe Kids/Teens für 8- bis 16-Jährige. *Palliativmedizin* **2020**, *21*, 253–259. [CrossRef]
18. Kuckartz, U.; Grunenberg, H.; Dresing, T. (Eds.). *Qualitative Datenanalyse: Computergestützt: Methodische Hintergründe und Beispiele aus der Forschungspraxis*; VS Verlag für Sozialwissenschaften: Wiesbaden, Germany, 2007.
19. Malterud, K. Qualitative research: Standards, challenges, and guidelines. *Lancet* **2001**, *358*, 483–488. [CrossRef] [PubMed]
20. Tanzer, N.K.; Sim, C.Q.E. Adapting instruments for use in multiple languages and cultures: A review of the ITC Guidelines for Test Adaptions. *Eur. J. Psychol. Assess.* **1999**, *15*, 258–269. [CrossRef]
21. Hudson, P.; Thomas, T.; Quinn, K.; Cockayne, M.; Braithwaite, M. Teaching family carers about home-based palliative care: Final results from a group education program. *J. Pain Symptom Manag.* **2009**, *38*, 299–308. [CrossRef]
22. Hudson, P.L. How well do family caregivers cope after caring for a relative with advanced disease and how can health professionals enhance their support? *J. Palliat. Med.* **2006**, *9*, 694–703. [CrossRef]
23. Hacker, M.; Slobodenka, S.; Titzer, H. *Edukation in der Pflege*; Facultas: Wien, Austria, 2017.
24. Büscher, A. *Negotiating Helpful Action. A Substantive Theory on The Relationship between Formal and Informal Care.*; Tampere University Press: Tampere, Finland, 2007.
25. Mazanec, S.R.; Daly, B.J.; Douglas, S.L.; Lipson, A.R. Work productivity and health of informal caregivers of persons with advanced cancer. *Res. Nurs. Health* **2011**, *34*, 483–495. [CrossRef]
26. McNamara, B.; Rosenwax, L. Which carers of family members at the end of life need more support from health services and why? *Soc. Sci. Med.* **2010**, *70*, 1035–1041. [CrossRef]
27. Hansen, L.; Archbold, P.G.; Stewart, B.; Westfall, U.B.; Ganzini, L. Family caregivers making life-sustaining treatment decisions: Factors associated with role strain and ease. *J. Gerontol. Nurs.* **2005**, *31*, 28–35. [CrossRef]
28. Escobar Pinzon, L.C.; Claus, M.; Zepf, K.I.; Letzel, S.; Fischbeck, S.; Weber, M. Preference for place of death in Germany. *J. Palliat. Med.* **2011**, *14*, 1097–1103. [CrossRef]
29. Gomes, B.; Calanzani, N.; Gysels, M.; Hall, S.; Higginson, I.J. Heterogeneity and changes in preferences for dying at home: A systematic review. *BMC Palliat. Care* **2013**, *12*, 7. [CrossRef] [PubMed]
30. Carrasco Heiermann, A.; Kiziak, T.; Hinz, C. *Auf Ein Sterbenswort: Wie Die Alternde Gesellschaft Dem Tod begegnen Will*; Berlin-Institut für Bevölkerung und Entwicklung: Berlin, Germany, 2020.
31. Bollig, G.; Meyer, S.; Knopf, B.; Schmidt, M.; Hayes Bauer, E. First Experiences with Online Last Aid Courses for Public Palliative Care Education during the COVID-19 Pandemic. *Healthcare* **2021**, *9*, 172. [CrossRef] [PubMed]

healthcare

MDPI

Article

A Survey of Attitudes and Beliefs about Care, Compassion and Communities Networks in Palliative Care. A Preliminary Study for the Development of a Compassionate University

Silvia Librada Flores [1,*,†], Sonia Herminia Roa Trujillo [2,†], Nurlian Torrejano Gonzálex [2,†], María del Pilar García Buitrago [2,†,‡] and Miguel Ángel Lucas Díaz [1,†,‡]

1 New Health Foundation, 41014 Sevilla, Spain; miguelangel.lucas@newhealthfoundation.org
2 Welfare Department, Sanitas University Foundation, Bogota 111321, Colombia; shroa@unisanitas.edu.co (S.H.R.T.); unisanitascompasiva@unisanitas.edu.co (N.T.G.); mpgarcia@unisanitas.edu.co (M.d.P.G.B.)
* Correspondence: silvia.librada@newhealthfoundation.org
† These authors contributed equally to this work.
‡ These authors share last authorship.

check for updates

Citation: Librada Flores, S.; Roa Trujillo, S.H.; Torrejano Gonzálex, N.; García Buitrago, M.d.P.; Lucas Díaz, M.Á. A Survey of Attitudes and Beliefs about Care, Compassion and Communities Networks in Palliative Care. A Preliminary Study for the Development of a Compassionate University. *Healthcare* **2021**, *9*, 946. https://doi.org/10.3390/healthcare9080946

Academic Editor: Paolo Cotogni

Received: 19 June 2021
Accepted: 23 July 2021
Published: 27 July 2021

Abstract: The aim of this study was to know the level of knowledge, sensitivities and training needs regarding care of people at the end of life in medicine, nursing and psychology students/academic and administration university personnel; and to identify skills to perceive and expressed values related to compassion it in their living environment. Method: a descriptive observational study was conducted among undergraduate medical, nursing and psychologist students, academic and administration personnel of the University of Bogotá in Colombia the survey was based on a web-based questionnaire (November 2019–April 2020). Levels of knowledge and sensitivities about care of people at the end of life, educational needs and compassion were assessed. Descriptive and comparative measures and statistical significance tests used, Student's t and ANOVA ($\alpha = 0.05$). Results: 465 people answered the survey; students (82.4%), academic (13.1%) and administration personnel (4.5%). 81.6% knew about palliative care concepts. 64.7% had not cared for other people with advanced or terminal illness. 44.7% talked about death without problems. The most evaluated training competences were humanity, dignity and compassion. Mean levels for compassion by Gilbert's scale were 70.55 for self-compassion, 72.61 for compassion for others and 60.47 for compassion from others. Significant differences were found by age and gender in self-compassion values. Conclusions: the level of knowledge, sensitivities and training needs regarding care of people at the end of life in the University and the values related to compassion enables the development of Compassionate Universities.

Keywords: palliative care; Compassionate University; empathy; community networks; student health services; education

1. Introduction

Care, compassion and community are considered essential elements for the care of people with advanced disease and/or at the end of life and it's necessary to incorporate these concepts progressively in the Universities that also affect the quadruple aim in health from the benefits of compassion: patients´ benefits, population health, professional's wellbeing's and effective organizations. [1,2]. As expressed by Lown et al. [3] "care without compassion cannot be provided and compassion without an element of empathy and help towards the other cannot be well applied". Community involvement is an essential element for person-centered care where care can be redistributed among a range of members involved in care [4].

University is an institution that seeks to generate a series of competencies towards the best practices of professional development and in its relationship with people. In recent years, training in palliative care has been gradually implemented in Universities in Latin America [5]. Among the main topics included in the curricular proposals for the training of doctors, nurses and psychologists in Palliative Care (PC) are: (1) basics concepts of PC, (2) pain and symptom management, (3) psychosocial and spiritual aspects, (4) ethical and legal issues, (5) communication and (6) teamwork and self-reflection [6]. Being fundamental elements of the curriculum, there is a lack of knowledge about students and professionals´ perceptions about palliative care, its relationship with death, its will to care for someone close to them or if they have skills to be empathetic or compassionate with people around them [5].

A "Compassionate University" is an organization that is committed to developing and facilitating the practice of compassion in students and health professionals for the creation of more humane, dignified and compassionate health systems.

"Compassion" can be defined as a sensitivity to the suffering of self and others with a commitment to prevent it and relieve it. As a complex and multifaceted response to suffering, compassion involves sensitivity, recognition, understanding, emotional resonance, empathic concern and distress tolerance for another's pain or suffering, coupled with motivation and relational action to ameliorate it [2]. So, as starting point, it is necessary to identify how each of us relates to care, compassion and community involvement. The best way to build ourselves as compassionate beings is to have our own experience that we are going to die, that we are going to need to be cared for and that surely in our lives we are going to have to take care of a relative or some other close person.

A recent study carried out in Ecuador has shown that the identification of these factors and the actions implemented to promote compassion in the university and create a compassionate university have been beneficial in terms of greater satisfaction of students and teachers thanks to the skills and values acquired during this stage at the University [7].

From this perspective, it is essential to offer students and professionals the best tools and skills to provide this quality care, incorporating these concepts into the curriculum and developing awareness-raising actions towards care that are spread throughout the educational community.

The Sanitas University Foundation of Bogotá, Colombia is committed not only to the quality of teaching, but also to the dignity of people, humanization and compassion. Thus they decided to launch a project of "Compassionate University" together with the New Health Foundation, which has its own methodology for the development of Compassionate Communities (All with you® method) [8] which is also being applied to Universities with the main objective of building a University that recognize for its culture of cultivating empathy, compassion and caring for people who face difficult situations inside and outside the organization, as well as fostering the development of community networks at the University to help from within and without those who are with a situation of advanced disease and/or at the end of life.

Based on this objective of becoming a Compassionate University, a preliminary study has been carried out with the purpose of:

- Identifying the level of knowledge and sensitivities that professionals and students have regarding the care and attention of people at the end of life.
- Detecting the training needs—according main topics included in the curricular proposals for the training of doctors, nurses and psychologists in Palliative Care-, within the university teaching programs related to the care of people with advanced disease and/or at the end of life.
- Identifying the abilities of professionals and students to perceive values related to compassion and express it in their life environment.

2. Materials and Methods

2.1. Study Design and Population

Descriptive observational study. A 63-item web-based questionnaire was design by New Health Foundation. An invitation letter with the link to the survey were emailed to all undergraduate medical, nursing and psychologist students from first to sixth year of education, academics and professionals of the University (N = 650). Data collection was carried out Since November 2019 to April 2020.

2.2. Variables and Measures

The survey was designed in 4 blocks:

- Block 1. Sociodemographic and academic characterization: sex, age, household structure, academic relationship with the University.
- Block 2. Level of knowledge and sensitivities of the population about care of people at the end of life.
- Block 3. Training needs of students related to care of people with advanced disease and/or at the end of life. The competencies were classified according to the European Association for Palliative Care (EAPC) curriculum [6] on PC in Universities.
- Block 4. Assessment of Compassion in students and professionals on self-compassion, compassion for others and compassion from others. The validated Gilbert´s scale was used [9].

2.3. Statistical Analysis

Descriptive and comparative frequency measures were used by blocks of contents of the survey and by type of profile of respondents. Student's t-statistical significance tests and one-way ANOVA were performed to compare the mean values on the compassion scale in the distribution by sex, age and professional profile. An α value of 0.05 was established to determine statistical significance. The SPSS program was used for statistical analyzes.

All respondents agreed to the use and treatment of the data for the research.

2.4. Ethical Considerations

Participation and acceptance of the survey was requested through written consent for the use of the data for research purposes, guaranteeing the anonymity and confidentiality of the information to all participants. The study took into account the Declaration of Helsinki and resolution 008430 of the Ministry of Health [10]. The data used were for the exclusive use of the investigation and the identity of the individuals was protected according to Law 1581 [11].

3. Results

3.1. Sociodemographic and Academic Characterization of the Study Population

A total of 465 surveys corresponding to university students, academics and professionals of University were collected, representing a response rate of 71.5%. 74% women, 26% men. Mean age: 24 years (standard deviation: 10,003). 74.6% couple without children.

The highest participation in the surveys were students with a total of 383 participants (82.4%). 167 were nursing students (43.6%), 128 medical students (33.4%) and 77 psychology students (20.2%). The highest representation of students corresponded to first-year students (48.8% of cases), followed by third-year students (20.6%).

The university academics and others professionals were represented by 61 academics (13.1% of the population), of which 26.2% were nursing academics, 24.6% psychology academics and 23% medicine academics. The professional corresponding to administration represented 4.5% of the professionals. The Mean dedication of the academics at the university was 4.5 years. The sociodemographic and academic characterization of study population is represented in Table 1.

Table 1. Sociodemographic and academic characterization of the study population.

Variables	Total Sample *N*: 465	%
Sociodemographic characterization		
Sex		
Male	121	26%
Female	344	74%
Age group		
• 18–39 years	412	88.6%
• 40–59 years	49	10.5%
• Over 60 years	4	0.9%
Mean age	24	
Standard deviation	10,003	
Household structure		
Couple without children	347	74.6%
Married with children	29	6.2%
Single with children	25	5.4%
Cohabitant without children	22	4.7%
Cohabitant with children	17	3.7%
Married without children	14	3%
Separated with children	6	1.3%
Separated without children	5	1.1%

Students

Students *n* = 383 (82.4%)	**Total students (%)**	**(Semester 1/2)**	**(Semester 3/4)**	**(Semester 5/6)**	**(Semester 7/8)**	**(Semester 9/10)**	**(Semester 11/12)**
Medicine Students	**128** (33.4%)	69 (53.8%)	24 (18.5%)	10 (7.6%)	8 (5.9%)	9 (6.7%)	10 (7.6%)
Psychology Students	77 (20.2%)	51 (65.8%)	10 (13.2%)	9 (11.8%)	7 (9.2%)	0 (0.0%)	0 (0.0%)
Nursing Students	**167** (43.6%)	62 (37.1%)	27 (16.2%)	58 (34.7%)	20 (12.0%)	0 (0.0%)	0 (0.0%)
No specification	**11** (2.8%)						
Total	**383 (100%)**	181 (48.8%)	61 (16.3%)	77 (20.6%)	35 (9.3%)	9 (2.3%)	10 (2.6%)

Teachers	**Total Sample**	**%**
Professor of the University of Nursing	16	26.2%
Professor at the University of Psychology	15	24.6%
Professor at the University of Medicine	21	23.0%
No job specification	9	14.8%
Total Teachers	***n* = 61**	**13.1%**
Other professionals at the University		
Academic directors	7	33.3%
Operational area	5	23.9%
Academic support executive and authority area	4	19.0%
Administration area	3	14.3%
No job specification	2	9.5%
Total Other University professionals	*n* = 21	4.5%

3.2. Level of Knowledge and Sensitivities of the Population about Care of People at the End of Life

363 people (81.6%) knew palliative care concepts, most of them as part of their university education or their profession (67.2%), followed by family members (13.6%), friends (9.1%), social media (8.8%), personal experience (7.4%) or other reasons (3.1%).

The people who reported knowing how to give a definition of palliative care associated this concept with the provision of palliative care for adults and pediatric population in a situation of chronic, advanced and/or end-of-life disease, to the decrease in suffering, improvement of the quality of life, state of agony and end of life, and the privilege of caring and being cared for people.

72.9% (339 people) reported having had previous contact with palliative care due to the experiences of patients or close relatives. Of these, 255 (77.3%) received palliative care. In 79.3% of the cases, they were valued as useful both for the person at the end of their life and for their family and their entire care network.

64.7% of the study population had not cared for people with advanced or terminal illness. 91.2% would be willing to take care of a person who was not a relative or close friend. 50.8% of those surveyed indicated that they felt capable of accompanying a person at the end of their life.

Among the 465 people who answered the question: "How many people do you think would be able to take care of you if an illness were to overtake you at this time in your life?" 67.5% (313) indicated that fewer than 5 people would be involved in their care, 24.6% (114) between 5 and 9 people and 7.9% (38) more than 10 people.

49.2% did not feel capable of accompanying a person at the end of their life. Those who indicated feeling capable were those who had received some training in CP.

44.7% of those surveyed (n = 208) referred to talking about death without a problem, 24.5% do so very rarely, 20.9% sometimes, but with people from the environment and professional profile, 6.7% when it occurs in a way close and 3.2% never.

The level of knowledge and sensitivities of the population about the care of people at the end of life is represented in Table 2.

Table 2. Level of knowledge and sensitivities of the population about the care of people at the end of life.

Knowledge and Sensitivities towards Palliative Care	YES						NO					
	Medicine	Psychology	Nursing	Teachers	Other Professionals	Total	Medicine	Psychology	Nursing	Teachers	Other Professionals	Total
Do you know what palliative care is? (*n*: 445)	110 30.3%	50 13.8%	139 38.3%	46 12.7%	18 5.0%	**363 *** **81.6%**	18 4.8%	27 7.1%	28 7.4%	6 1.6%	3 0.8%	**82 **** **18.4%**

Who Do You Consider They are Aimed at (*n*: 442)	Medicine	Psychology	Nursing	Teachers	Other Professionals	Total
- To the entire population (adult and pediatric population) with advanced disease and/or at the end of life	110 24.9%	62 14.0%	150 33.9%	47 10.6%	15 3.4%	**384** **86.9%**
- Only to the adult population with advanced disease and/or at the end of life	17 3.8%	13 2.9%	16 3.6%	4 0.9%	2 0.5%	**52** **11.8%**
- Only to the pediatric population with advanced disease and/or at the end of life	1 0.2%	2 0.5%	1 0.2%	1 0.2%	1 0.2%	**6** **1.4%**

Concepts Associated with Palliative Care (*n* = 1115 Multiple Responses)

	If you know palliative care (*n* = 950)	Does not know palliative care (*n* = 165)
- Death	105 (11.1%)	22 (13.3%)
- State of agony and end of life	164 (17.3%)	37 (22.4%)
- Decrease in suffering	276 (29.1%)	41 (24.8%)
- Quality of life	263 (27.7%)	38 (23%)
- The privilege of caring and being cared for	138 (14.5%)	26 (15.8%)
- Other concepts	4 (0.4%)	1 (0.6)

Experiences of Contact with People in Palliative Care

Temporality	Yes = 339 (72.9%)				No = 126 (27.1%)
	Nowadays	**In the last month**	In the last year	More than 1 year ago	
	41 (12.1%)	**27 (8.0%)**	97 (28.6%)	174 (51.3%)	

Relationship	Patient	Grandparent	Uncle	Father mother	Friend	Work partner	Sibling	Spouse/Partner	Other
	95 (28.9%)	92 (28.0%)	52 (15.8%)	30 (9.1%)	25 (7.6%)	7 (2.1%)	4 (1.2%)	2 (0.6%)	22 (6.7%)

Received Palliative Care

Usefulness of CP	Yes = 255 (77.3%)				No = 75 (22.7%)
	Yes and I only considered it useful for the person who was going through this disease process	Yes, and I considered them useful both for the person with the disease, as well as for their family and their entire care network.	Yes and I considered them useful, but only for the family and their care network.	Do not consider them useful	
	36 (145.9%)	191 (79.3%)	4 (1.7%)	10 (4.1)	

Table 2. *Cont.*

Knowledge and Sensitivities towards Palliative Care	YES						NO					
	Medicine	**Psychology**	**Nursing**	**Teachers**	**Other Professionals**	**Total**	**Medicine**	**Psychology**	**Nursing**	**Teachers**	**Other Professionals**	**Total**
Experiences of Caring for Someone at the End of Life												
Have cared for a person at the end of life						**Yes = 164 (35.3%)**						**No = 301 (64.7%)**
Hours of dedication to care Mean of 7 h of dedication	<6 h		6–11 h			12–17 h		18–23 h		24 h		
	41 (51.7%)		27 (23.1%)			(18.2%)		97 (1.4%)		(5.6%)		
People involved in care Mean of 8 people involved	<5 people		5–9 people			10–14 people		15–19 people		> 20 people		
	55 (41.4%)		52 (39.1%)			10 (7.5%)		5 (3.8%)		11 (8.3)		
Willingness and Ability to Care												
Willingness to take care of a person other than the closest family or circle of friends				**Si = 424 (91.2%**						**No = 41 (8.8%)**		
You feel able to care for a person with advanced disease				**Yes = 236 (50.8%)**						**No: 229 (49.2%)**		
Care Network (*n* = 465)	**Less Than 5 People**		**Between 5 and 9 People**		**Eetween 10 and 14 People**		**Between 15 and 19 People**		**Between 20 and 24 People**		**More Than 25 People**	
	313 (67.5%)		114 (24.6%)		28 (6.0%)		2 (0.4%)		6 (1.3%)		2 (0.2%)	
Talk about death (*n* = 465)			**Yes, Since I Have No Problem and I Talk About it When I Want**		**Yes, But When It Happens to Me Closely**		**Sometimes, but with People from my Environment and Professional Profile**		**Seldom**		**Never**	
			208 (44.7%)		31 (6.7%)		97 (20.9%)		114 (24.5%)		15 (3.2%)	

* Without data specification (15). ** Without data specification (5).

3.3. Students Training Needs Related to Caring of People with Advanced Disease and/or at the End of Life

47.7% of the students reported not having previous training in palliative care. 52.3% whom had training in palliative care, 32.8% had attended it through training at the university, 8.7% through continuous training, 3.4% in postgraduate courses and 7.4% other training outside the university.

The highest training in Palliative Care at the University was received by nursing students (50%), followed by medical students (26.7%) and psychology students (13%).

Nursing students indicated that they would prefer to dedicate themselves professionally to PC (58.1%), followed by medicine (43%) and very closely by psychology (42.9%).

The subjects received in palliative care and the interest in receiving training in these subjects among the students of the different faculties and the professors are represented in the Table 3.

The training competences most valued by students, academics and professionals of the university was Humanity, Dignity and Compassion, which was considered by 70.5% of those surveyed as a high priority. (Figure 1).

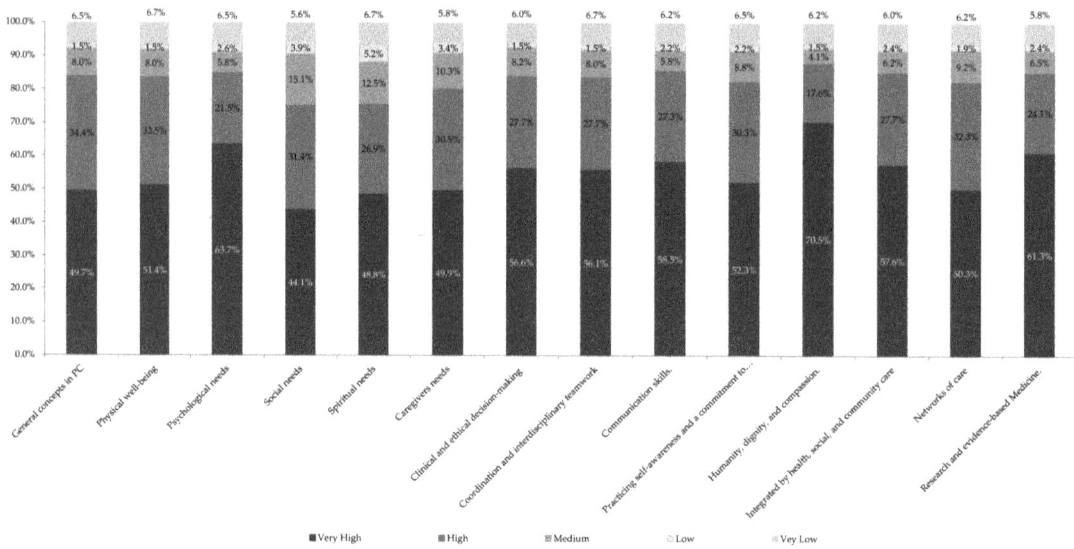

Figure 1. Priority level for competences to be developed in training related to Palliative Care.

Table 3. Topics received and interest in palliative care.

	Training Received in PC						Interest in PC Themes					
	Medicine n = 119		Psychology n = 76		Nursing n = 167		Academics n = 61			Total Students n = 383		
	YES	NO	YES	NO	YES	NO	High	Medium	Low	High	Medium	Low
General concepts	69 (58.0%)	50 (42.0%)	36 (47.4%)	40 (52.6%)	116 (69.5%)	51 (30.5%)	70.5%	27.9%	1.6%	80.9%	16.7%	2.3%
Rights, Policies	42 (35.3%)	77 (64.7%)	36 (47.4%)	40 (52.6%)	108 (64.7%)	59 (35.3%)	55.7%	36.1%	8.2%	70.5%	25.6%	3.9%
Oncological PC	28 (23.5%)	91 (76.5%)	9 (11.8%)	67 (88.2%)	84 (50.3%)	83 (49.7%)	54.1%	31.1%	14.8%	77.5%	17.5%	5.0%
Non-Oncological PCs	29 (24.4%)	90 (75.6%)	12 (15.8%)	64 (84.2%)	89 (53.3%)	78 (46.7%)	59.0%	32.8%	8.2%	75.2%	20.6%	4.2%
Pediatric PC	19 (16.0%)	100 (84.0%)	9 (11.8%)	67 (88.2%)	35 (21.0%)	132 (79.0%)	55.7%	29.5%	14.8%	80.4%	15.4%	4.2%
Needs people end of life	47 (39.5%)	72 (60.5%)	26 (34.2%)	50 (65.8%)	104 (62.3%)	63 (37.7%)	62.3%	32.8%	4.9%	80.2%	15.9%	3.9%
Physical symptoms	34 (28.6%)	85 (71.4%)	12 (15.8%)	64 (84.2%)	105 (62.9%)	62 (37.1%)	62.3%	27.9%	9.8%	83.8%	12.3%	3.9%
Nursing care	21 (17.6%)	98 (82.4%)	10 (13.2%)	66 (86.8%)	126 (75.4%)	41 (24.6%)	42.6%	27.9%	29.5%	66.3%	26.1%	7.6%
End of life emergencies	20 (16.8%)	99 (83.2%)	6 (7.9%)	70 (92.1%)	67 (40.1%)	100 (59.9%)	50.8%	31.1%	18.0%	80.7%	14.1%	5.2%
Last days	24 (20.2%)	95 (79.8%)	9 (11.8%)	67 (88.2%)	88 (52.7%)	79 (47.3%)	62.3%	29.5%	8.2%	76.2%	18.3%	5.5%
Death and mourning	41 (34.5%)	78 (65.5%)	26 (34.2%)	50 (65.8%)	109 (65.3%)	58 (34.7%)	70.5%	27.9%	1.6%	79.9%	14.1%	6.0%
Psychological aspects, communication	39 (32.8%)	80 (67.2%)	21 (27.6%)	55 (72.4%)	107 (64.1%)	60 (35.9%)	72.1%	26.2%	1.6%	79.9%	15.4%	4.7%
Social aspects	30 (25.2%)	89 (74.8%)	16 (21.1%)	60 (78.9%)	100 (59.9%)	67 (40.1%)	62.3%	34.4%	3.3%	72.3%	22.5%	5.2%
Cultural and spiritual aspects	29 (24.4%)	90 (75.6%)	16 (21.1%)	60 (78.9%)	95 (56.9%)	72 (43.1%)	66.9%	27.3%	5.8%	67.6%	26.6%	5.7%
Community aspects and networks	33 (27.7%)	86 (72.3%)	14 (18.4%)	62 (81.6%)	102 (61.1%)	65 (38.9%)	63.9%	32.8%	3.3%	70.5%	23.5%	6.0%
Social awareness	36 (30.3%)	83 (69.7%)	20 (26.3%)	56 (73.7%)	86 (51.5%)	81 (48.5%)	60.7%	36.1%	3.3%	70.2%	24.5%	5.2%
Volunteer programs	31 (26.1%)	88 (73.9%)	11 (14.5%)	65 (85.5%)	55 (32.9%)	112 (67.1%)	52.5%	39.3%	8.2%	74.2%	19.1%	6.8%
Integrated care	30 (25.2%)	89 (74.8%)	8 (10.5%)	68 (89.5%)	73 (43.7%)	94 (56.3%)	60.7%	34.4%	4.9%	69.5%	24.5%	6.0%
Tools to care	28 (23.5%)	91 (76.5%)	11 (14.5%)	65 (85.5%)	97 (58.1%)	70 (41.9%)	70.5%	24.6%	4.9%	79.4%	15.7%	5.0%
Compassionate, active listening, emotional	48 (40.3%)	71 (59.7%)	20 (26.3%)	56 (73.7%)	106 (63.5%)	61 (36.5%)	75.4%	23.0%	1.6%	84.3%	11.0%	4.7%
Investigation and evaluation	17 (14.3%)	102 (85.7%)	12 (15.8%)	64 (84.2%)	79 (47.3%)	88 (52.7%)	62.3%	29.5%	8.2%	77.5%	17.2%	5.2%
Management and organization	17 (14.3%)	102 (85.7%)	5 (6.6%)	71 (93.4%)	76 (45.5%)	91 (54.5%)	50.8%	41.0%	8.2%	71.3%	22.5%	6.3%
Networks and Compassionate Communities	20 (16.8%)	99 (83.2%)	8 (10.5%)	68 (89.5%)	67 (40.1%)	100 (59.9%)	55.7%	41.0%	3.3%	71.8%	23.0%	5.2%
Public politics	19 (16.0%)	100 (84.0%)	7 (9.2%)	69 (90.8%)	79 (47.3%)	88 (52.7%)	59.0%	34.4%	6.6%	67.9%	25.3%	6.8%
Rights of care	38 (31.9%)	81 (68.1%)	16 (21.1%)	60 (78.9%)	103 (61.7%)	64 (38.3%)	68.9%	29.5%	1.6%	80.7%	14.1%	5.2%

3.4. *Self-Compassion, Compassion for Others, Compassion from Others; Gilbert's Scale*

For a total of 465 people who answered the compassion survey, a Mean value of 72.61 was obtained for compassion for others, 70.55 for self-compassion and 60.47 for compassion from others.

Mean values on the compassion scale are represented on the Figure 2.

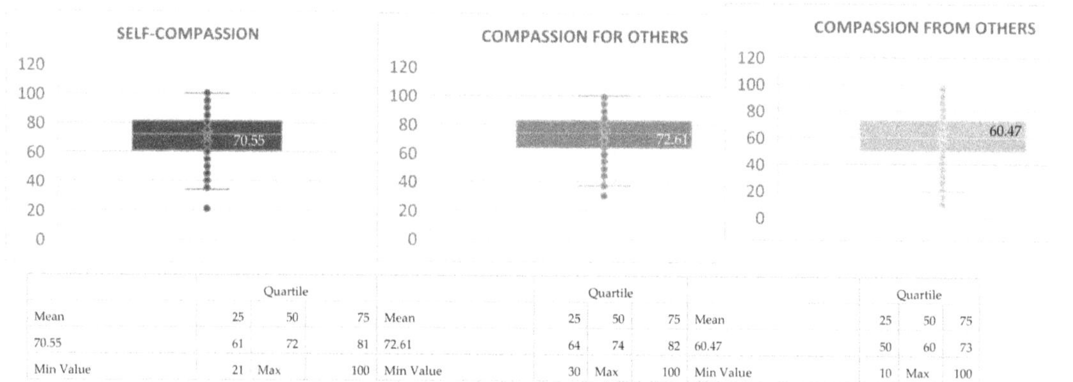

Figure 2. Gilbert´s compassion scale.

Men scored higher on self-compassion (Mean 73.04), compassion for others (73) and compassion from others (61.30).

Self-compassion, compassion for others and compassion from others were most valued in people aged 60 and over.

Compassion for others was the most valued among psychology students (74.94), self-compassion the most valued among teachers (73.77) and compassion from others among nursing students (61.82).

Significant differences were found for gender and age in self-compassion values ($p = 0.028$, $p = 0.039$, respectively). No significant differences were obtained in the values of compassion by academic profile. The results of the compassion and p-values surveys are represented in Table 4.

Table 4. Compassionate engagement and actions scale.

Sex	**Self-Compassion**			**Compassion for Others**			**Compassion from Others**		
	Mean	**Eng**	**Act**	**Mean**	**Eng**	**Act**	**Mean**	**Eng**	**Act**
Male	73.04	41.75	31.28	73	42.74	30.25	61.30	35.57	25.73
Female	69.67	39.91	29.75	72.47	42.03	30.44	60.18	34.71	25.46
	SELF-COMPASSION			COMPASSION FOR OTHER $t = -0.356$ p-value = 0.722			COMPASSION FROM OTHERS $t = -0.612$ p-value = 0.541		
Age	**Self-Compassion**			**Compassion for Others**			**Compassion from Others**		
	Mean	**Eng**	**Act**	**Mean**	**Eng**	**Act**	**Mean**	**Eng**	**Act**
18–39 years	70.32	40.19	30.13	72.29	41.98	30.30	60.46	34.86	25.59
40–59 years	71.71	41.69	30.02	74.53	43.81	30.71	59.83	35.12	24.71
> 60 years	79.75	45.5	34.25	81.75	46.25	35.5	69.75	40	29.75
	SELF-COMPASSION F = 1.012 p-value = 0.039 *			COMPASSION FOR OTHER F = 2.138 p-value = 0.119			COMPASSION FROM OTHERS F = 1.331 p-value = 0.265		

Table 4. *Cont.*

	Self-Compassion			Compassion for Others			Compassion from Others		
	Mean	**Engagement**	**Action**	**Mean**	**Engagement**	**Action**	**Mean**	**Engagement**	**Action**
Academics	73.77	43.14	30.62	72.93	43.09	29.83	59.01	34.42	24.59
Medicine Student	69.03	39.23	29.79	72.36	42.10	30.25	59.95	34.04	25.91
Psychology Student	71.59	40.23	31.35	74.94	43.42	31.52	58.89	33.98	24.90
Nursing Student	69.41	39.86	29.55	71.29	41.08	30.20	61.82	35.92	25.89
	Self-Compassion F = 3.327 *p*-value = 0.364 *			Compassion for Other F = 1.423 *p*-value = 0.242			Compassion from Others F = 0.607 *p*-value = 0.545		

* statistically significant.

4. Discussion

We offer some data on compassion and palliative care among university students, academics and other professionals that can help on improving the skills and self-awareness of future health care professionals [12]. One of two doctors and patients reports that care is not compassionate despite being a preferred element in the care and relief of suffering [13]. The practice of compassion is beneficial and even more so in the most vulnerable moments such as advanced disease and at the end of life. The benefits of compassion in PC have been evidenced by Brito and Librada [2], impacting the quadruple health goal: patients´ benefits, population health, professional's wellbeing's and effective organizations. In this way, the University is the most suitable environment to create compassionate professionals and leaders who act through a more humane, dignified and compassionate treatment in the care of people, especially at the end of life.

This study has been carried out with the objective of identifying the sensitivities and knowledge of the university community towards care, compassion and the community. The development of this baseline diagnosis in students, academics and professionals of the University it´s the first stages for the development of a Compassionate University. Results will allow designing actions at the University aimed at raising awareness, training and research in this field.

Training in Palliative Care is an essential component in the faculties of health sciences, even more so when death is a natural process of life that all people are going to encounter. According to Latin American Atlas of PC [14], only 30% of the Universities in Latin American countries teach these topics, and there is also a disproportion of the contents taught or teaching hours. In our study, the greatest knowledge about palliative care in students comes from studies at the University. Even so, up to 18.4% of those surveyed indicated that they did not know what palliative care is, associating this concept in a greater proportion with death, with the state of agony and care. Those who expressed having knowledge in PC, associated it with the decrease in suffering, the improvement of the quality of life, care and to a lesser extent with the state of agony and death [15].

91.2% of those surveyed would be willing to take care of a person who was not a relative or close friend, although up to 49.2% indicated that they would not feel capable of doing so. Sometimes half of the graduates do not feel prepared to attend the end of life as shown by the studies by Fraser et al. [16]. There are also references that up to 35% of medical students have not observed a patient at the end of life [13]. This can cause fear in students in the face of death due to the feeling of not having enough tools to deal with this situation. This question was deliberately asked to reflect later with the students in these analyzes and to emphasize that care should not be directly related to the profession, but to the willingness and commitment to help, which is an inherent condition of the human being.

In the same way, it is worth highlighting the answer to the question, how many people do you think would be able to take care of you if an illness were to overtake you at this point in your life? This question is being asked by the New Health Foundation to all types of people of all age groups and usually the Mean number of people who identify themselves is 4 people. In our population, up to 67.5% indicated that less than 5. The concept of care is usually related to the development of tasks related to the basic activities of daily life and with first and second degree people involved in care. In a study carried out on 99 terminally ill people, other profiles that may be involved in caring for people at the end of life were identified and that they can develop other types of tasks [17]. In this way, as Julian Abel expresses in his model of care circle [4], it is necessary to sensitize the population to the presence of other profiles (friends, co-workers, neighbors, etc.) that can carry out tasks that are complementary to those of a main caregiver. The increase in these care networks improves the quality of life of the person, reduces the burden of the main caregiver and improves the satisfaction of patients and their families. These results are already being analyzed in a community intervention process through the RedCuida protocol for the creation and management of care networks [18,19].

Death is not entirely present in the Universities. 44.7% of those surveyed indicated that they talk about it without problem. However, professional practice should bring us closer to talking about death since experiences with patients can bring us closer to these sensitivities towards it. Not talking about death makes us not empathize with the death of the other, and this has caused health professionals frustrations on many occasions. In other studies, carried out on the approach to death of students, communication needs about death with close people, patients or children have also been identified [20]. It´s necessary to implement in the University themes about death and programs such as Death Café [21] in the university are being implemented along this line to bring together not only health sciences students, but also the rest of the university community.

The topics least covered in the faculties of medicine, psychology and nursing are Management and Organization, Public Policies, Pediatric Palliative Care, Network Management and Compassion. These results coincide with those of Billings et al. [22] in 1455 medical students where the lack of communication and compassion aspects is expressed in the training curriculum in end of life care. There is a tendency to focus the topics on the most specialized areas of the profession, leaving vacant topics related to organization, management, research, death, emotional skills and values of humanization, compassion and dignity. Therefore, the results of this first study indicate that these areas must be reinforced in the curriculum and in the rest of the awareness-raising actions that are carried out at the university and that have to do with the development of the Compassionate University.

Humanization, dignity and compassion were the skills most valued by the students. 70.5% considered it a high priority for adequate care of people at the end of life. These results coincide with those of Borgstrom et al. [23], Centeno et al. [24] and Hurwitz et al. [25] that indicate the competences of dedicated time with patients, learning about wider elements of treatment and holistic care, communications skills and learning about themselves through reflective writing.

The Gilbert Compassion Scale [9] applied to students and professionals it values components of action and commitment of compassion towards oneself, towards others and the compassion that we receive from others. The survey has been applied with the aim of evaluating compassion on a personal level, although the students may have been conditioned in their responses according to the career they were studying or their personal relationship with palliative care.

The results are remarkable in each one of the blocks, being the least valued the one of compassion of the others. In the interpretations made later at the University with the professors and students about these answers, it was concluded that we usually relate more with the help to the other than with the help we receive from the other. As expressed by Brito et al. [2], the benefits of compassion in palliative care can bring us closer to improving care for people at the end of life.

The results of this first diagnosis at the University coincide with those of Dávalos et al. [7], where the same research was carried out within the framework of the Compassionate University for a sample of 459 students and 77 members of the University. The development of this line of research is allowing Universities to advance in response to a series of needs and motivations in students and professors: there is a willingness to care, the values of compassion are notable in the students and professors of the faculties of health sciences and it is necessary to include more topics on care, compassion and the community as transversal axes of training in the curriculum.

This study has been carried out with the objective of knowing the sensitivities and knowledge towards the end of life at a personal rather than an academic level and from here to propose a training curriculum together with a series of complementary actions in the development of a Compassionate University. It integrates the elements of care, compassion and community to work from its analysis in the development of a Compassionate University based on its own methodology of diagnosis, research and action that is being applied to other universities in Spain and Latin America. Thanks to the methodology and the results that are extracted from this study, the development of a Compassionate University is allowed since the surveys and analyzes of training needs regarding care, compassion and the community allow the development of initiatives that make a Compassionate University.

5. Limitations

The surveys that were carried out in this first diagnosis were carried out anonymously, so it has not been possible to make a comparison before and after launching a series of actions at the University that promote the values of care.

6. Conclusions

The development of this survey, which contains a high reflective component on care, compassion and the way we behave with our own environment at the end of life, has allowed students to approach the knowledge of the subject in a way closer and compassionate, mobilized by action and not considered as a theoretical subject.

Thanks to the results of this first diagnostic study, a Compassionate University project is being developed at the University that sensitizes, trains and mobilizes students and professionals to develop care networks around people at the end of life.

Compassion must be extended beyond professional competencies, making care for the people around us extend from the University.

Author Contributions: Conceptualization and design: S.L.F. methodology, database, surveys; S.L.F., S.H.R.T., N.T.G. and M.d.P.G.B.; statistical analysis: M.Á.L.D. writing; review and editing: S.L.F. All authors have read and agreed to the published version of the manuscript.

Funding: This research received no external funding.

Institutional Review Board Statement: Not applicable.

Informed Consent Statement: Not applicable.

Data Availability Statement: Data are available from Unisanitas data sources.

Acknowledgments: We thanks all students, academics participants in the survey.

Conflicts of Interest: The authors declare no conflict of interest. The funders had no role in the design of the study; in the collection, analyses or interpretation of data; in the writing of the manuscript or in the decision to publish the results.

References

1. Block, S.; Billings, J.A. Nurturing humanism through teaching palliative care. *Acad. Med.* **1998**, *73*, 763–765. [CrossRef] [PubMed]
2. Brito, G.; Librada, S. Compassion in palliative care: A review. *Curr. Opin. Support. Palliat Care* **2018**, *12*, 472–479. [CrossRef] [PubMed]
3. Lown, B.; McIntosh, S.; Gaines, M.; McGuinn, K.; Hatem, D.S. Integrating Compassionate, Collaborative Care (the "Triple C") into health professional eductaion to advance the triple aim of heath care. *Acad. Med.* **2016**, *91*, 310–316. [CrossRef] [PubMed]

4. Abel, J.; Bowra, J.; Walter, T.; Howarth, G. Compassionate community networks: Supporting home dying. *BMJ Support. Palliat. Care* **2011**, *1*, 129–133. [CrossRef] [PubMed]
5. Vindrola-Padros, C.; Mertnoff, R.; Lasmaría, C.; Gomez-Batiste, X. Palliative care education in Latin America: A systematic review of training programs for heathcare professionals. *Palliat. Support. Care* **2018**, *16*, 107–117. [CrossRef] [PubMed]
6. Recommendations of the European Association for Palliative Care (EAPC) for the Development of Undergraduate Curricula in Palliative Medicine to the European Medical Schools; Report of the EAPC Steering Group on Medical Education and Training in Palliative Care. EAPC, 2013. Available online: https://dadun.unav.edu/bitstream/10171/34516/1/Recommendations%20of%20the%20EAPC%20for%20the%20Development%20of%20Undergraduate%20Curricula%20in%20Palliative%20Medicine%20At%20European%20Medical%20Schools.pdf (accessed on 26 July 2021).
7. Davalos-Batallas, V.; Vargas-Martínez, A.-M.; Bonilla-Sierra, P.; Leon-Larios, F.; Lomas-Campos, M.-d.-l.-M.; Vaca-Gallegos, S.-L.; de Diego-Cordero, R. Compassionate Engagement and Action in the Education for Health Care Professions: A Cross-Sectional Study at an Ecuadorian University. *Int. J. Environ. Res. Public Health* **2020**, *17*, 5425. [CrossRef] [PubMed]
8. Librada, S.; Herrera, E.; Boceta, J.; Vargas, R.M.; Vicuna, M. All with You: A new method for developing compassionate communities and cities at the end of life. Experiences in Spain and Latin-America. *Ann. Palliat. Med.* **2018**, *7*, S15–S31.
9. Gilbert, P.; Catarino, F.; Duarte, C.; Matos, M.; Kolts, R.; Stubbs, J.; Ceresatto, L.; Duarte, J.; Pinto-Gouveia, J.; Basran, J. The development of compassionate engagement and action scales for self and others. *J. Compassionate Health Care* **2017**, *4*, 4. [CrossRef]
10. Colombia. Ministry of Health. Resolution 8430 of 1993. By which the scientific, technical and administrative standards for health research are established. 1993. Available online: https://www.urosario.edu.co/Escuela-Medicina/Investigacion/Documentos-de-interes/Files/resolucion_008430_1993.pdf (accessed on 26 July 2021).
11. Statutory Law 1581 of 2012, on the General Regime for the Protection of Personal Data: Article 6.e and article 10.d. Available online: http://www.fundacionmicrofinanzasbbva.org/revistaprogreso/en/international-collection-of-personal-data/ (accessed on 26 July 2021).
12. Lown, B.A.; Rosen, J.; Marttila, J. An Agenda for Improving Compassionate Care: A Survey Shows About Half of Patients Say Such Care Is Missing. *Health Aff.* **2011**, *30*, 1772–1778. [CrossRef] [PubMed]
13. Sinclair, S.; Beamer, K.; Hack, T.F.; McClement, S.; Bouchal, S.R.; Chochinov, H.M.; Hagen, N.A. Sympathy, empathy, and compassion: A grounded theory study of palliative care patients' understandings, experiences, and preferences. *Palliat. Med.* **2017**, *31*, 437–447. [CrossRef] [PubMed]
14. Pastrana, T.; De Lima, L.; Pons, J.J.; Centeno, C. *Atlas de Cuidados Paliativos de Latinoamérica*; Edición Cartográfica; IAHPC Press: Houston, TX, USA, 2013.
15. Hui, D.; Nooruddin, Z.; Didwaniya, N.; Dev, R.; De La Cruz, M.; Kim, S.H.; Kwon, J.H.; Hutchins, R.; Liem, C.; Bruera, E. Concepts and definitions for "actively dying", "end of life", "terminally ill," Terminal care ", and" transition of care ": A systematic review. *J. Pain Symptom Manag.* **2014**, *47*, 77–89. [CrossRef] [PubMed]
16. Fraser, H.C.; Kutner, J.S.; Pfeifer, M.P. Senior Medical Students' Perceptions of the Adequacy of Education on End-of-Life Issues. *J. Palliat. Med.* **2001**, *4*, 337–343. [CrossRef] [PubMed]
17. Díaz, F.; Redondo, M.J.; Librada, S. Networks of Care at the End of Life people in a palliative care population. In Proceedings of the XI Congress of the Spanish Palliative Care Society, SECPAL, Seville, Spain, 12–14 May 2016.
18. Librada Flores, S.; Herrera Molina, E.; Díaz Díez, F.; Redondo Moralo, M.J.; Castillo Rodríguez, C.; McLoughlin, K.; Abel, J.; Jadad Garcia, T.; Lucas Díaz, M.Á.; Trabado Lara, I.; et al. REDCUIDA Development and Management of Networks of Care at the End of Life (the REDCUIDA Intervention): Protocol for a Nonrandomized Controlled Trial. *JMIR Res. Protoc.* **2018**, *7*, e10515. [CrossRef] [PubMed]
19. Librada, S.; Castillo, C.; Trabado, I.; Lucas, M.A. REDCUIDA protocol: Development and Management of Networks of Care at the End of Life. Preliminary results. In Proceedings of the XII Congress of the Spanish Palliative Care Society, Vitoria, Spain, 7–9 June 2018.
20. Pérez-de la Cruz, S.; García-Luengo, M.V. Comparative study among Spanish students of heatlh sciences degrees: Facing death. *Nurs. Health Sci.* **2018**, *20*, 380–386. [CrossRef] [PubMed]
21. Miles, L.; Corr, C.A. Death Cafe. *Omega* **2017**, *75*, 151–165. [CrossRef] [PubMed]
22. Billings, M.; Engelberg, R.; Randall, C.; Block, S.; Sullivan, A.M. Determinants of medical students´perceived preparation to perform end of life care, quality of end of life care education, and attitudes toward end of life care. *J. Palliat. Med.* **2010**, *13*, 319–326. [CrossRef] [PubMed]
23. Borgstrom, E.; Morris, R.; Wood, D.; Cohn, S.; Barclay, S. Learning to care: Medical students' reported value and evaluation of palliative care teaching involving meeting patients and reflective writing. *BMC Med. Educ.* **2016**, *16*, 1–9. [CrossRef] [PubMed]
24. Centeno, C.; Ballesteros, M.; Carrasco, J.M.; Arantzamendi, M. Does palliative care education matter to medical students? The experience of attending an undergraduate course in palliative care. *BMJ Support. Palliat. Care* **2014**, *6*, 128–134. [CrossRef] [PubMed]
25. Hurwitz, S.; Kelly, B.; Powis, D.; Smyth, R.; Lewin, T. The desirable qualities of future doctors—A study of medical student perceptions. *Med. Teach.* **2013**, *35*, e1332–e1339. [CrossRef] [PubMed]

healthcare

MDPI

Article

Winners and Losers in Palliative Care Service Delivery: Time for a Public Health Approach to Palliative and End of Life Care

Samar M. Aoun [1,2,*], Robyn Richmond [1], Leanne Jiang [1,2] and Bruce Rumbold [2]

1 Perron Institute for Neurological and Translational Science, Nedlands, WA 6009, Australia; robyn.richmond@perron.uwa.edu.au (R.R.); leanne.jiang@latrobe.edu.au (L.J.)
2 Public Health Palliative Care Unit, School of Psychology and Public Health, La Trobe University, Melbourne, VIC 3086, Australia; b.rumbold@latrobe.edu.au
* Correspondence: samar.aoun@perron.uwa.edu.au

Abstract: Background: Consumer experience of palliative care has been inconsistently and selectively investigated. Methods: People in Western Australia who had experienced a life limiting illness in the past five years were recruited via social media and care organisations (2020) and invited to complete a cross sectional consumer survey on their experiences of the care they received. Results: 353 bereaved carers, current carers and patients responded. The winners, those who received the best quality end-of-life care, were those who were aware of palliative care as an end-of-life care (EOLC) option, qualified for admission to and were able to access a specialist palliative care program, and with mainly a cancer diagnosis. The losers, those who received end-of-life care that was adequate rather than best practice, were those who were unaware of palliative care as an EOLC option or did not qualify for or were unable to access specialist palliative care and had mainly a non-cancer diagnosis. Both groups were well supported throughout their illness by family and a wider social network. However, their family carers were not adequately supported by health services during caregiving and bereavement. Conclusions: A public health approach to palliative and end of life care is proposed to integrate tertiary, primary, and community services through active consumer engagement in the design and delivery of care. Therefore, suggested strategies may also have relevance in many other international settings.

Keywords: palliative care; end of life care; consumer perspectives; equity; public health approach; compassionate communities; caregiving; bereavement

Citation: Aoun, S.M.; Richmond, R.; Jiang, L.; Rumbold, B. Winners and Losers in Palliative Care Service Delivery: Time for a Public Health Approach to Palliative and End of Life Care. *Healthcare* **2021**, *9*, 1615. https://doi.org/10.3390/healthcare9121615

Academic Editors: Georg Bollig and John Rosenberg

Received: 1 October 2021
Accepted: 18 November 2021
Published: 23 November 2021

1. Introduction

A recent literature review on consumers' needs and preferences [1] found that consumer experience of palliative care has been inconsistently and selectively investigated. The review highlighted that, in addition to competent treatment, information about the illness experience and strategies for managing that experience in everyday life are important to patients and their family carers. It also indicated that end-of-life needs usually include needs that have already arisen earlier in patients' illness journeys. For some patients, transfer to an end-of-life care setting to meet fresh needs that arise can have the unintended consequence that important continuing needs are no longer adequately met [1]. It has been suggested that such inconsistencies and disruptions in care could be addressed by implementing a patient journey perspective that requires services to be integrated across the illness course [2,3].

Tools assessing how patients prefer to engage in healthcare are of variable quality [4] and need further consumer involvement in their development. Consumer experience studies that indicate the process of engagement and negotiation are in themselves helpful in building relationships and reinforcing support [5–7].

Most palliative care programs collect some form of internal consumer data, but few publish their findings. Consumer satisfaction scores are often collected by palliative care peak bodies, but this activity tends to be more a marketing measure than a focused enquiry into quality. To date, the only program that has consistently collected consumer data in granular detail across a health system is the Views Of Informal Caregivers Evaluation of Services (VOICES), commissioned by the UK Department of Health [8], and badged as the National Survey of Bereaved People once managed by the Office for National Statistics. This UK survey investigated the quality of care delivered in the last three months of life for adults who died in England, using a sample of approximately 30% of all deaths over a four-month period selected from the death registration database. One of the strengths of the national survey has been its contribution to quality at the local level, although these local projects seldom lead to peer-reviewed publications.

The closest equivalent to VOICES in Australia is the FAMCARE-2 tool (Family Satisfaction with Palliative Care), which measures satisfaction across four domains, management of physical symptoms and comfort, provision of information, family support, and patient psychological care. The validation study [9] indicated lower levels of satisfaction in response to the subscales 'provision of information' and 'family support', consistent with VOICES findings. FAMCARE-2 has been adapted to MND Care to evaluate consumer satisfaction [10]. FAMCARE-2 is administered periodically in selected services by Australia's Palliative Care Outcomes Collaboration (PCOC). A survey of 1592 caregivers across 49 palliative care services in 2016 [11] found generally high levels of satisfaction and positive experiences of care. Scores were higher for in-patient care on three of the four domains, provision of information being the exception. Dissatisfaction with information provision was higher for older carers, while home carers reported that information to support them with practical caring tasks was inadequate. Similar results were found with the Australian EOL and Bereavement Study [12].

The literature review on consumer needs and preferences also found that, while contributions from consumer engagement were virtually absent from policy documents and service guidelines documents a decade ago, they have in recent years been consistently included [1]. These contributions are, however, uneven. Recent documents acknowledge the importance of community involvement or engagement although few expand on how this engagement might take place. Despite support for community engagement and involvement of informal carers, most current models still fall short because their integration is limited to formal health services, with consumers consulted as clients rather than partners in the co-design of services. The review proposed public health approaches to palliative care as a framework for addressing these shortfalls [1]. The aim of this article is to report on what matters most to consumers (patients and informal carers) in the delivery of palliative care in Western Australia.

2. Objectives

This study was commissioned by the Western Australian Department of Health's End of Life Care (EOLC) Program as an independent review (i) to gain a consumer perspective on palliative care, (ii) to identify key challenges/gaps in the provision of EOLC, and (ii) to determine how service delivery can adapt and improve to meet community needs and expectations. The independent review took place from May to November 2020 and comprised three phases with the same three above-mentioned objectives: a literature review, a cross sectional consumer survey, and consultation forums with service providers. This article reports on the findings of the consumer survey where the winners and losers in palliative care service delivery are highlighted regardless of the care setting. A forthcoming article will focus on experiences specific to care settings such as home, hospice, hospital, and nursing home.

3. Methodology

A cross sectional consumer survey was designed to respond to the six priorities of the Western Australia (WA) End of Life Strategy [13] for developing and improving palliative care services across WA:

Priority 1. Care is accessible to everyone, everywhere
Priority 2. Care is person-centred
Priority 3. Care is coordinated
Priority 4. Families and carers are supported
Priority 5. All staff are prepared to care
Priority 6. The community is aware and able to care

The survey contained sets of questions grouped under the six priorities and related to the following: patient and carer demographics; experience with and quality of care in separate settings (home, hospice, hospital, and nursing home); formal and informal support before death, at the time of death, and after death. A number of questions in the sections on experiences in the four settings were adapted from the UK VOICES annual survey [8].

The survey was available in six formats for six different target consumer groups who had experienced a life limiting illness in the last five years: Consumers (patients and family carers) who are current or past users and non-users of palliative care services, were invited to report on what is working and not working well (or what has or has not worked well or could have worked better) for them in their end-of-life experience.

The survey was made primarily available as an online survey using Redcap. Hard copy surveys were also provided on request. Complementing the survey tool were additional documents for respondents to clarify several aspects of the survey: definitions of several terms used in the field; a list of palliative care service providers in WA categorised by setting; information on palliative care information and services; information on grief and bereavement, including how to contact services should the respondent become distressed completing the survey; and a participant information sheet. The survey was promoted extensively, but over a short six-week period, via service providers and relevant social media pages.

Ethics approval was granted by La Trobe University Research Ethics Committee (HEC20232). As this was an anonymous online survey, returning the completed survey was considered as implied consent. The information sheet that accompanied the survey emphasised that participation was entirely voluntary.

Descriptive analyses were undertaken. Statistical tests for significant differences in quality indicators between users/non-users and cancer/non-cancer groups could not be performed as participants contributed multiple responses for settings of care and therefore violated the statistical assumption of independence. However, we have indicated in Figures 1 and 2 where differences are large enough to be worth considering.

4. Results

4.1. Profile of Survey Respondents

In total, 430 surveys were received, with only three as paper copies. Following data cleaning the final number suitable for analyses was 353: 71% of total respondents were bereaved carers; 68% of total respondents had used a palliative care service; The most reported setting for care was home (43%) followed by hospital (26%), hospice (23%), and nursing home (8%). The majority of respondents used one care setting. There were no significant differences in the demographic characteristics of the users and non-user groups. Focusing on the largest respondent group, the bereaved carers, for both users and non-users, about 90% were female, average age was 55 years, over 50% had university level education, and over 60% were working. There were some slight differences in marital status (34% widowed users vs. 22% widowed non-users), rural/regional residence (28% users vs. 18% non-users), and relationship to patient (spouse/partner 34% users vs. 24% non-users). However almost twice the number of non-users had non-cancer diagnoses, mainly MND, dementia, and lung disease (27% users vs. 56% non-users). Table 1 presents the distribution of survey respondents across the groups. Table 2 presents selected demographic characteristics of users and non-users of palliative care services.

Table 1. Distribution of survey respondents.

Number of Respondents	Used Palliative Care (Users)	Did Not Use Palliative Care (Non-Users)	Total
Bereaved Carer	204	45	249 (71%)
Current Carer	27	45	72 (20%)
Patient	8	24	32 (9%)
TOTAL	239 (68%)	114 (32%)	353 (100%)

Table 2. Demographic characteristics of survey respondents.

	Users						Non-Users					
	Bereaved Carer (*n* = 204)		Current Carer (*n* = 28)		Patient (*n* = 8)		Bereaved Carer (*n* = 45)		Current Carer (*n* = 45)		Patient (*n* = 24)	
	n	%	*n*	%	*n*	%	*n*	%	*n*	%	*n*	%
Gender												
Male	21	10.3	6	21.4	2	25	4	8.9	6	13.3	9	37.5
Female	181	88.7	22	78.6	6	75	41	91.1	39	86.7	15	62.5
Missing	2	1	0	0	0	0	0	-	0	-	0	-
Age, year												
Mean (SD)	54.6 (13.2)		46.5 (12.3)		66.7(9.3)		57.4 (12.2)		56.8 (11.3)		65.7(7.5)	
Median (Range)	55.0 (26–89)		46 (20–69)		69 (47–75)		57 (30–83)		58 (33–73)		66 (53–81)	
Marital Status												
Married/de facto	91	44.6	19	67.9	5	62.5	26	57.8	36	80	13	54.2
Widowed	70	34.3	1	3.6	0		10	22.2	2	4.4	3	12.5
Other	38	18.6	8	28.6	3	37.5	8	17.8	6	13.3	8	33.3
Missing	5	2.5	0	-	0	-	1	2.2	1	2.2	0	-
Education Level												
University	102	50.5	14	50	2	25	24	53.3	26	57.8	14	58.3
Below University	98	49	13	46.4	6	75	21	46.7	17	37.8	10	41.7
Missing	3	14.8	1	3.6	0	-	0	-	2	4.4	0	-
Employment Status												
Working	128	62.7	20	71.4	0	-	29	64.4	21	46.7	4	16.7
Not Working	24	11.8	6	21.4	2	25	5	11.1	11	24.4	3	12.5
Retired	49	24	1	3.6	6	75	11	24.4	11	24.4	17	70.8
Missing	3	1.5	1	3.3	0	-	0	-	2	4.4	0	-
Residential Postcode												
Metropolitan	140	68.6	18	64.3	4	50	34	75.6	35	77.8	17	70.8
Regional/Rural	56	27.5	9	32.1	3	37.5	8	17.8	10	22.2	6	25
Interstate	1	0.5	0	0	0	0	1	2.2	0	0	0	0
Missing	7	3.4	1	3.6	1	12.5	2	4.4	0	0	1	4.2
Relationship to Patient												
Spouse/Partner	70	34.3	5	17.9	-		11	24.4	24	53.3	-	
Daughter/Son	79	38.7	11	39.3	-		21	46.7	16	35.6	-	
Other	48	22.5	11	39.3	-		13	28.9	5	11.1	-	
Missing	7	3.4	1	3.6	-		0	-	0	-	-	
Disease												
Cancer	118	57.8	14	50.0	5	62.5	17	37.8	14	31.1	20	83.3
Non–Cancer	55	27	12	42.9	3	37.5	25	55.6	30	66.6	4	16.7
Motor Neurone Dis.	19	-	3	-	1	-	5	-	2	-		-
Dementia	14	-	4	-	0	-	7	-	18	-	0	-
Other neurological	3	-	1	-	1	-	8	-	8	-	2	-
Lung/Heart/Kidney	24	-	6	-	1	-	7	-	7	-	2	-
Missing/Unknown	31	15.2	2	7.1	0	0	3	6.7	1	2.3	0	0

4.2. Non-Users' Reasons for Not Receiving Palliative Care

Fifty eight out of 114 non-users gave reasons as to why they did use palliative care services with 72 multiple responses. The most common responses were: Unaware of what was available (17%); Satisfied with the care we received from general health and community services (12%); Tried but could not access them (11%); No-one initiated a referral to these services (11%); We were told it was not close enough to dying/end of life stage (10%); We were told it was too soon in the illness trajectory (8%); Unaware how it could help (8%).

4.3. Differences in Quality Indicators within the Six Priorities

Table 3 summarizes what worked well and not so well for consumers. Aspects of care services were delivering very well (at 90% satisfaction) were the competence of staff, working well together within a care setting and treating consumers with respect/dignity and compassion/kindness. Taking into account culture, values, and beliefs, access to care, relief of pain, being involved in decision making at end of life came next (at 80% satisfaction), followed by relief of symptoms, practical assistance, patient included in care decisions (70%). However, consumers reported more needs not being adequately met in questions relating to priority four, about families and carers not being supported before and after death of their relative. Most quality indicators for non-users of palliative care services were lower than those of users and those for non-cancer conditions rated lower than those for cancer, as described in detail below.

Table 3. Differences in quality indicators within the six priorities.

What Is Working Well	What Is Not Working So Well
Priority one: Care is accessible to everyone, everywhere	
78% rated quality of care excellent to good	60% reported receiving as much support as wanted before death.
84% could access care as soon as they needed.	50% felt they received enough help after their relative's death
76% rated relief of pain excellent to good	All indicators lower for non-cancer conditions
70% for relief of symptoms other than pain and practical assistance.	All indicators lower for non-users of palliative care
80% rated quality of EOL care excellent/good and reported they received enough help at time of death (definitely/ to some extent).	
Priority Two: Care is person-centred	
83% rated values respected always/most of the time	58% felt they could discuss worries/fears as much as they wanted
87% rated cultural background respected always/most of the time	61% rated spiritual support as excellent/good
82% rated spiritual beliefs respected always/most of the time	64% rated emotional support as excellent/good
69% reported that the services checked if they have EOL wishes documents	All indicators lower for non-cancer conditions
78% felt their wishes were taken into account	All indicators lower for non-users of palliative care
72% of patients felt included in care decisions (excellent/good)	
80% of carers reported being involved in decision making at EOL as much as they wanted	
Priority Three: Care is coordinated	
75% found the referral process easy/very easy	60% reported that services worked well with GP and external services
87% thought staff worked well within each setting (definitely/to some extent)	10% of ED admissions were planned or coordinated
74% rated out of hours services as excellent/good	All indicators lower for non-cancer conditions
Priority Four: Families and carers are supported	
78% reported patients were involved in decisions about their EOL care as much as they wanted	62% rated emotional support to family carer as excellent/good
	60% were provided information on their relative's condition
	47% of carers reported being able to talk about experience of illness and death to services
	53% of carers were offered information on grief by palliative care services
	42% of carers were contacted by palliative care services 3–6 weeks after death and only 16% six months after death of their relative

Table 3. *Cont.*

What Is Working Well	What Is Not Working So Well
	All indicators lower for non-cancer conditions
	All indicators lower for non-users of palliative care
Priority Five: All staff are prepared to care	
88% thought they were treated with respect/dignity always/most of the time	All indicators lower for non-cancer conditions
89% thought they were treated with compassion/ kindness always/most of the time	
90% rated staff as very competent/competent	
78% said they could obtain information when needed always/most of the time	
86% of carers reported being dealt with in a sensitive manner at death/end of life	
Priority Six: The community is aware and able to care	
96% reported they received informal support before death and 92% found this informal support very/quite helpful	Lower rates of helpfulness before and after death for non-users
94% reported they received informal support after death and 87% found this informal support very/quite helpful	

4.4. Differences in Care between Users and Non-Users of Palliative Care Services

The most pronounced differences were in the following quality indicators where the non-users fared worse (Figure 1): quality of end of life care (83% users vs. 38% non-users); receiving enough help at the time of death (84% users vs. 59% non-users); receiving practical assistance (75% users vs. 56% non-users); relief of pain (77% users vs. 62% non-users) and other symptoms; carer involved in decisions as wanted (80% users vs. 45% non-users); inclusion of patient in care decisions (72% vs. 58%); spiritual support of patient (61% vs. 37%); could discuss worries/fears (58% vs. 40%), being asked if they had EOL wishes documentation (69% vs. 48%); twice as many non-users had decisions made that were not wanted (16% users vs. 38% non-users); receiving as much help as needed before the death (61% vs. 40%); However, the support received after death was equivalent in both groups (47% vs. 45%). The referral process to services was not as easy for the non-users (75% users vs. 52% non-users).

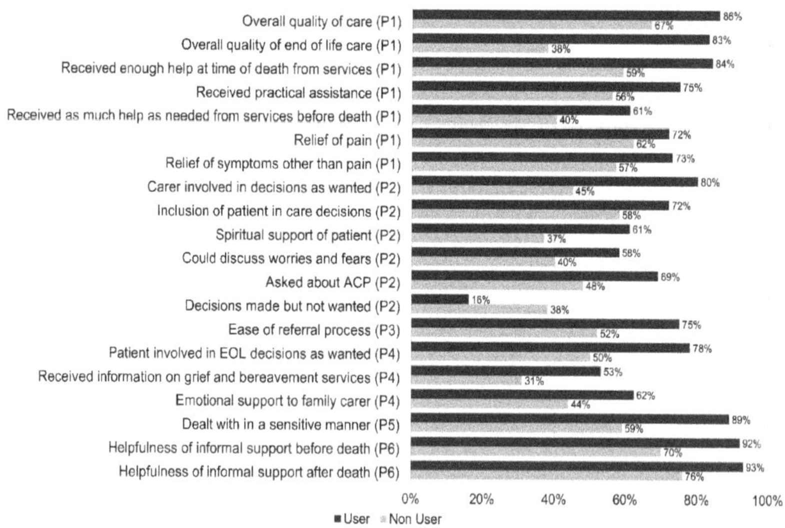

Figure 1. Differences in care between users and non-users of palliative care services (with EOL strategy priority number).

Only 50% of non-users reported that the patient was involved in decisions at EOL compared to 78% of users; 31% of non-users received information on grief and bereavement services compared to 53% of users; 44% of non-users reported family carer receiving emotional support compared to 62% of users; being dealt with in a sensitive manner (89% users vs. 59% non-users). Both groups received the same extent of informal support. The non-users however reported lower ratings for the helpfulness of informal support before death (70% vs. 92%) and after death (76% vs. 93%). These differences could be accounted for by the way palliative care services tend to be intentional about encouraging caregivers to look and ask for support, including from not-for-profit organisations, in a way that other services may not [12].

4.5. Differences in Care between Cancer and Non-Cancer Conditions

Across most indicators, quality indicators for non-cancer rated lower than cancer (Figure 2), especially overall quality of care (65% vs. 84%), quality of EOLC (72% vs. 89%), respecting values (71% vs. 87%), culture (79% vs. 94%), spiritual beliefs (68% vs. 89%), could discuss worries/fears (49% vs. 62%), spiritual support for patient (45% vs. 68%), patient involved in decisions as wanted (67% vs. 83%), ease of referral process (63% vs. 79%) and staff worked better together (76% vs. 91%), staff competence (82% vs. 94%), being treated with respect/dignity (78% vs. 93%).

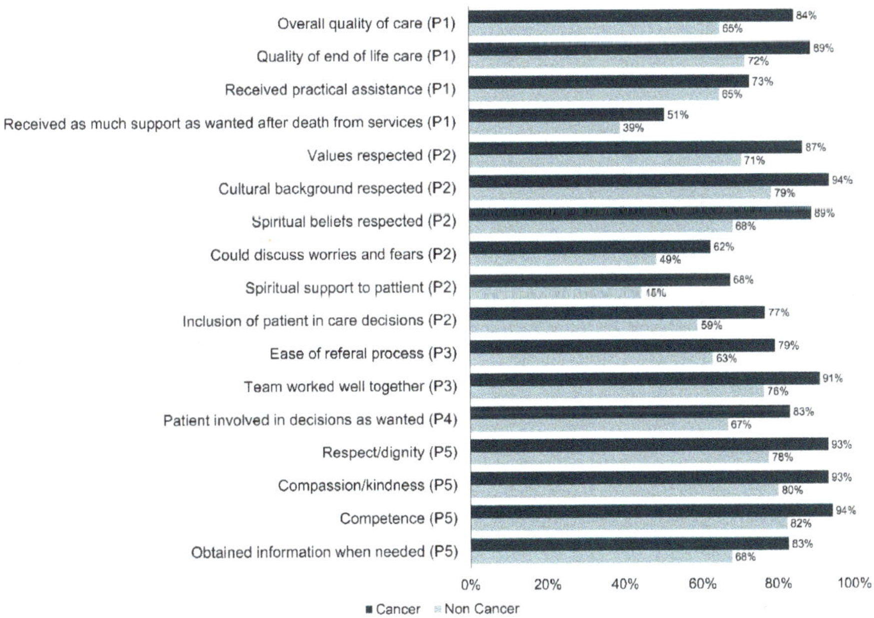

Figure 2. Differences in care between cancer and non-cancer conditions (with EOL strategy priority number).

4.6. What Could Have Worked Better for Consumers?

Suggestions for improvement from respondents included the following: being provided with earlier access to palliative care, assistance completing relevant documentation on advance care planning and having this followed by staff, improving consumer knowledge, improving referral processes, better delivery of pain medication, improving staff training and staffing levels, better after-hours access and support to stay at home, increasing the level of family carer support and consumer involvement in decision making and care choices, improving delivery of palliative care for non-malignant diseases and more specifically for neurodegenerative conditions such as MND and dementia, and better access to palliative care in rural and remote areas.

5. Discussion

This survey was a first of its kind in Australia in terms of its depth and breadth of community engagement. Of the six priorities, quality indicators for Priority Four (families and carers are supported) lag behind the others. Families are not well supported before and after bereavement. Of user respondents, 40% reported that emotional and spiritual support to their patient was not adequate. This is considerably lower than other indicators such as symptom management. Emotional support to family carers and ability to discuss worries and fears were not adequate for 40% of respondents, as also reported by Wang [14]. About 40% of bereaved respondents felt that they did not receive as much support as they wanted from palliative care services during the illness and 50% did not after the patient's death. Support after death was generally not adequate [12,15]. Although these aspects (emotional and spiritual support for patient and family before death, and bereavement support) are promoted as part of the holistic approach of palliative care, there seems to be in practice a disconnect between what the sector portrays and encourages the community to expect and what is actually delivered by services. This may be in part due to time and resource constraints on service capacity, and in part because some of these end-of-life needs are by their very nature unable to be met by professional support [16].

One strategy to address this deficit in support is to develop better referral pathways to not-for-profit support organisations who can, with better resourcing, dedicate the time to have these conversations and provide this support [17]. However, alongside this is the need to upskill the community networks that support people throughout the illness journey. It is evident that family carers assumed the vital role of 'connecting the dots' in liaising with several treating teams and maintaining communication around coordination of care. In the absence of formal case managers, family carers must be supported to develop their capacity in this role if care is to be as effective as possible. Family carer support needs to be at two levels: to help family carers care for the ill person but also to help care for themselves [18–20]. This can be achieved by instigating a system that assesses and addresses carer support needs, collects regular consumer feedback, and co-designs service improvements.

By way of contrast, responses to Priority Six (the community is aware and able to care) gave high ratings to the care provided by informal networks. Over 90% of respondents (both users and non-users) relied on the community (family/friends/neighbors/community organizations) to support them before and after bereavement and reported that this informal support was helpful in attending to practical, social, emotional, and spiritual support needs. Other studies support this finding [19–21]. The primacy of support from social networks is at the heart of public health approaches to palliative and end of life care which have the potential to enhance integration of services and provide a comprehensive approach that engages the assets of local communities [1,22]. The disease-specific not-for-profit support organisations have an important role to play in this space and their role too should be bolstered [17].

A particular innovation in this project was to seek responses from non-users as well as users of palliative care in order to explore sources of help received by non-users and how these compared in quality to the help users received from palliative care services. In general, the quality indicators reported by non-users were lower than those of the users. However, it should be noted that non-cancer conditions made up nearly 60% of non-users and their quality indicators were consistent with those with non-cancer conditions who used palliative care services. This would seem to reflect that palliative care services tend, as a result of their evolution, to be expert in cancer care but may lack expertise in other life-limiting conditions [23]. Another recent retrospective study of cancer and non-cancer patients in a Canadian tertiary palliative care setting did not find any major distinction between the needs of the two groups [24], but they did note that the non-cancer patients, a small proportion of the sample, were admitted precisely because their physical needs matched the expertise of the service. Of course, patients with a cancer history have on average significantly greater engagement with the health system, usually through hospitalisation, than non-cancer patients [25], and this may also shape expectations of care.

It is encouraging to know that palliative care services make the experience of patients and families considerably better in most aspects of care and also that the palliative approach to care provided by general services can be effective [26]. However, the issue remains that palliative care services select patients on the basis of the services' capacity to respond to physical symptoms most commonly found in advanced cancer patients [27], not the broader spectrum of end-of-life need found across the general population [14,28].

Given that equity in end-of-life care provision is a goal of government policy [1], a key finding of the survey is the lower standard of care for non-cancer conditions across all six priorities. Because the survey relied on social connections to gather data, it did not receive responses relating to people who were socially disconnected in their dying, where their quality measures on family and community support measures would be expected to be even lower than those measured here. Inequity arising from disease type should be addressed within the health system. Inequity arising from inadequate social support must be addressed by local communities. Both aspects are taken into account by a public health approach.

Non-cancer conditions would benefit from a more inclusive palliative approach based on partnerships between specialist and generalist services to ensure that expert end-of-life care is added to, but does not replace, expert care for the illness with which the person is dying [26]. Non-cancer conditions should be given specific attention in new models of integrated end-of-life care. Current service provision should be bolstered by systematic and consistent education and training for general health professionals to ease the pressure on specialist palliative care services, and to broaden the non-cancer expertise available to these services.

Models of integrated care need also to be grounded in community upskilling/knowledge, supported consistently by generalist palliative care, with specialist palliative care providing 'episodic' care as particular needs arise during the illness journey [29]. This includes mobilising community options/better primary care engagement and potentially episodic care to broaden the reach of palliative care, case coordination, and improved communication/clinical handover. The role of not-for-profit organisations is vital in this space.

A public health approach to palliative and end of life care is able to achieve an integration of tertiary, primary, and community services through active consumer engagement in designing and delivering care to provide a comprehensive approach that engages the assets of local communities. This approach constructs a framework in which partnerships can be developed with patient communities with distinctive end of life needs, such as those with non-cancer conditions, thus providing a more inclusive approach to EOLC [30]. To implement this approach, we need to hear directly from the consumers about their experiences of unmet needs and how these could be met with better partnerships between the health services and the community, with the consumer involved in the co-design.

This approach is illustrated in Figure 3 and recognises the 'patient and social network' (Circles of Care) [31]. The 'inner' and 'outer' circles of care, and neighbourhood supports are the main foundation of resilient networks caring for people at home. Together they form a Compassionate Community. However, these systems must also ensure that professional care, service delivery and policy enhance the care provided by the person's social network. The model can be used as a practical guide about how care can be provided in communities and how different formal and informal services coordinate with each other and the communities they serve. The model looks at integration of the disability, health, and aged care sectors (tertiary, primary, and community services, specialist palliative care, generalist palliative care, disease specific clinics, and primary and allied health care services). The enablers for this integration include digital and assistive technologies, telehealth, advance care planning, education and training for health professionals and the community, not for profit organizations, and a compassionate community approach to care which enhances social networks.

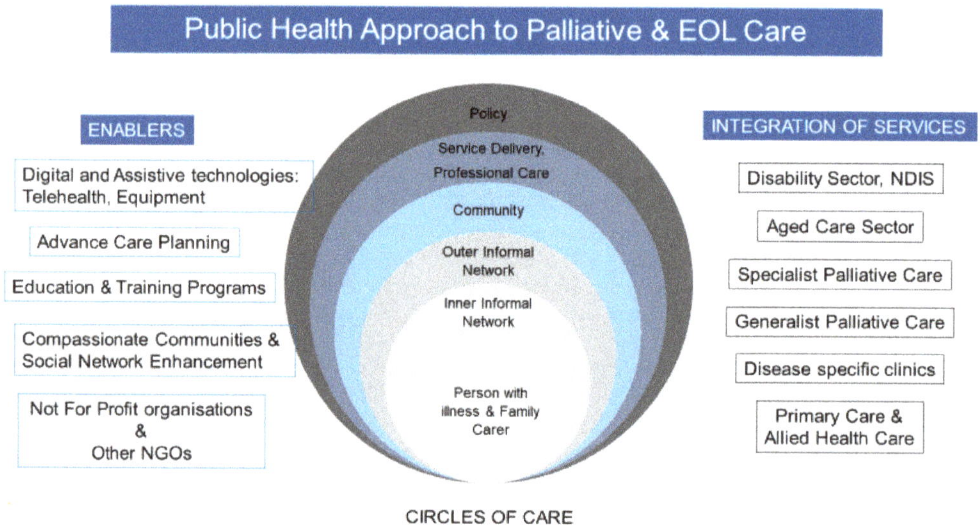

Figure 3. Public Health approach to palliative and EOL care.

Strengths and Limitations

The sample that responded to the survey is not representative of all those who received specialist palliative care services in WA. A random or stratified sample would have been necessary to be truly representative but not at all achievable, especially given the methodological, ethical, and logistical challenges of conducting palliative care research [6,32], and the limited time available to produce findings from the three phases of this statewide review. Nevertheless, the findings where unmet needs exist are in line with those reported in the national and international literature [14,33]. The respondents to this survey have quite distinctive characteristics: 51% had a university education, 60% had one or more documents on EOL wishes, the majority with non-cancer conditions had dementia, MND or lung disease. That 60% of survey respondents who used palliative care services had a document on EOL wishes is encouraging as the rate of uptake in the general population is only 10% in WA. Perhaps there is a selection bias here in that those with an EOL wishes document may be more inclined to give their opinion on their experiences. Additionally, there is evidence that people using palliative care services are twice as likely to have an EOL wishes document completed [12]. Two-thirds of rural respondents were from a regional area close to the capital which consequently is better resourced than others, which is why rural–urban comparisons have not been included in this article. Nevertheless, there was good representation of 30% of rural consumers and those with non-cancer conditions, both of which tend to be under-represented in other studies. The respondents who self-selected to participate seemed to be well informed, had a keen interest to improve experiences for other people in their situation and were constructive with their suggestions for improvement.

There were five Aboriginal and Torres Strait Islander respondents, eight from culturally and linguistically diverse backgrounds and five from the paediatric population (<18 years). Given the low number of respondents in these three groups, separate analyses for them were not possible. While these population groups have been the subject of a more recent tailored national review into their needs [34], further efforts are needed to document and incorporate consumer feedback from these groups in prospective frameworks on end-of-life care.

6. Conclusions

This consumer survey has provided a detailed exploration of experiences during the caregiving journey through to bereavement, identifying strategies that worked well and strategies that could have worked better. The survey also provided useful feedback to services as to where they are meeting the six priorities of the Strategy and where there are still unmet needs as experienced by their consumers. It also provided some insight into those who die without accessing their services.

It is admittedly stretching the point to characterise respondents to the survey as winners or losers, but clearly differences in quality of end-of-life care emerged. The winners—those who received the best quality end-of-life care—were those who were aware of palliative care as an EOLC option; qualified for admission to, and were able to access, a specialist palliative care program; and were supported throughout their illness by family and a wider social network. They were for the most part people with a cancer diagnosis. The losers—those who received care at end-of-life that was adequate rather than best practice—were those who were unaware of palliative care as an EOLC option or did not qualify for or were unable to access specialist palliative care, and for the most part had a non-cancer diagnosis. They too were supported by family who responded to the survey. In the losers' category are also family carers not being supported during caregiving and during bereavement.

A public health approach to palliative and end of life care is proposed to integrate tertiary, primary, and community services through active consumer engagement in the design and delivery of care. A public health approach to palliative and end of life care in the broadest sense encompasses a primary care approach involving generalist healthcare workers in providing initial assessment, support, intervention, and ongoing support; a tertiary care approach involving specialist healthcare providers and inpatient facilities such as hospitals, clinics, or hospices; and a population health approach involving education and community development. The latter is the least-developed aspect of palliative care service development. Hence the distinctive focus of a public health approach to end-of-life care today is that it views the community as an equal partner in the long and complex task of providing quality healthcare at the end of life.

This WA initiative of surveying consumer responses to EOLC, not simply palliative care, is an important step forward both in understanding quality of care at the end of life, and some sources of inequity in accessing end-of-life care. While the focus of attention in this article has been consumer experience in the state of Western Australia, the correlation of the findings with the international literature [1] suggests that strategies and solutions put forward for Western Australia may also have relevance in many other settings around the world. Further research including more socially diverse samples is required to identify the scope of need to be addressed by community care.

Author Contributions: Conceptualization, S.M.A. and B.R.; Data curation, S.M.A., R.R. and L.J.; Formal analysis, S.M.A., R.R. and L.J.; Funding acquisition, S.M.A.; Investigation, S.M.A., R.R., L.J. and BR; Methodology, S.M.A., R.R. and B.R.; Project administration, S.M.A.; Resources, S.M.A. and R.R.; Software, S.M.A. and L.J.; Supervision, S.M.A.; Validation, S.M.A., L.J. and B.R.; Visualization, S.M.A., R.R. and B.R.; Writing—original draft, S.M.A. and B.R.; Writing—review & editing, S.M.A., B.R., R.R. and L.J. All authors have read and agreed to the published version of the manuscript.

Funding: This study was funded by the End-of-life and Palliative Care Program, Department of Health Western Australia.

Institutional Review Board Statement: The study was conducted according to the guidelines of the Declaration of Helsinki, and approved by La Trobe University research ethics committee, approval number HEC20232.

Informed Consent Statement: Consent was implied by the return of the completed survey. The information sheet that accompanied the survey emphasised that participation was entirely voluntary.

Data Availability Statement: Ethical approval precludes the data being used for another purpose or being provided to researchers who have not signed the appropriate confidentiality agreement. Specifically, the ethical approval specifies that all results are in aggregate form to maintain confidentiality and privacy and precludes individual level data being made publicly available. All aggregate data for this study are freely available and included in the paper. Interested and qualified researchers may send requests for additional data to Samar Aoun at s.aoun@latrobe.edu.au.

Acknowledgments: The authors acknowledge the input and advice of the project reference group and Lauren Breen and the advice of biostatistician Natasha Bear.

Conflicts of Interest: The authors declare no conflict of interest.

References

1. Rumbold, B.; Aoun, S.M. Palliative and End-of-Life Care Service Models: To What Extent Are Consumer Perspectives Considered? *Healthcare* **2021**, *9*, 1286. [CrossRef]
2. Sercu, M.; Beyens, I.; Cosyns, M.; Mertens, F.; Deveugele, M.; Pype, P. Rethinking End-of-Life Care and Palliative Care: Learning From the Illness Trajectories and Lived Experiences of Terminally Ill Patients and Their Family Carers. *Qual. Health Res.* **2018**, *28*, 2220–2238. [CrossRef]
3. Sanson-Fisher, R.; Fakes, K.; Waller, A.; MacKenzie, L.; Bryant, J.; Herrmann, A. Assessing patients' experiences of cancer care across the treatment pathway: A mapping review of recent psychosocial cancer care publications. *Support. Care Cancer* **2019**, *27*, 1997–2006. [CrossRef]
4. Jerofke-Owen, T.; Garnier-Villarreal, M.; Fial, A.; Tobiano, G. Systematic review of psychometric properties of instruments measuring patient preferences for engagement in health care. *J. Adv. Nurs.* **2020**, *76*, 1988–2004. [CrossRef]
5. Bellamy, G.; Gott, M.; Frey, R. 'It's my pleasure?': The views of palliative care patients about being asked to participate in research. *Prog. Palliat. Care* **2011**, *19*, 159–164. [CrossRef]
6. Aoun, S.; Slatyer, S.; Deas, K.; Nekolaichuk, C. Family Caregiver Participation in Palliative Care Research: Challenging the Myth. *J. Pain Symptom Manag.* **2017**, *53*, 851–861. [CrossRef]
7. Cotterell, P.; Harlow, G.; Morris, C.; Beresford, P.; Hanley, B.; Sargeant, A.; Sitzia, J.; Staley, K. Service user involvement in cancer care: The impact on service users. *Health Expect.* **2010**, *14*, 159–169. [CrossRef]
8. Hunt, K.; Shlomo, N.; Richardson, A.; Addington-Hall, J. *VOICES Redesign and Testing to Inform a National End of Life Care Survey*; University of Southampton: Southampton, UK, 2011.
9. Aoun, S.; Bird, S.; Kristjanson, L.J.; Currow, D. Reliability testing of the FAMCARE-2 scale: Measuring family carer satisfaction with palliative care. *Palliat. Med.* **2010**, *24*, 674–681. [CrossRef]
10. Aoun, S.M.; Hogden, A.; Kho, L.K. "Until there is a cure, there is care": A person-centered approach to supporting the wellbeing of people with Motor Neurone Disease and their family carers. *Eur. J. Pers. Centered healthc.* **2018**, *6*, 320–328. [CrossRef]
11. Pidgeon, T.M.; Johnson, C.E.; Lester, L.; Currow, D.; Yates, P.; Allingham, S.F.; Bird, S.; Eagar, K. Perceptions of the care received from Australian palliative care services: A caregiver perspective. *Palliat. Support. Care* **2018**, *16*, 198–208. [CrossRef] [PubMed]
12. Aoun, S.M.; Rumbold, B.; Howting, D.; Bolleter, A.; Breen, L. Bereavement support for family caregivers: The gap between guidelines and practice in palliative care. *PLoS ONE* **2017**, *12*, e0184750. [CrossRef] [PubMed]
13. Government of Western Australia. *WA End-of-Life and Palliative Care Strategy 2018–2028*; Government of Western Australia: Perth, Australia, 2018.
14. Wang, T.; Molassiotis, A.; Chung, B.P.M.; Tan, J. Y. Unmet care needs of advanced cancer patients and their informal caregivers: A systematic review. *BMC Palliat. Care* **2018**, *17*, 1–29. [CrossRef] [PubMed]
15. Aoun, S.M.; Keegan, O.; Roberts, A.; Breen, L.J. The impact of bereavement support on wellbeing: A comparative study between Australia and Ireland. *Palliat. Care Soc. Pract.* **2020**, *14*, 2632352420935132. [CrossRef]
16. Donnelly, S.; Prizeman, G.; Coimín, D.Ó; Korn, B.; Hynes, G. Voices that matter: End-of-life care in two acute hospitals from the perspective of bereaved relatives. *BMC Palliat. Care* **2018**, *17*, 1–13. [CrossRef]
17. Aoun, S.M.; Cafarella, P.A.; Hogden, A.; Thomas, G.; Jiang, L.; Edis, R. Why and how the work of Motor Neurone Disease Associations matters before and during bereavement: A consumer perspective. *Palliat. Care Soc. Pract.* **2021**, *15*, 26323524211009537. [CrossRef] [PubMed]
18. Aoun, S.; Toye, C.; Deas, K.; Howting, D.; Ewing, G.; Grande, G.; Stajduhar, K. Enabling a family caregiver-led assessment of support needs in home-based palliative care: Potential translation into practice. *Palliat. Med.* **2015**, *29*, 929–938. [CrossRef] [PubMed]
19. Aoun, S.M.; Ewing, G.; Grande, G.; Toye, C.; Bear, N. The Impact of Supporting Family Caregivers before Bereavement on Outcomes After Bereavement: Adequacy of End-of-Life Support and Achievement of Preferred Place of Death. *J. Pain Symptom Manag.* **2018**, *55*, 368–378. [CrossRef] [PubMed]
20. Luymes, N.; Williams, N.; Garrison, L.; Goodridge, D.; Silveira, M.; Guthrie, D.M. "The system is well intentioned, but complicated and fallible" interviews with caregivers and decision makers about palliative care in Canada. *BMC Palliat. Care* **2021**, *20*, 1–12. [CrossRef]
21. Abel, J. Compassionate communities and end-of-life care. *Clin. Med.* **2018**, *18*, 6–8. [CrossRef]

22. Rumbold, B.; Aoun, S. An assets-based approach to bereavement care. *Bereave. Care* **2015**, *34*, 99–102. [CrossRef]
23. Boland, J.; Johnson, M.J. End-of-life care for non-cancer patients. *BMJ Support. Palliat. Care* **2013**, *3*, 2–3. [CrossRef] [PubMed]
24. Bandeali, S.; Ordons, A.R.D.; Sinnarajah, A. Comparing the physical, psychological, social, and spiritual needs of patients with non-cancer and cancer diagnoses in a tertiary palliative care setting. *Palliat. Support. Care* **2020**, *18*, 513–518. [CrossRef] [PubMed]
25. Reeve, R.; On behalf of the EOL-CC study authors; Srasuebkul, P.; Langton, J.M.; Haas, M.; Viney, R.; Pearson, S.-A. Health care use and costs at the end of life: A comparison of elderly Australian decedents with and without a cancer history. *BMC Palliat. Care* **2018**, *17*, 1. [CrossRef] [PubMed]
26. Aoun, S.M. The palliative approach to caring for motor neurone disease: From diagnosis to bereavement. *Eur. J. Pers. Centered Heal.* **2018**, *6*, 675–684. [CrossRef]
27. Russell, B.; Vogrin, S.; Philip, J.; Hennessy-Anderson, N.; Collins, A.; Burchell, J.; Le, B.; Brand, C.; Hudson, P.; Sundararajan, V. Triaging the Terminally Ill—Development of the Responding to Urgency of Need in Palliative Care (RUN-PC) Triage Tool. *J. Pain Symptom Manag.* **2020**, *59*, 95–104.e11. [CrossRef] [PubMed]
28. Hirshberg, E.L.; Butler, J.; Francis, M.; Davis, F.A.; Lee, D.; Tavake-Pasi, F.; Napia, E.; Villalta, J.; Mukundente, V.; Coulter, H.; et al. Persistence of patient and family experiences of critical illness. *BMJ Open* **2020**, *10*, e035213. [CrossRef] [PubMed]
29. Van Beek, K.; Siouta, N.; Preston, N.; Hasselaar, J.; Hughes, S.; Payne, S.; Radbruch, L.; Centeno, C.; Csikos, A.; Garralda, E.; et al. To what degree is palliative care integrated in guidelines and pathways for adult cancer patients in Europe: A systematic literature review. *BMC Palliat. Care* **2016**, *15*, 26. [CrossRef] [PubMed]
30. Aoun, S.M.; Abel, J.; Rumbold, B.; Cross, K.; Moore, J.; Skeers, P.; Deliens, L. The Compassionate Communities Connectors model for end-of-life care: A community and health service partnership in Western Australia. *Palliat. Care Soc. Pract.* **2020**, *14*, 1–9. [CrossRef]
31. Abel, J.; Walter, T.; Carey, L.; Rosenberg, J.; Noonan, K.; Horsfall, D.; Leonard, R.; Rumbold, B.; Morris, D. Circles of care: Should community development redefine the practice of palliative care? *BMJ Support. Palliat. Care* **2013**, *3*, 383–388. [CrossRef]
32. Blum, D.; Inauen, R.; Binswanger, J.; Strasser, F. Barriers to research in palliative care: A systematic literature review. *Prog. Palliat. Care* **2015**, *23*, 75–84. [CrossRef]
33. Moghaddam, N.G.; Coxon, H.; Nabarro, S.; Hardy, B.; Cox, K. Unmet care needs in people living with advanced cancer: A systematic review. *Support. Care Cancer* **2016**, *24*, 3609–3622. [CrossRef] [PubMed]
34. Australian Healthcare Associates. *Australian Department of Health, Exploratory Analysis of Barriers to Palliative Care Summary Policy Paper*; Australian Healthcare Associates: Melbourne, Australian, 2020.

healthcare

MDPI

Article

A Salutogenic Perspective on End-of-Life Care among the Indigenous Sámi of Northern Fennoscandia

Lena Kroik [1,2,*], Carol Tishelman [3,4], Krister Stoor [5,6] and Anette Edin-Liljegren [1,2,3]

1 Department of Nursing, Umeå University, 901 87 Umeå, Sweden; anette.liljegren@regionvasterbotten.se
2 The Center for Rural Medicine, Region Västerbotten, 923 31 Storuman, Sweden
3 LIME/Division of Innovative Care Research, Karolinska Institutet, 171 77 Stockholm, Sweden; carol.tishelman@ki.se
4 Stockholm Health Care Services, 171 77 Stockholm, Sweden
5 Department of Language Studies, Umeå University, 901 87 Umeå, Sweden; krister.stoor@umu.se
6 Centre for Sámi Studies-Várdduo, Umeå University, 907 87 Umeå, Sweden
* Correspondence: lena.kroik@regionvasterbotten.se

Abstract: There is limited empirical data about both health and end-of-life (EoL) issues among the Indigenous Sámi of Fennoscandia. We therefore aimed to investigate experiences of EoL care and support among the Sámi, both from the Sámi community itself as well as from more formalized health and social care services in Sweden. Our primary data source is from focus group discussions (FGDs) held at a Sámi event in 2017 with 24 people, complemented with analysis of previously collected data from 15 individual interviews with both Sámi and non-Sámi informants familiar with dying, death and bereavement among Sámi; "go-along" discussions with 12 Sámi, and individual interviews with 31 Sámi about advance care planning. After initial framework analysis, we applied a salutogenic model for interpretation, focusing on a sense of community coherence. We found a range of generalized resistance resources in relation to the Sámi community, which appeared to support EoL care situations, i.e., Social Organization; Familiarity with EoL Care, Collective Cultural Heritage; Expressions of Spirituality; Support from Majority Care Systems; and Brokerage. These positive features appear to support key components of a sense of community coherence, i.e., comprehensibility, meaningfulness and manageability. We also found relatively few, but notable deficits that may diminish the sense of community coherence, i.e., lack of communication in one's own language; orientation, familiarity and/or agreement in contacts with formal health and social care systems; and/or support from extended family. The results suggest that there is a robust basis among Sámi for well-functioning EoL care; a challenge is in developing supportive interactions with the majority health and social care systems that support and complement these structures, for partnership in developing care that is meaningful, comprehensible and manageable even in potentially difficult EoL situations.

Keywords: indigenous research; salutogenesis; end-of-life; ethnic groups; Sámi; Sweden; sense of community coherence

Citation: Kroik, L.; Tishelman, C.; Stoor, K.; Edin-Liljegren, A. A Salutogenic Perspective on End-of-Life Care among the Indigenous Sámi of Northern Fennoscandia. *Healthcare* **2021**, *9*, 766. https://doi.org/10.3390/healthcare9060766

Academic Editors: Georg Bollig and John Rosenberg

Received: 29 April 2021
Accepted: 15 June 2021
Published: 19 June 2021

1. Introduction and Aim

This article derives from a larger program of research, DöBra (DöBra is a pun in Swedish, literally meaning "dying well" and figuratively used as "awesome"), based on a public health approach to end-of-life (EoL) care. DöBra is composed of several specific projects which share the general goal of aiming to promote constructive change to support a better quality of life and death among the general population, in specific subgroups, and interventions directed to professional groups caring for dying individuals, their friends and families. These projects also share some methodological features, working with innovative approaches in partnership with different publics and disciplines. Prompted by the limited empirical data about both health and EoL issues, the article presented here is one of several in a project focusing on EoL issues among the Indigenous Sámi people in Sweden [1–3]. While there is increasing international attention paid to Indigenous health issues, most EoL-related research still derives from Australia, New Zealand and Canada [4,5].

The Sámi have their origin in Sápmi, an area in Northern Fennoscandia. In Sweden today the Sámi population is estimated at between 17,000–40,000 people [6,7]; lack of clarity is a result of ethnic background not being explicitly documented in the country. About 70% of Sámi live in the rural and remote northern half of Sweden [8], with over 4600 involved in reindeer husbandry to some extent [9]. This involves "mobile pastoralism" [10], as the owners follow the reindeer in seasonal wandering across extensive areas. This way of life does not always mesh with the organization of Swedish society [11].

Particular regional and municipal areas in which many Sámi live have a formal mandate to support Sámi opportunities to develop and preserve their culture [12]. This means that government agencies in these areas must actively promote the maintenance and continued development of the Sámi identity, including the Sámi language. In theory, this could include the opportunity for a Sámi person to receive EoL support from health care providers with cultural understanding, knowledge of what it means to live as a Sámi in Sweden today, and with Sámi language skills.

Although limited, the existing research from Sápmi and from other Indigenous contexts gives reason to question the quality of interactions between formal services and Sámi in need of health and social care [13,14]. The overall aim of this article is therefore to investigate experiences of EoL care and support among the Sámi, both from the Sámi community itself as well as from formalized services in the majority society. This includes exploring questions such as who and what is described as providing support in relation to the EoL, what forms of knowledge are referred to, and how the interplay between formal and informal support systems is portrayed.

2. Background

A review of palliative care service delivery for Indigenous Peoples' in Australia, New Zealand, Canada and the U.S. points to commonalities, despite cultural differences, in the importance of cultural aspects, family and network, as well as access to EoL care close to or in the home environment [15,16]. However, this and other research also point to a range of difficulties, often due to living in geographically remote regions, in realizing care provision that incorporates these aspects [17].

Recent research from Canada on cancer treatment decisions further highlights the unique health needs of Indigenous peoples, but also how disparities and other difficulties in contact with the health care system are common, with historical origins from colonial times [18]. Difficulties in contact with mainstream care, notably a lack of satisfaction, were also observed with regard to Norwegian Sámi's contacts with both health and social care systems [19,20]. Numerous factors were found to play a role, i.e., not feeling included in care that was provided without consideration to Sámi language or culture, differences in ways of communicating, particularly around care needs, as well as preconceived notions about Sámi self-sufficiency and reluctance to seek formal care [21]. Blix [22] notes that Sámi may avoid speaking directly about sickness, by using metaphors and other indirect references, a type of indirect communication also addressed by Duggelby et al. [23] in their meta-synthesis of research on Indigenous people's EoL experiences in English-speaking countries. However, Blix [22] also warns about the risk of over-generalization about indirect communication.

In her Swedish doctoral thesis, Daerga [24] found that the Swedish health care system does not fit well with the needs of Sámi migrating reindeer herders who are not able to enroll as patients in a particular care facility. These facilities are also often accessible only at times that are not suitable for them. The needs of reindeer husbandry thus were found to lead to delays in care-seeking and therefore a lack of reliable statistics about health issues. Blix [22], while noting few differences in health status and use of care services between the Norwegian Sámi and the rest of the population, also points to a lack of satisfaction with services among the Sámi, but warns about over-generalizations that may result from describing the Sámi as a homogeneous group.

Even Ness et al. [25] emphasize that the Sámi are not necessarily homogenous even when sharing a specific local background. In their recent Swedish study of older South Sámi people in home care, they found that individuals in this group could have contradictory expectations of nursing care provided by Sámi-speaking staff [25].

While relevant, little Sámi-related research, including that named above, focuses on EoL issues. In our previous EoL-specific research [23], we critically examined Kastenbaum's model of death systems [26] in relation to Swedish Sámi. We found a number of features we call Sámi-relevant, in that they could also be shared by other parts of Swedish society and were often linked to the particular environment in the rural and remote far north. However, we also found Sámi-specific features, closely related to community identity that played a role in relation to dying, death and bereavement. Relationships to nature and seasons linked people, place and time, with the role of the extended family for enculturation of central importance. In contrast to many assumptions, we found that by using a variety of conversational-based data collection and analysis approaches, Sámi people were willing to share their experiences and knowledge related to EoL issues with us. However, the research we conducted previously did not focus on the part of Kastenbaum's death system related to "care for dying" [1–3]; in this article, we make an effort to fill this knowledge gap.

3. Methods

3.1. Research Team Investigating Sámi Perspectives on EoL

The research group consists of four people, with both Sámi and non-Sámi backgrounds. Both Sámi researchers, a south Sámi woman PhD student and registered nurse L.K, and K.S, a northern Sámi man with a PhD in Sámi studies, have strong roots in the reindeer-herding community. The non-Sámi researchers are a non-Swedish woman, CT who is a registered nurse PhD living in the capital region of Sweden and a woman PhD, AEL, from northern Sweden, with experience of research involving Sámi health issues. LK, KS, and CT participated in all or part of the data collection underlying this article, along with OL, a non-Sámi RN PhD researcher and project PI until his death in 2018.

3.2. Data Collection

The bulk of the data was collected in 2017 at the Sámi Church Days, an event arranged every fourth year by Sámi church organizations in the Nordic countries and Barents region—that is, the whole area considered to be Sápmi, the original home of the Sámi people. This event brings many Sámi together, irrespective of whether they identify as religious or secular, as it is one of few occasions to meet, even across country borders. In 2017, Sweden hosted the Church Days in a small town in Lapland in Northern Sweden. This event focused on Sámi church life, with worship services, talks, lectures and cultural presentations covering a wide range of Sámi-relevant topics. Issues such as Sámi rights, self-determination, sustainable development in the Arctic, reconciliation and further development of Sámi church life were some of the areas discussed. The first author contacted the organizers about their interest in her presenting research findings from the group's initial studies as a means for both providing feedback to the community and inspiring new group discussion as a form of data collection. Information about the 90-min initiative consisting of both a lecture "When the well of life dwindles-care at the end of life" with subsequent focus-group discussions (FGDs) was disseminated through the program for the Sámi Church Days.

Approximately 50 people attended the lecture, and 24 participated in the following FGDs with all providing informed consent to use the data generated. No pre-registration to this program point was needed. Participants were predominately Sámi with a variety of backgrounds, most from Sweden, but also from Norway and Finland, working with, e.g., reindeer husbandry, in churches, with handcrafts and other forms of Sámi culture, in the health/social care system and as academics and linguists. No demographic data were systematically collected at this event.

Four FGDs with 5–7 participants plus a moderator in each, were held simultaneously in a large room, with each table focusing on a different topic and moderated by one member of the research team. Participants themselves chose which topic they wished to discuss. The four topics were: "Is yoik (a form of Sámi a cappella song, see below) a natural part of dying, death and bereavement (FGD 1, moderator KS)?"; "What role does the landscape/nature play in dying, death and bereavement (FGD 2, LK)?"; "How do the health and social care systems work today for Sámi at the end-of-life (FGD 3, OL)?" and "Who does what in Sámi families at the end-of-life and in its aftermath (FGD 4, CT)?"

The FGDs lasted for about 30 min, with a 15-min joint closing discussion including a summary of the discussion at each table. Each FGD was audio-recorded, as was the joint discussion, and the event photo-documented after receiving permission from all participants.

While the bulk of the data used for analysis was generated as described above, this was complemented with a directed content analysis [27] to find additional relevant data from our combined, previously generated data with 58 other individuals derived from (a) individual interviews (n = 15, see [1] for detail) from 2016–2017 with both Sámi and non-Sámi informants with experience of dying, death and bereavement among Sámi; (b) storytelling in go-along group discussions to gravesites at the tree-line with cultural and historical significance for the Indigenous Sámi peoples held in 2017 (n = 12 Sámi participants [2]); and (c) brief explorative advance care planning (ACP) discussions with 31 Sámi people with participants at Sámi events in 2019–2020 [3], see Table 1. While the data collection approaches varied, they shared the characteristic of addressing EoL issues in conversational form, and the combined database for this analysis focused on transcript excerpts related to EoL care only.

Table 1. Overview of previous data collections.

	Individual Interviews [1]	Go-Along Focusgroup Discussions [2]	Individual Interviews [3]
Age (year)	25–83	19–78	26–84
Participants, number (n)	15	12	31
Women (n)	8	7	18
Men (n)	7	5	13

See references. [1] [1] [2] [2] [3] [3].

3.3. Ethics

In addition to formal ethical permission granted (2016/02-31, 2016/252-32), we also contacted the Church of Sweden's research unit and received their permission for data collection at the Sámi Church Days. Prior to ethical review, we composed an information letter and informed consent form for participants. These were professionally translated from Swedish to Norwegian and to the three major Sámi languages.

3.4. Data Analysis

Analysis initially followed Framework Analysis, focusing on the care of the dying. Framework analysis is an iterative approach [28] that makes use of previous knowledge by questioning its relevance and developing it further in relation to new data, thus heightening its usefulness in practice and policy. The analysis was performed in the 5 steps described by Ward [28]: 1. Familiarization—through immersion in the data, 2. Developing a theoretical framework by identifying recurrent and important themes, 3. Indexing and pilot charting, 4. Summarizing data in analytical framework, and 5. Synthesizing data by mapping and interpreting. These steps are shown in the graphic illustration of the analysis process depicted in Figure 1.

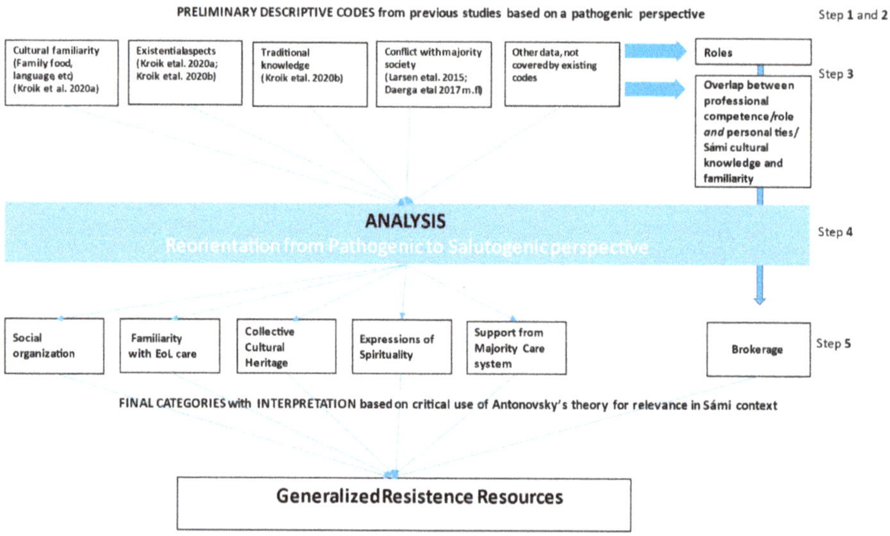

Figure 1. Graphic description of the analytic process.

LK, who led data analysis with the support of the co-authors, began by familiarizing herself with all data, listening to audio recordings and rereading verbatim transcripts repeatedly. In the next stage, she extracted all data relating to the care of the dying up until the time of the funeral and compiled it in a new database. Based on the existing literature, both from this research group's prior studies and the international literature, preliminary codes were developed and used in initial indexing and pilot charting onto a matrix for each data segment about EoL care. The initial preliminary descriptive codes can be found in Figure 1.

At this point, we began to recognize that the research team, emulating much of the literature, had been expecting a problem-orientation in the data. We instead observed that this focus led us to circular reasoning, without generating new knowledge and did not seem to match the substance of the empirical data. We began to transition from description to analysis and observed several salient features in the data. One feature was that the distinction between professional or formal health and care services versus informal caregiving was not found to be as distinct as expected, resulting in new preliminary codes relating to overlap and integration of formal and informal care systems through the roles people had (Figure 1). The second feature of importance was that much of the data described how difficult situations were dealt with in manners evaluated as positive by the participants.

This latter feature led to a new stage in the analysis process, illustrated in Figure 1, in which we questioned our own pathogenic assumptions as researchers and made an effort to focus on what new knowledge could be found in these data, which led us to be inspired by Antonovsky's salutogenic framework [29] for interpretation. This phase was guided by a new question we addressed to the data during analysis: "What is described as leading to positive outcomes in EoL care situations among the Sámi, according to these data?"

As we continued the coding/recoding process, we observed that most of our final categories could be conceptualized according to what Antonovsky described as Generalized Resistance Resources (GRRs) in his early work [30]. GRRs are defined as "any characteristic of the person, the group, or the environment that can facilitate effective tension management" and are described along a continuum with the opposite pole called Generalized Resistance Deficits (GRDs) when such resources are lacking (p. 28). Antonovsky means that GRRs are important in that they provide life experiences that promote the development and maintenance of what he calls a strong Sense of Coherence (SOC), whereas GRDs provide experiences that wear away at a SOC (p. 129).

While a SOC is generally discussed in relation to individuals, several researchers also argue its relevance in more collective situations, e.g., families and communities [31]. According to Peled, Sagy and Braun-Lewensohn [32], a sense of community coherence is based on the same three key components as individual SOC. In this context, they define *comprehensibility* as the "sense of predictability and security felt by the members of a community and the extent of which the community is comprehensible"; *manageability* as "the ability of the community to assist its members in times of need"; and *meaningfulness*, the motivational component, as "the ability of the members of the community to express themselves in order to feel a higher level of satisfaction and interest within the community".

The final interpretative phase illustrated in Figure 1, involved again perusing all data in relation to GRRs, GRDs and the components of a SOC on a community level. The relationships among these are presented in Figure 2 and described below in relation to findings from the empirical data. In the final section of the paper, we discuss how this is relevant in relation to a sense of collective coherence. As there is only limited literature using a salutogenic perspective in a Sámi context [33–35], we also made an effort to distinguish data that might question the theory's applicability or relevance in this context.

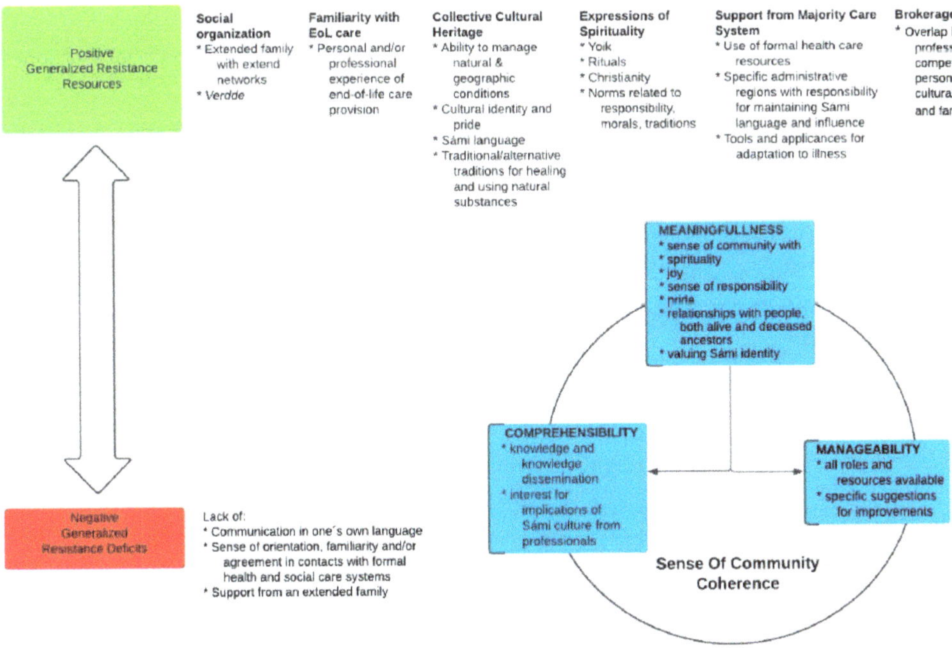

Figure 2. Graphic representation of a description and interpretation of the results.

4. Findings

The findings are presented in relation to the illustration in Figure 2. GRRs, at the positive end of a continuum, are shown on the upper half of Figure 2, and conceptualized in relation to the Sámi community as Social Organization; Familiarity with EoL Care, Collective Cultural Heritage; Expression of Spirituality; Support from Majority Care Systems; and Brokerage, with related factors found in the data, under each heading; note that these codes are not mutually exclusive but presented separately for the sake of clarity. These positive features support the key components of a sense of community coherence, i.e., Comprehensibility, Meaningfulness and Manageability. The lower left side of the figure shows the opposite, negative end of the GRR-GRD continuum, with the relatively few features that work to diminish a sense of community coherence that were found in these data.

All individuals cited below are Sámi, if not otherwise noted.

4.1. Generalized Resistance Resources

4.1.1. Social Organization

The most central organizational form in these data relating to EoL is the extended family, a feature of Sámi life that is self-evident and taken for granted, as this woman says, "*Family is just there. It's just there.*" (FGD 4) There were also many stories about its' importance; one woman working as a home health aide, said:

In some way I feel like I think we have stronger ties to each other in some strange way. They [non-Sámi] say, usually say like "*yes, you Sámi, you're so attached to your family [. . .] I think that . . . at times of death . . . it gives us strength when there is serious disease. And it's something, I think, that we should boast about . . .* " (FGD 4)

This comment exemplifies a number of important resources, i.e., social support, commitment, and cohesion to one's cultural roots, and suggests others, i.e., cultural stability and coping strategies, with a sense of pride and happiness apparent in her voice.

Cultural stability is also demonstrated through traditions that are incorporated into an existing and functioning extended family system, which becomes particularly evident in EoL situations. A lawyer speaks of his own role in his extended family, but also refers to the informal *Verdde* (North Sámi spelling) system, for reciprocity between reindeer-herding Sámi families and non-reindeer-herding families, both Sámi and non-Sámi [36]. *Verdde* involves the mourning family being helped and supported with practical aspects of life, particularly around the time of burial:

> *I'm participating here [at the churchdays] because I think I have . . . as a member of this clan I have experienced lots of . . . I have been part of this family system, relation . . . this care in the end-of-life. There are some...lots of things to think about. Lots of traditions in my area and also in the other Sámi areas. And also dealing with this . . . subject in my profession.* (FGD 3)

4.1.2. Familiarity with End-Of-Life Care

The importance of self-determination with the ability to steer resources—physical, practical and psychosocial—appeared often to be related to having knowledge and experience oneself or access to it through others that were trusted. This is evident in a conversation between two women, a nursing assistant (D6) and a Norwegian church functionary (D2, non-Sámi) about in-patient care for D6's dying relative:

> D6: *I felt like my workmates were a support during that time.*
>
> D2: *But then you were steering it a bit when you decided what you would need . . . it was you who was the closest as well, and so it was you who pressed the button when they [staff] should come in.*
>
> D6: *yes, but I . . . but you know what it was? I'm both an assistant nurse and a relative, and then I could sometimes feel 'what is what'? But I didn't feel badly about it. I had to call you know, when I felt like I couldn't manage, then I called and so another workmate came in.* (FGD 4)

This situation illustrates a positive collaboration between formal care provision and family, simplified by an overlap with a family member with professional competence and familiarity, not only with care but also with the care providers. However, this was not always the case, and perhaps the most striking GRDs were those describing the negative effects of lacking such familiarity. The following quote illustrates a situation in which a woman describes her sense of being lost in an unfamiliar care system, which also defined the role of family differently than was the norm in her community:

Because we were very lost, both mama and me, in the health care system. And these words that are so important, care-planning and ... if you ... you know what you can get and not get from the health care system when you are in ... you know, death's waiting room, that was very confusing for us. And as Sámi, we are very close to our extended family and it is, it was very confusing because we're used to doing everything ourselves and then suddenly the health care system tells me "you shouldn't be the care provider, you should be family, you should brighten up her last phase of life". And it was really hard to figure out where the line should be drawn. And I realized afterwards that I maybe should have asked for help earlier. As an only child and as a Sámi, it was very ... And finally Mama said stop, she said "we reached the limit, it's no longer dignified for you, as my child, to care for me" And that feeling of being lost in the health care system as a Sámi, in death's waiting room, I feel that so strongly, that a little book or something is needed. (FGD 4)

This woman is unusually clear about a need for guidance for her, as a Sámi, in dealing with EoL issues. This unfamiliar situation demanded a departure from that which she was used to and which was tradition for her. She expresses a clear sense of vulnerability, for both her mother and herself, in as she says " ... *death's waiting room*". (FGD 4)

4.1.3. Collective Cultural Heritage

While the description above relates to problems arising as Sámi norms clash with the majority health care system, many stories instead spoke to the importance of and pride in Sámi traditions and cultural features such as food, nature, and reindeer-herding as providing both structure and support at the EoL. A woman working for a municipality told a story of noting the importance of familiar sensory experiences during her visit to a residential care home for the elderly, relating it to information from a local government survey of older Sámi:

And I pushed that 'skåerrie' [a piece of treated reindeer skin with a recognizable scent] across the table to the two ladies sitting there. And they just went 'mmm, skåerrie, ohhhhh'. So you can see how much it means, things you may think are trivial, but they are memories and they are childhood and they are family and they are just the culture, they are so much ...

There were three things everyone wanted [refers to the survey]. And these were that when they got older and moved to a care home, they wanted to still have their language with staff that could speak Sámi, and Sámi food, and they wanted to be able to be with other Sámi. (from data collection 2, go-along group discussions)

Sámi languages were mentioned repeatedly in discussions and stories, as both an important aspect of care, as well as a means to deal with grief. A non-Sámi priest, experienced in working with Sámi congregations, exemplifies this, saying:

And you know, it's not possible to carry those feelings across in a second or third language, and so therefore we need to use our mother tongue in such times, that is at a death bed or at the funeral [...] as an important part of the process, the healing process or the grieving process. (FGD 1)

Another, less frequently described and, as observed below, often silenced, phenomenon, that of using traditional Sámi medicines, was spoken of by a young woman who had her own experience of life-threatening disease:

And then there's a lot, you might say alternative medicine, that is not drugs, but how you earlier maybe drank chaga-birch tea and blueberry, that is these things that are around, that have been used for a long time. So this knowledge exists. But it's very very ... hush hush and secretive. (From data collection 3, ACP discussions)

As she continues, the intertwined relationship between traditional treatments and spirituality also becomes evident:

> *They [the family] called 'govhlar', what's it called, kind of healers, shamans, who you believe in, in the Sámi culture and who still remain. And you call them and ask them for help so that they can heal and make it take a turn for the better now [. . .] No one has visited me in person, but it's about these strong forces that work through the mind.* (From data collection 3, ACP discussions)

4.1.4. Expressions of Spirituality

As observed in the above quote from the young Sámi woman, spirituality was evidenced in many aspects of life, and not only isolated in formal religious rituals. One Sámi-specific means of dealing with feelings such as grief, but also a means of making death both comprehensible and meaningful, is *yoik*, a traditional Sámi a cappella song. Yoik is both a verb and a noun, and one yoiks not to someone or something, one becomes what one yoiks [37]. This man speaks of how he commemorates his connection to his ancestors through "person yoik": *"It is very important when it's related to death. Just to be able to go on and remember or spend time with someone through their person yoik."* (FGD 1)

Yoik is also a means for communicating joy. A social worker tells about her sister's funeral and its' effect on others less familiar with Sámi traditions:

> *But during the funeral there was yoik and everything. And then these people, her workmates, she said it was fantastic to be at a Sámi funeral. We're there with koltar* [traditional clothing in the national colors of red, blue, yellow and green] *and all, it's not all in black and so, but it was, yes it was so very nice.* (FGD 4)

In these data, expressions of spirituality often reflected a way of life. Based on her experience of EoL situations, this non-Sámi woman who had worked with Sámi churches for many years described how animals could be a form of protection, as well as support:

> *I'm thinking about if I experienced anything [. . .] the animals had such . . . importance [. . .]. And everyone had their own animal that watched over them and that they were preoccupied with, and then I thought, that this is a Sámi thing. Understanding animals and that way of being observant, it comes from their way of living . . .* (FGD 2)

However, Christianity was dominant in the descriptions of formal religion at the EoL, with many variations between individuals and families, but as a self-evident part of many Sámi's identities. As a woman said: *"We are so influenced by it* [Christianity] *and we're Christian of course, we are more Christian than Swedish in general."* (FGD 4)

Another aspect of our data we categorize as relating to spirituality regards an immaterial legacy of Sámi values and norms. Many ways of dealing with responsibilities in EoL situations were spoken of, and this male, non-Sámi church parson speaks of dangers in neglecting such responsibilities:

> *even though you are related [. . .] there are these moral obligations. There is also a . . . it's also dangerous to say no [. . .], yes, it is unheard of, so to speak. You can also bring misfortune over yourself then [. . .] since it is such a very strict norm* (FGD 3)

Sámi norms thus demand both engagement and continuity with one's cultural roots, with many speaking of responsibilities at the EoL as indisputable. While Sámi people are often depicted in stereotypes, i.e., *"strong and solitary"*, *"uncomplaining"*, and *"quiet and self-sufficient"* (FGD 4) we also find descriptions that challenge these clichés, for example as told by this woman from a remote area:

> *I've grown up with X siblings, and if one is sick, we are all sick and everyone wants to contribute [. . .] Father always said 'it's important to show your feelings'. And we have cried together and I have a sibling who died in an accident [. . .] I thought when my brother died [. . .] then that it was punishment from God. But then my grandmother said 'it's not punishment from God, but we have different trials, because life is a school that can be hard sometimes, and maybe his time had come'. And that has given me strength in my grief process, thinking that [. . .] his time had come. [. . .] it's a trial but not a punishment. There's no shame. No sense of shame.* (FGD 4)

However, shame and silence are spoken about by several participants as a way of dealing with sickness and death. A woman speaks of this in relation to her own experiences of caring for a close family member at the EoL:

> *Yes, and in the Sámi world, there is a zipper here. You shouldn't talk about feelings, you shouldn't ... you feel shame if you are sick because then there is something evil you have ... sort of ... You have maybe ... it is a punishment from God. And there is a lot of shame connected to talking about it and opening yourself up.* (FGD 4)

Despite these traditional norms, several participants, as observed above, expressed a desire for more openness. As the woman quoted directly above continues: "*But I also have to say thank you for people daring to talk ... It feels so very ... very beneficial*". (FGD 4)

4.1.5. Support from Majority Care Systems

In the text above, there are illustrations of problems arising at the intercept of the majority health care system and the Sámi community. However, there were also descriptions of well-functioning support. One woman, living in a remote area, describes how she, along with her sisters, struggled to move their mother from inpatient care to her home during the last days of her life. While there was the conflict with the hospital, she described the support they felt from the primary health care system:

> *If you only knew how stubborn we had to be. Everyone came and said, 'do you really understand what kind of responsibility you are taking on, the responsibility you have?' But then I call the community nurse [mentioning her by first name] and so I said ... I told about how it was and that we were thinking of bringing Mama home, but that they advised us not to. "Take [mentions mother by name] home, I'll come and help you" she just said. So my sister went to her [the community nurse] and brought back a load of things to help ...* (from data collection 2, go-along group discussions)

Help was also provided by representatives of voluntary organizations, described as enthusiasts, working with municipalities. In the following quote, ongoing work in an area in which government agencies appear to take their mandate to support Sámi culture seriously is referred to, here in relation to residential care homes for the elderly. A woman who works with traditional handcrafts says:

> *and there are always some fantastic enthusiasts who work for the Sámi population, the elders, who should be able to have a place in residential care homes, on special units where they feel at home, where staff who applies for those positions, they are able to study Sámi language to be able to meet their needs [...]. And then you need some enthusiasts who, along with their maternal and paternal grandparents, get a foot in and have the strength to get the municipalities to ... so that this unit ... it should be reserved for ... it should just be for Sámi.* (FGD 2)

While in the above quotes, participants describe actual help received from majority social care systems in collaboration with Sámi support systems, a woman who had worked in home health care speaks of her visions for the future, pointing to a sense of security and cultural context in daily life as crucial:

> *...for us Sámi, our own TV and group room, so we can see Ođđasat* [Sámi news program] *without the laedtieh* [non-Sámi] *who question 'what's that you're watching?' ... no, I say, we should have our own* [...], *we can be in the same unit* [...] *but then when we should have our food and such, then we can go and eat in their dining room. But we should have our own ... it should be the kind of cooking that we cook, so we can make bovtsen bearkoe* [reindeer meat] *and we can guelie voessjedh jih maelie laejpie bissedh jih numhtie* [cook fish and fry blood bread and all that] ... (FGD 2)

4.1.6. Brokerage as a Bridge between Cultures

The ability to deal with EoL care is strongly supported by the extended family system, which activates a wide range of resources in a broad network. In our data, we found frequent mention of how a variety of people with formal education and/or experience who were within the reach of the extended family, were used as resources, able to fill different roles. We found examples of people acting as advocates for the ill person and family, assistant nurses, community nurses, deacon/deaconess, home help aides, hospital clergy, hospital translators, physicians, priests, registered nurses, and representatives of volunteer organizations. Most notable is that these people act as a bridge, i.e., as brokers, between the Sámi community and resources and knowledge about EoL from the majority society.

In the preceding text, we provided one example showing how a Sámi woman negotiated her double role as a family member and an assistant nurse and also described how the extended family and Sámi culture are an organizational form resting on both a strong sense of responsibility and sharing such responsibility in particular manners. Another participant spoke about how EoL home care for his Sámi mother was made possible through the help of a relative he describes as *"a woman who had sure-fire competence and was able to take the bulk of responsibility."* (FGD 3)

A woman reflects on the benefit her father had in having a Sámi-speaking community nurse during his last phase of life: *"I know my father had a community nurse who spoke Sámi, and she was the one he had most trust in ... it was her that he ... he waited for her to come, so he could talk."* (from data collection 1, individual interviews)

A non-Sámi priest describes the effect of a psalm the priest sung in a familiar language in the last days of a Sámi man's life:

> *And then I sang, and so suddenly, the nurse, she happened to be there and suddenly he [the dying Sámi man] lifted one of his hands and so he began ... you could even hear it, how he started to hum along, and then she [the nurse] said 'that's never happened before', she said. Yes, but now it happened. It touched something inside him ...* (from data collection 1, individual interviews)

The Sámi lawyer summarizes well the importance of the broker role, bridging different systems and types of knowledge needed to deal with EoL issues among Sámi communities:

> *And most people don't have the energy and the knowledge that they have [in the formal health care system]. So that's why it's so important that someone in the church and in the health care system knows what's important to Sámi, and asks about it, isn't it? And it is ... that we know too little, really both the church and health care and all those places. That's why it's so important, what you see here [in this research].* (FGD 3)

4.2. Generalized Resistance Deficits

We have already mentioned most of the GRDs found in our data in the above text, contrasting them with the positive qualities of GRRs, for example, lack of communication in one's own language, as well as a sense of disorientation or lack of familiarity with, or at its' most extreme, conflicts with health and social care systems. In addition, one other GRD found in our data concerns the lack of an extended family. This is evident in this comment by a priest:

> *I was thinking, horrors of horrors is one of ... if there is a Sámi who doesn't have a strong family who can stop, then you are ... abandoned to a system that has it's bureaus and doesn't have time or space or possibility or the desire to let the family go in and be involved. And the people of the church even have [refers to internal lack of understanding for Sámi culture and needs even within the church]. Because we wanted the family to ride with the casket but 'no that's not what we usually do' ...* (FGD 3)

The priest ended his comment by pointing out that even with strong family ties, conflicts can occur not only with the health or care systems but also with the church when norms and traditions collide.

5. Discussion

In this study, we see a new perspective of the extended family in Sámi EoL contexts as including a broad network with far-reaching arms. This family/network functions as a social organizational system and form of support in which those involved have clear roles and responsibilities. Through this network, a wide range of GRRs are accessed and various resources can be activated when needed. This extended system plays a central role in linking both what is often called an "informal" community-based care system with the formal care provided by the majority society, in best cases appearing to support EoL care becoming meaningful, comprehensible, and manageable.

Despite some potential limitations in our data, e.g., the selective nature of our three samples with most informants self-defined Sámi from Northern Sweden, and a substantial portion of data deriving from Sámi church Days, we still find that many of the GRRs we see in our data that are accessed through extensive network systems are well in line with those described by Horsburgh and Ferguson [38]. To use their terms, we see GRRs related to material resources; knowledge and intelligence (e.g., knowing the world and acquiring skills); coping strategies rooted in tradition; social support, commitment, and cohesion with one's cultural roots; cultural stability; rituals; religion; and philosophy. In combination, these comprise a world view and way of life which seems to often provide a "stable set of answers to life's perplexities" [39], and also includes relationships with nature and animals. While Horsburgh and Ferguson [38] also name personal attributes, those are beyond the scope of this study, as we focus on a sense of community coherence here.

However, as observed previously, the characteristics of a sense of community coherence are collective versions of components important on an individual level [32]. We found only limited prior research based on Antonovsky's work in Sámi populations, with all focusing on the individual level using the SOC instrument [33–35]. Abramsson et al. [33] found that while there were relatively few differences between the majority Swedish sample and the Sámi sample in their study, Sámi working with the traditional occupation of reindeer-herding were found to have lower SOC, particularly in regard to comprehensibility, but had notably high levels of meaningfulness. Hassler and Eklund [34] compared self-reported health with results from the short version of the SOC instrument, finding that the studied Sámi had low levels of mental health and experiences of structural discrimination similar to another official minority group in Sweden, the Roma people. Alex [35] studied resilience among old Sámi women. The Sámi women's narratives generally described a high degree of resilience; discrimination was described as negatively affecting their resilience. This leads to several questions, previously raised by Tishelman [40], e.g., how can the same manner of instrumentalizing SOC, as in the existing questionnaire, be both supra-cultural and gender-neutral, particularly as it aims to investigate "a succinct formulation of a world view, of the web of linkages between the person and his or her world" [41]. We note the importance of this linkage clearly in our data. While our data may be considered limited in that we apply no measurement of SOC on the individual level, through analysis of our qualitative data and consideration of the components of community coherence, we have instead provided a variety of examples leading to a new understanding of what supports the components of community SOC. We find that comprehensibility is heightened by a clear understanding of both roles and responsibilities, as well as norms and values that have permeated the Sámi culture across generations. This knowledge, and its dissemination through processes of enculturation [1,2] seem to help make EoL care both meaningful, comprehensible and manageable. Meaningfulness is indeed one of the most prominent aspects of these data, and difficult to disentangle from comprehensibility and manageability, as both concrete and general descriptions could be permeated with pride and joy in Sámi traditions and culture. What is striking in these data, is the importance of familiarity with and respect for this from professionals. Manageability is also heightened by familiarity, which means that contacts with the majority health care system may involve potential risks to the sense of community coherence, if cultural values, traditions and norms are not respected.

In these data we found a variety of people who acted as cultural brokers, seeming to help negotiate risks, access resources in both material and immaterial forms, and avoid distress. These individuals appear to have a key role in mediating contact between the majority health and care systems, and those based in the Sámi community. In these data, cultural brokers were trusted people with knowledge about how the majority care system worked and familiarity and/or sensitivity about the Sámi context. These people were often but not always Sámi themselves, as even others, e.g., non-Sámi community care nurses, could act to bridge cultures. We have however found few descriptions of cultural brokers specifically for EoL care. One exception is Aboriginal or Indigenous Liaison Officers who work in various ways to support culturally appropriate EoL care [17].

One role of such cultural brokers can be seen as promoting cultural safety. Mehus et al. [42] found that bilingual health care staff in Norway were able to use their competency in Western medicine and familiarity with the majority health care system to provide culturally safe care for the Sámi population, illustrating a form of cultural brokerage. Other examples of cultural brokerage for Sámi in Norway through use of Sámi staff are illustrated by Andreassen Devik and Olsen 2020 [43] based on municipal care for elderly Sámi, and Larsen [13], as who studied relatives to Sámi patients with dementia.

Mehus et al. [42] mean that in order to achieve cultural safety on a group level, all health professionals who meet Sámi patients and families should reflect on the extent to which cultural competence and sensitivity are present in their workplaces. Andreassen Devik and Olsen [43] conclude that cultural sensitivity is even a prerequisite for person-centered care for Sámi. While the term cultural sensitivity is most often used in English-language literature, its use is not always consistent [44], and in our prior work, we have used the term cultural humility [45] instead. Whichever term is used, we argue based on this study, that most important is that these qualities lead to cultural safety for Sámi or other Indigenous groups in contact with majority health and social care systems. As Schill and Caxaj [46] highlight from their review of palliative care in rural Indigenous settings in several countries, cultural competency may lead to a framework of cultural safety but is not sufficient in itself. They also emphasize that strategies leading to cultural safety contribute to decolonization of care, by heightening awareness of colonialism, racism and discrimination, and thus supporting partnership building and sharing of power and decision-making in care situations.

6. Conclusions

In conclusion, according to Antonovsky, a prerequisite for discussing SOC on a community level is the existence of an "identifiable collectivity", with sense of shared identity [30], pointing out that a group SOC can be a characteristic of an oppressed or self-aware minority. The insight achieved through this study suggests that there is a robust basis among self-defined Sámi for well-functioning EoL care; a challenge is in developing supportive interactions with the majority health and social care systems that further support and complement these structures, for partnership in developing care that is meaningful, comprehensible and manageable even in potentially difficult EoL situations.

Author Contributions: Conceptualization, L.K., C.T., K.S. and A.E.-L.; methodology, L.K., C.T., K.S.; formal analysis, L.K., C.T., K.S. and A.E.-L.; writing—original draft preparation, L.K., C.T.; writing—review and editing, L.K., C.T., K.S., and A.E.-L.; supervision, A.E.-L., C.T., K.S. funding acquisition, C.T. All authors have read and agreed to the published version of the manuscript.

Funding: This research was funded by: the Swedish Research council for Health, Welfare and Working Life (FORTE) (grant # 2014-4071) for the DöBra Research Programme; Umeå University Department of Nursing and the Centre for Rural Medicine, Region Västerbotten.

Institutional Review Board Statement: The study was conducted according to the guidelines of the Declaration of Helsinki, and approved by the Ethics Committee of Umeå University (2016/02-31, 2016/252-32).

Informed Consent Statement: Informed consent was obtained from all subjects involved in the study; no patients or persons in vulnerable situations have taken part in the study.

Data Availability Statement: For original data, please contact the corresponding author; ethical approval does not cover making data openly accessible.

Acknowledgments: We would like to thank Olav Lindqvist, who died suddenly in the spring of 2018, for his important contributions to the initial ideas and data collection underlying this article, as well as the participants who so generously shared their knowledge and perspectives with us.

Conflicts of Interest: The authors declare no conflict of interest. The funders had no role in the design of the study; in the collection, analyses, or interpretation of data; in the writing of the manuscript, or in the decision to publish the results.

References

1. Kroik, L.; Lindqvist, O.; Stoor, K.; Tishelman, C. The past is present: Death systems among the Indigenous Sámi in Northern Scandinavia today. *Mortality* **2020**, *25*, 470–489. [CrossRef]
2. Kroik, L.; Stoor, K.; Edin-Liljegren, A.; Tishelman, C. Using narrative analysis to explore traditional Sámi knowledge through storytelling about End-of-Life. *Health Place* **2020**, *65*, 102424. [CrossRef]
3. Kroik, L.; Eneslätt, M.; Tishelman, C.; Stoor, K.; Edin-Liljegren, A. Values and Preferences for Future End-of-Life Care among the Indigenous Sámi. *DiVA* **2021**, diva2:1542796.
4. Kelley; Prince, H.; Nadin, S.; Brazil, K.; Crow, M.; Hanson, G.; Maki, L.; Monture, L.; Mushquash, C.J.; O'Brien, V.; et al. Developing palliative care programs in Indigenous communities using participatory action research: a Canadian application of the public health approach to palliative care. *Ann. Palliat. Med.* **2018**, *7*, S52–S72. [CrossRef]
5. Caxaj, C.S.; Schill, K.; Janke, R. Priorities and challenges for a palliative approach to care for rural indigenous populations: A scoping review. *Health Soc. Care Community* **2018**, *26*, e329–e336. [CrossRef] [PubMed]
6. Wängberg, H.Å. Samerätt och samiskt språk: slutbetänkande. In *Statens Offentliga Utredningar*; Allmänna förl.: Stockholm, Sweden, 1990; ISSN 0375-250X.
7. Sametinget. Samerna i Sverige. Available online: https://www.sametinget.se/samer (accessed on 17 June 2021).
8. Hassler; Johansson, R.; Sjolander, P.; Gronberg, H.; Damber, L. Causes of death in the Sami population of Sweden, 1961–2000. *Int. J. Epidemiol.* **2005**, *34*, 623–629. [CrossRef] [PubMed]
9. Sametinget. Statistik Rennäring. Available online: https://www.sametinget.se/renstatistik (accessed on 17 June 2021).
10. Ingold, T. *Hunters, Pastoralists and Ranchers: Reindeer Economies and Their Transformations*; Cambridge U.P.: Cambridge, UK, 1980.
11. FAO. Understanding Mobile Pastoralism Key to Prevent Conflict. Available online: http://www.fao.org/pastoralist-knowledge-hub/news/detail/en/c/449730/ (accessed on 22 January 2021).
12. Lag (2009:724) om Nationella Minoriteter och Minoritetsspråk. Available online: https://www.riksdagen.se/sv/dokument-lagar/dokument/svensk-forfattningssamling/lag-2009724-om-nationella-minoriteter-och_sfs-2009-724 (accessed on 17 June 2021).
13. Larsen, L.S.; Normann, H.K.; Hamran, T. Collaboration between Sami and non-Sami formal and family caregivers in rural municipalities. *Ethn. Racial Stud.* **2015**, *39*, 821–839. [CrossRef]
14. Daerga; Sjolander, P.; Jacobsson, L.; Edin-Liljegren, A. The confidence in health care and social services in northern Sweden—A comparison between reindeer-herding Sami and the non-Sami majority population. *Scand. J. Public Health* **2012**, *40*, 516–522. [CrossRef]
15. Bernardes, C.M.; Diaz, A.; Valery, P.C.; Sabesan, S.; Baxi, S.; Aoun, S.; Thompson, S.C.; Lashbrook, M.; Garvey, G. Unmet supportive care needs among Indigenous cancer patients across Australia. *Rural Remote Health* **2019**, *19*, 4660. [CrossRef] [PubMed]
16. Shahid, S.; Taylor, E.V.; Cheetham, S.; Woods, J.A.; Aoun, S.M.; Thompson, S.C. Key features of palliative care service delivery to Indigenous peoples in Australia, New Zealand, Canada and the United States: A comprehensive review. *BMC Palliat. Care* **2018**, *17*, 72. [CrossRef] [PubMed]
17. Waran, E.; O'Connor, N.; Zubair, M.Y.; May, P. 'Finishing up' on country: Challenges and compromises. *Intern. Med. J.* **2016**, *46*, 1108–1111. [CrossRef] [PubMed]
18. Roberts, R.A.; Groot, G.; Carr, T. Decisions on cancer care by Indigenous peoples in Alberta and Saskatchewan: A narrative analysis. *Rural Remote Health* **2020**, *20*, 5610. [CrossRef] [PubMed]
19. Hansen, K.L. Ethnic discrimination and health: the relationship between experienced ethnic discrimination and multiple health domains in Norway's rural Sami population. *Int. J. Circumpolar Health* **2015**, *74*, 25125. [CrossRef] [PubMed]
20. Nystad, T.; Melhus, M.; Lund, E. Sami speakers are less satisfied with general practitioners' services. *Int. J. Circumpolar Health* **2008**, *67*, 116–123. [CrossRef]
21. Blix, B.H.; Hamran, T. "They take care of their own": Healthcare professionals' constructions of Sami persons with dementia and their families' reluctance to seek and accept help through attributions to multiple contexts. *Int. J. Circumpolar Health* **2017**, *76*. [CrossRef]
22. Blix, B.H. Helse- og Omsorgstjenester til den Samiske Befolkningen i Norge. Available online: https://core.ac.uk/download/pdf/335076695.pdf (accessed on 17 June 2021).
23. Duggleby, W.; Kuchera, S.; MacLeod, R.; Holyoke, P.; Scott, T.; Holtslander, L.; Letendre, A.; Moeke-Maxwell, T.; Burhansstipanov, L.; Chambers, T. Indigenous people's experiences at the end of life. *Palliat. Supportive Care* **2015**, *13*, 1721–1733. [CrossRef]

24. Daerga, L. Att Leva I Två Världar: Hälsoaspekter Bland Renskötande Samer. Ph.D. Thesis, Umeå Universitet, Umeå, Sweden, 2017.
25. Ness, T.M.; Soderberg, S.; Hellzen, O. 'Contradictions in having care providers with a South Sami background who speak South Sami': older South Sami People in Sweden's expectations of home nursing care. *Scand. J. Caring Sci.* **2020**, *34*, 436–445. [CrossRef]
26. Kastenbaum, R.; Moreman, C.M. *Death, Society, and Human Experience*, 12nd ed.; Routledge: New York, NY, USA, 2018.
27. Hsieh, H.-F.; Shannon, S. Three Approaches to Qualitative Content Analysis. *Qual. Health Res.* **2005**, *15*, 1277–1288. [CrossRef]
28. Ward, D.J.; Furber, C.; Tierney, S.; Swallow, V. Using Framework Analysis in nursing research: a worked example. *J. Adv. Nurs.* **2013**, *69*, 2423–2431. [CrossRef]
29. Mittelmark, M.B.; Sagy, S.; Eriksson, M.; Bauer, G.F.; Pelikan, J.M.; Lindström, B.; Espnes, G.A. *The Handbook of Salutogenesis*, 1st ed.; Springer International Publishing: Cham, Switzerland, 2017. [CrossRef]
30. Antonovsky, A. *Unraveling the Mystery of Health: How People Manage Stress and Stay Well*, 1st ed.; Jossey-Bass: San Francisco, CA, USA, 1987.
31. Idan, O.; Eriksson, M.; Al-Yagon, M. The Salutogenic Model: The Role of Generalized Resistance Resources. In *The Handbook of Salutogenesis*; Sagy, M.B.M.S., Pelikan, M.E.G.F.B.J.M., Espnes, B.L.G.A., Eds.; Springer: Cham, Switzerland, 2017; pp. 62–65.
32. Peled, D.; Sagy, S.; Braun-Lewensohn, O. Community perceptions as a coping resource among adolescents living under rockets fire: A salutogenic approach. *J. Community Posit. Pract.* **2012**, *4*, 681–702.
33. Abrahamsson, A.; Lindmark, U.; Gerdner, A. Sense of coherence of reindeer herders and other Samis in comparison to other Swedish citizens. *Int. J. Circumpolar Health* **2013**, *72*, 20633. [CrossRef]
34. Hassler, S.; Eklund, L. Sense of coherence and self-reported health among Roma people in Sweden—A pilot study. *Int. J. Circumpolar Health* **2012**, *71*, 18438. [CrossRef]
35. Alex, L. Resilience among old Sami women. *Ageing Soc.* **2016**, *36*, 1738–1756. [CrossRef]
36. Nordin, Å. *Relationer i ett Samiskt Samhälle: En Studie av Skötesrensystemet i Gällivare Socken under Första Hälften av 1900-talet*; Umeå University: Umeå, Sweden, 2002.
37. Stoor, K. Juoiganmuitalusat-Jojkberättelser: En Studie av Jojkens Narrativa Egenskaper. Ph.D. Thesis, Umeå Universitet, Umeå, Sweden, 31 August 2007.
38. Horsburgh, M.E.; Ferguson, A.L. Salutogenesis: Origins of helath and sense of coherence. In *Handbook of Stress, Coping, and Health: Implications for Nursing Research, Theory, and Practice*, 2nd ed.; Rice, V.H., Ed.; Sage Publications: Thousand Oaks, CA, USA, 2012; pp. 180–198.
39. Idan, O.; Eriksson, M.; Al-Yagon, M. The salutogenic model: The role of generalized resistance resources. In *The Handbook of Salutogenesis*; Springer: Cham, Switzerland, 2017; pp. 57–69.
40. Tishelman, C. Några kritiska reflektioner över vårt okritiska bruk av mätinstrument: Exemplet Känsla av Sammanhang frågeformulär. *Vård i Norden* **1996**, *16*, 33–37. [CrossRef] [PubMed]
41. Antonovsky, A.; Sagy, S. Confronting developmental tasks in the retirement transition. *Gerontologist* **1990**, *30*, 362–368. [CrossRef] [PubMed]
42. Mehus, G.; Bongo, B.A.; Engnes, J.I.; Moffitt, P.M. Exploring why and how encounters with the Norwegian health-care system can be considered culturally unsafe by North Sami-speaking patients and relatives: A qualitative study based on 11 interviews. *Int. J. Circumpolar Health* **2019**, *78*, 1612703. [CrossRef] [PubMed]
43. Devik, S.A.; Olsen, R.M. Trygghet uten særomsorg? *Tidsskr. Omsorgsforskning* **2020**, *6*, 70–86. [CrossRef]
44. Evans, N.; Meñaca, A.; Koffman, J.; Harding, R.; Higginson, I.J.; Pool, R.; Gysels, M. Cultural Competence in End-of-Life Care: Terms, Definitions, and Conceptual Models from the British Literature. *J. Palliat. Med.* **2012**, *15*, 812–820. [CrossRef] [PubMed]
45. Foronda, C.; Baptiste, D.-L.; Reinholdt, M.M.; Ousman, K. Cultural Humility: A Concept Analysis. *J. Transcult. Nurs.* **2016**, *27*, 210–217. [CrossRef]
46. Schill, K.; Caxaj, S. Cultural safety strategies for rural Indigenous palliative care: A scoping review. *BMC Palliat. Care* **2019**, *18*, 21. [CrossRef]

healthcare MDPI

Concept Paper

Implementation of Compassionate Communities: The Taipei Experience

Chia-Jen Liu [1,2], Sheng-Jean Huang [1] and Samuel Shih-Chih Wang [2,*]

1 Taipei City Hospital, Taipei City 10341, Taiwan; liu920411@livemail.tw (C.-J.L.); sjhuang1@ntu.edu.tw (S.-J.H.)
2 Department of Health and Welfare, Tian-Mu Campus, College of City Management, University of Taipei, Taipei City 111036, Taiwan
* Correspondence: scwang@utaipei.edu.tw; Tel.: +886-979-311255

Abstract: A worldwide movement to empower communities to support their members to care for each other at the end of life (EoL) has emerged since Kellehear published the Compassionate City Charter. This current report discusses the implementation experiences and preliminary outcomes of Compassionate Communities (CC) in Taipei City. Using the guidance of the Charter and international experiences, we have developed and multiplied a culturally sensitive, sustainable, and holistic CC program that composes municipal hospital, social, and other services, partnering with community leaders, non-governmental organizations, university students, and volunteers. Innovative campaigns, such as workshops, conferences, and the Life Issue Café, have been delivered to facilitate engagement, public education, and leadership with reverence to folk beliefs and the use of existing social networks. We have identified a model with strong collaborative leadership, high participation rates, and ongoing commitment. The gaps between asking/accepting and providing help were bridged when social connectedness was strengthened. We also integrated home-based medical care, home-based palliative care, and advance care planning to help the vulnerable who live alone, with poor status, or with limited resource access, and continue to support the community throughout the COVID-19 pandemic.

Keywords: health promoting palliative care; home death; compassionate communities; cultural sensitive; integrated; public-private-partnership

Citation: Liu, C.-J.; Huang, S.-J.; Wang, S.S.-C. Implementation of Compassionate Communities: The Taipei Experience. *Healthcare* 2022, 10, 177. https://doi.org/10.3390/healthcare10010177

Academic Editors: Georg Bollig and John Rosenberg

Received: 9 December 2021
Accepted: 12 January 2022
Published: 17 January 2022

1. Introduction

Many international professionals and scholars have recognized the significance of end-of-life care and grief as a public health issue [1–5]. As a result, a global movement, Compassionate City/Community (CC), has been formed. This paradigm shift is occurring in medical systems. It necessitates community partnerships and community energy to build mutual support, providing a supportive environment for palliative care and grief counseling [6]. Inspired by the Healthy Cities or Healthy Communities program of the World Health Organization (WHO), CC is a concept pioneered by Professor Allan Kellehear of the University of Bradford in the United Kingdom. This public health notion first emerged in the 1980s, and policies and practices in the field of health education can be dated back even further [7,8]. According to this, health is more than just disease-free. The new concept urged the general population to recognize that health is no longer the sole responsibility of doctors and hospitals but everyone. Hospitals can assist patients suffering from accidents, disabilities, or acute or chronic diseases. However, prevention and early intervention are the most effective treatments.

The spirit of this new wave of public health is prevention, harm reduction, and early intervention [7,8]. This health city movement has urged the government, workplaces, schools, and other social organizations to offer relevant policies. Mass media and legislation have discouraged people from using harmful substances or staying in harmful conditions, thereby adopting a healthy lifestyle. Kellehear built the principles of health promotion, particularly the Ottawa Charter (1986), advocating that health promotion and well-being should be complimentary. He integrated these two ideas to develop a Health Promoting Palliative Care (HPPC) paradigm.

Kellehear also criticized the narrowing of the traditional palliative care approach of medical treatment and the care of dying patients. He thought that palliative care should include the following components: improving self-care and support for patients with chronic or terminal illnesses; providing education and information regarding health, death, and end-of-life care; providing personal and community social support; encouraging rethinking palliative care; and fostering the collaboration between health promotion and palliative care [9]. Currently, palliative care is defined by the WHO as a crucial part of integrated and people-centred health services. It is a global ethical responsibility to relieve severe health-related suffering, be it physical, psychological, social, or spiritual [10].

Since then, hospices and palliative care providers have encouraged medical organizations to accept death as a natural part of the human experience. These ideas had been advocated gradually from the late 1990s to the early 2000s. They have now been expanded to public health and medicine [6]. Professor Kellehear took the lead to bring the concept of health promotion into hospice and palliative care because anxiety, despair, social isolation, social prejudice, social exclusion, family disintegration, unemployment, financial restrictions, spiritual distress or crisis, and even suicide may occur in terminal patients, as well as the surrounding relatives and friends [11]. These are essential aspects that influence quality of life. Many social, psychological, and spiritual issues are too complex for medical institutions to address effectively and become even more difficult in the patients' final days of life.

A new wave of CC movements is emerging [12–15]. In 1993, Kozhikode, India, was the first funded CC in Asia. The project included marginalized groups such as the elderly and the mentally ill who were compassionately cared for through community participation. In 2015, the local administration decided to expand its efforts by establishing a platform called Compassionate Kozhikode. Currently, psychiatric institutions receiving frequent community support, community-based rehabilitation plans for chronic mental disorders, and various disadvantaged groups have also been included in Compassionate Kozhikode, with students being permitted to participate [16].

CC in different countries or communities adopts different strategies and develops different programs. The CC in Vic, Spain, embraces positive cultural, social attitudes and activities toward the end of life, provides a comprehensive and integrated care system, and avoids and minimizes suffering [13]. Due to the Medical Assistance in Dying (MAiD) legislation and the growing elderly population, the Canadian government began to provide leadership, education, and promotion programs to help communities across the country understand and establish their CC, with reverence to the local culture to support community members going through the experience [14]. Canada has a national-level promotion organization, e.g., Pallium Canada, a non-profit organization established in 2001 to promote cross-disciplinary palliative care education [15]. Through education courses, the provision of tools and resources, the improvement of the fairness of obtaining palliative care, and the empowerment of front-line workers and non-professional caregivers, the organization promotes the health of the entire population and supports patients and their families by fostering community energy, resilience, and community transformation [17]. The Medical Orders for Life-Sustaining Treatment (MOLST) in New York, a patient-centered shared medical decision-making program, successfully collaborated medical treatment with the community [12]. In Osaka, Japan, a social welfare organization has constructed a community daycare center to help patients manage their daily lives. They expect collaboration from the community and social service departments to help people comprehend the concept of CC, develop problem-solving skills, enhance the experience of dying, the loss of relatives and friends, and meet their welfare needs [11]. According to the above literature review, we have seen CC built by different groups and organizations and different levels of government administration in the context of different cultural and historical backgrounds.

However, there is still a lack of discussion of value dissemination, what strategies are adopted, and how people, organizations, and the government should work together.

This project report discusses the CC implementation experiences and preliminary outcomes in the capital of Taiwan, Taipei City. We will describe the CC's core values and strategies, such as humanistic care, social network, holistic care, and life wisdom. Through specific health care interventions, including home health care services, workshops, conferences, and the Life Issue Cafe in cooperation with a hospital and other social services, a CC has been implemented in the Shilin Old Street neighborhood and later, multiplied in other communities. The following sections explain how we developed the Shilin Old Street community by applying international theory and experience and blending with the local culture, and how we constructed a public–private–partnership framework by connecting government agencies, communities, social welfare institutions, businesses, charitable and religious organizations, and other non-governmental organizations (NGOs).

2. Implementation Methods

The CC in Taipei is a significant effort initiated by the city government and a community hospital. It was developed from year-long efforts of community health promotion [18] and health literacy for Shilin Old Street. Professor Allan Kellehear inspired the idea of building Shilin Old Street into a compassionate community when he was invited as a keynote speaker at the Compassionate City Workshop entitled "Age-friendly, dementia friendly, palliative friendly-Supporting a comfortable and independent life for the elderly" in November 2017 hosted by the Health Promotion Administration, Ministry of Health and Welfare (MHW), Taiwan. After a discussion with Professor Allan Kellehear, the administrators of the Taipei City Hospital thought that the Shilin Old Street community was a perfect spot to promote the CC program. Death literacy, which CC promotes [19], can combine with health literacy and become a complete life literacy program that should be provided in community care from life to death.

The MHW began encouraging community health promotion in 1999, facilitating collaboration between the community, public, and private sectors to tackle health problems and improve the quality of life for people in the community. Asset-Based Community Development was then added in 2017 for long-term development, utilizing a resource inventory, emphasizing community participation, and empowering to solve problems and implement strategies to jointly promote the health of community residents.

The Shilin Old Street neighborhood refers to the region surrounding Shilin Shennong Temple, which is currently known as the Jiujia village of Shilin District and was the oldest historically developed place. Located in the centre of the community, Shilin Shennong Temple is a listed historical heritage (since 1812) and folk belief center. Nearby lies the Guo Yuanyi cake museum, a century-old bakery where visitors can learn about history and traditions. Shilin Old Street community represents a mixture of modern and nostalgic culture because of a nearby Mass Rapid Transit (MRT) station. The majority of the population has lived there for decades, with only a handful relocating from elsewhere. According to population statistics (2021), the current population is 6201 (2954 males and 3247 females), with those aged over 65 accounting for 33.29% of the population, which is higher than the Taipei City average of 19.22%, and the national average of 14.05% [20].

A health intervention known as the Shennong LOHAS Station was established through a collaboration between the Taipei City Hospital and the village head. This station is characterized by the local culture and folk religion—where people gather worship regularly—and is integrated with healthcare services. Twice a month, the LOHAS station provides meals, healthcare counseling, and health talks on the first and fifteenth days of the lunar calendar. The nearby Taipei City Hospital Yangming branch also offers home medical care and meals-on-wheels services. The station also works with local NGOs for the disabled and the disadvantaged. All activities included the components of community heritage and culture, e.g., Shennong in folk belief as to the ancestor of Chinese medicine and health seminars with Chinese medicine topic.

By pursuing the components of the International Compassionate City Charter (i.e., public education, community development, health promotion, participatory action, and social ecology), we solidified the core value of the Shilin Old Street CC and formed strategies that suit the reality (Figure 1). We aimed to build a culturally sensitive, sustainable, and holistic CC program by integrating municipal hospital, social, and other services and collaborating with community leaders, NGOs, university students, and volunteers. Innovative programs (such as workshops, conferences, and the Life Issue Café) were presented to enable engagement, public education, and leadership. Furthermore, we organized exhibitions of life aesthetics to raise community awareness of end-of-life issues and explained the evolution of end-of-life care. The four strategies: humanistic care, social network, holistic care, life wisdom, are explained as follows.

Figure 1. Core values and strategies of compassionate communities in Taipei.

2.1. Humanistic Care

We hold activities, such as the Festival of Life (death anniversary) to encourage people to share stories of their life, and use events such as Life Aesthetics (exhibition of the artwork or relics of the deceased) to preserve cultural legacy. We also host the Life Issue Café to talk about the issue of life, i.e., health literacy and death literacy. In doing so, we believe mutual trust, empathy, social connection, and solidarity within the community can be rebuilt.

2.2. Social Network

We use round table meetings to establish consensus among members of the community, and organize a Neighborhood Watch to improve safety and offer support, such as Meal together, Long Term Care Resources, and Assistant living for the disadvantaged, disabled, and the living alone, thus a friendly environment can be arranged. This can be conducted by collaborating with nearby groups and organizations.

2.3. Holistic Care

Our program utilizes home medical care, home pharmacists, home rehabilitation, home care, and home palliative care services of the Taipei City Hospital to offer health promotion and education, screening, prevention, to delay disabilities of the elderly, and increase health and death awareness. As such, people in every stage of life can receive proper support and care.

2.4. The Wisdom of Life and Death

The wisdom of pursuing a good life and good death is rooted in the folk. The purpose of palliative care is to promote a good death. We have created the Bucket List Fulfil Project to help the dying and their family to have an opportunity to love, say goodbye, thank, and apologize to each other. We offer Advance Care Planning section to help people finish their Advance Directive, and the home care team in Taipei City Hospital also offers grief counseling and spiritual care. We train community volunteers to care for the disadvantaged population. Pet-friendly services are offered since many people take pets as family members, and the loss of a pet should be considered grief. The Shilin Old Street CC formed a promotion committee and invited professionals, scholars, and social talents to advise the promotion initiatives. Various activities, such as the life issue café, lectures, life story micro-film competition, book clubs, aesthetic activities and exhibitions, drawing competitions, essay competitions, pet adoption reunion and memorial activities, environmentally friendly campaigns, and roundtable meetings, were held to create a trustworthy atmosphere and offer a sense of identity, belonging, and participation.

This community-building program involved many government agencies (Jiujia Village, Shilin District Office, Shilin Police Station, Fire Department Jiantan Branch, Shilin Social Welfare Service Center, Shilin Health Service Center, Shilin Elderly Service Center) and community-related organizations, such as Guo Yuanyi Cake Museum, Guangqing Foundation, Shilin MRT Commercial Association, and Shilinzhuang Culture and History Studio. Students from the University of Taipei, Taipei University of Marine Technology, and Taipei Adventist American School are among the young volunteers recruited by the program.

On 6 April 2018, the Shilin Old Street Compassionate Community was officially launched, and Taipei Mayor Dr. Ko Wenje personally unveiled the plaque. He also declared 6 April as the Taipei International Compassionate Community Day. Professor Allan Kellehear also invited Shilin Old Street CC to join the Public Health Palliative Care International (PHPCI). Currently, 20 villages have joined CC Taipei, and a Taiwan International Compassionate Community Development Association has been formed to promote further initiatives around the country.

3. Experience and Preliminary Outcome

Compared with previous CC models around the world, we would like to highlight some significance from our practical experiences, including communication with the end-users, collaboration with stakeholders, and education for service providers.

First, communication with end-users is critical because their understanding of the program and their willingness to be involved is crucial. However, it was considered impolite in traditional Taiwanese society to discuss death directly, especially with the elderly. In order to promote a culture of compassion with one another, especially regarding the issue of death and dying, people need to see that death is a natural part of life, and their death literacy needs to be improved. To establish a supportive network in the community, we first utilized existing social networks and held activities such as seminars, conferences, and the Life Issue Café to facilitate more public engagement.

One of the creative activities we often held was the intergenerational Life Issue Café. We brought the young and the old together to learn through mutual empathy and exchanges of life experience. These shared learning processes exposed the elderly to social energy and young people, which transformed the notions and beliefs of the older generations and injected the new concepts and ideas from the young while introducing self-identity, life objectives, and interpersonal connections to the elderly to improve community flexibility. The Life Issue Café aided the young to participate innovative thinking and the transmission of experience from the elderly. By participating in community activities, the elderly can reduce cognitive function deterioration through communication and mutual support.

The Life Issue Café is different from the Death Café in previous studies [21] because it does not directly touch the issue of death but instead rationalizes the importance of compassion firstly through discussion and engagement. It is inspired by the Milford Care Centre (MCC)'s Compassionate Communities Project that uses Café Conversation to engage their communities in discussion about death, dying, loss, and care [22]. The method explores collaborative creativity and thought through flexible small group talks. During the debate, one can interact to link diverse viewpoints, listen to reach consensus, think on the problem, and even devise a new course of action. Several life issue cafés have been held (Figure 2), allowing the aged to discuss the theme of life, death, and dying.

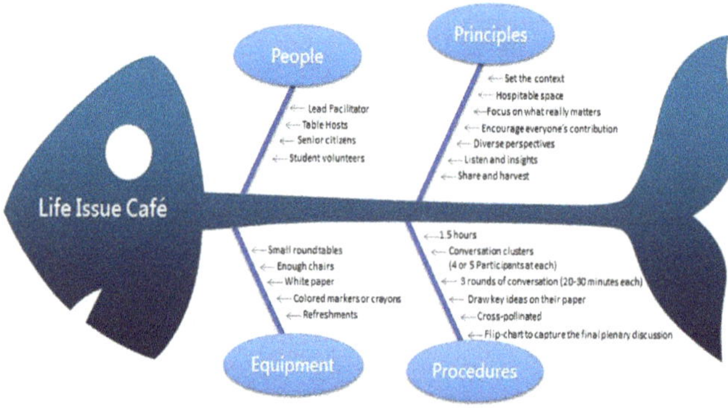

Figure 2. Method of Life Issue Café.

University students were invited to join with the elderly to explore these issues. The duration of the meeting is approximately 1.5 h, with each round of dialogue lasting for 20 min. There are three rounds in total, after which collective knowledge is visually generated and the content is shared. The Life Issue Cafe is a simple, adaptable, and efficient way to give people a sense of identification, belonging, and participation in the community in which they reside.

According to our preliminary study, four events were held in 2018, with 27 senior individuals and 60 students attending. The results of two questionnaire surveys showed the attitudes of the senior individuals versus young students toward death: 84.2% vs. 90.9% believe it is vital to address life and death matters with people; 57.9% vs. 45.5% expressed, however, that it is difficult to do so; 78.9% vs. 90.9% believed they have the ability to face death calmly [23].

Second, the collaboration among stakeholders within communities is also important to us. In order to encourage a sense of solidarity and establish a close friendship with all social groups and organizations, we held regular visits to the community care center to teach young students and help them realize the importance of healthy living and end-of-life care. The Shilin Old Street CC worked with university students who visited the elderly in good health, sub-health, disability, and end-of-life and followed-up regularly. Through conversations and activities with the seniors, students engaging in this project learn the fundamental meaning of life, and the elders can adopt healthy views. Community care visits allow college students to access the community, successfully combine school education theory with community practice, and improve social connections and the involvement of the elderly.

Third, we think education for service providers is essential for promoting this new idea of community movement. Succeeding the execution of the tactics mentioned above, we held lots of education and training programs for the hospital staff and community volunteers in order to establish understanding and consensus of the program vision and values. In doing so, community members can actively participate in social lives, share experiences and information, and help one another.

Following in the footsteps of the Shilin Old Street CC, Taipei City has recently developed CC in other administrative districts. The model has been replicated, and there are now 20 compassionate communities spread across the 12 districts of Taipei city. The scope from community participation in end-of-life care to the integration of medical treatment and community resources to improve health care quality. Communities with varying features were created, and each CC had its unique traits, e.g., the Huxing village CC in Neihu District with elderly beliefs, the Hulu village CC with a pet-friendly environment, the Changchun village CC with friendship, and other districts with their own regional characteristics.

4. Discussion

4.1. Glocalization of CC

Glocalization refers to a fusion of globalization and localization, signifying an increase in the relevance of continental and global levels, as well as an increase in the importance of local and regional levels, reflecting both local and global considerations [24]. According to Robertson, the genuine process of globalization includes the localization process within certain conditions and contexts. Robertson advocated a dual and mutual process that transforms localized models into global trends and goals [25]. When global universality is applied to other locations, it assimilates local traits and conditions and becomes locally exclusive. We believe the CC development is a glocalization process: theory, practice guidelines, and standards are distributed over an international network, while each CC was formed to meet local culture and community conditions.

4.2. Collaboration, Partnership, and Integration

The majority of CC organizations develop alliances by combining various types of public and private organizations, including those of education, medical care, social services, culture, religion, volunteer, business, and non-profit organizations. All fields of health and social care professions, such as palliative care, homes, communities and medical care, long-term care, physicians, and social workers, need to participate. All partners must work together through open communication and a shared vision, whichever launches the CC.

In Taipei, the CC evolved from a health promotion background and merged with palliative care. We believe in holistic care that integrates the personal needs for physical, psychological, and social well-being and the care needs ranging from healthy people to palliative care patients. The convergence of well-being and palliative care is critical for the entire community.

4.3. Communication and Public Education

A good communication plan is required to make people aware of the importance of open discourse concerning palliative care and death literacy. It is critical to boost communication and educate the people on the relevance of the government policies for end-of-life care. Communication is essential for a successful collaboration to achieve the same aims and speed up the promotion of CC. As people have taboos about dying, death, and grieving, and they are hesitant and fearful of addressing death, public education is critical to changing society, forming a culture of compassion, and sharing care obligations towards the end of life. There are also difficulties, such as a reluctance to ask for or accept help from others and provide assistance. Education should extend beyond campus and communities to improve social connectivity and death literacy. Professionals such as physicians, nurses, and caregivers may also need to incorporate death education into their curricula as dying, death, and mourning are not currently taught [4,26]. People of all ages and backgrounds must confront loss and experience death and bereavement, necessitating the provision of death and grief education.

4.4. Local Culture and Religions

Care, dying, death, and grieving occur in all aspects of our daily lives and human interactions, and they have always been impacted by local culture and religious beliefs [27].

Cultural or religious beliefs may influence one's reactions and subsequent behaviors [28]. It may help one to understand the difficulty of caring for the loved one who is seriously ill, recognize the cycle of life, and affirm the spirit of CC. Partnerships with religious groups are viable to create a compassionate and caring community [29]. Similar to other temples and Christian churches, the Shennong Temple helps promote palliative care and end-of-life education in the community, encourages its followers to cultivate and exercise compassion, and grasps the vocabulary and practices of palliative care.

4.5. COVID-19 Pandemics and CC

The outbreak of the COVID-19 pandemic has brought increased death and dying into communities, requiring new demands that significantly alter the social engagement patterns. Everywhere, social care and volunteering halted because they are deemed too dangerous. Despite this, people still want to connect, take action, and support those in need. The CC in Taipei is well-established and has not stepped back during the COVID-19 pandemic but continues to support its community members and presents strong solidarity and support to the health professionals. According to the advocate posted on the Public Health Palliative Care International website, compassionate streets and neighborhoods can respond to the COVID-19 pandemic by mobilizing community helpers, providing practical assistance and emotional support, and building local communications through information technology. Providing both physical and mental support is a demand of the heart and our compassionate response in the time of adversity brought by the COVID-19 pandemic [30]. CC can offer established support and social connections to those dealing with death, dying, loss, and caring.

5. Conclusions

CC has actively created a sense of solidarity, tranquility, and enjoyment in the community by capitalizing on the need for aged care and ageing in place. This strategy acquires worldwide and local support and collaboration with the medical teams, universities, and NGOs. We believe that the government and people working together can foster a friendly, caring community for the elderly and form a caring community model from birth to death.

This project report presents a paradigm of collaboration that combines health promotion, palliative care, and community assistance. Many education and training courses and community-building activities were conducted using a culturally sensitive approach, and appropriate health and end-of-life care were provided. The collaboration between hospital and community groups has resulted in positive and meaningful experiences for caregivers and patients. Community involvement lessens the workload of the hospital palliative care team and offers further service quality improvement.

The tentacles of palliative care and service can be extended to more persons in the community who have terminal diseases or require palliative care through activities. An ideal CC is a collaborative effort of caregivers, family members, friends, neighbors, volunteers, and the palliative care staff. The general public has diverse perspectives on death, dying, and grieving due to the diversity of cultural background, religious beliefs, and life experience. These are commonplace experiences for most people but may be difficult for medical experts to comprehend. The demands and difficulties necessitate community participation to prioritize the well-being of all community members. As a result, strengthening the collaboration is a viable option for CC.

Our practical experience has shown that empowering the community may effectively improve their capacity to deal with death, dying, and bereavement issues. By forming alliances and empowering the community, we can help bereaved families receive care from their community and eventually return to regular life. Spiritual care in our CC has become a regular topic of conversation among community members. The Shilin Old Street CC's experience intends to motivate more government agencies, hospitals, and communities to participate and improve the overall quality of end-of-life care. This culturally sensitive, sustainable, and holistic CC model bridges the bereavement support gap in palliative care by combining the municipal hospital, social, and other services and partnering with community leaders, NGOs, university students, and volunteers. Our intergenerational learning activity between the young and old is novel; it improves the sense of belonging of the elderly and creates a generation-friendly community. Participation of young students also allows them to apply what they have learned and return the favor to society, thus developing intergenerational reciprocity.

Author Contributions: Conceptualization, C.-J.L. and S.S.-C.W.; methodology, C.-J.L. and S.S.-C.W.; investigation, C.-J.L. and S.S.-C.W.; resources, C.-J.L., S.-J.H. and S.S.-C.W.; writing—original draft preparation, C.-J.L. and S.S.-C.W.; writing—review and editing, C.-J.L., S.-J.H. and S.S.-C.W.; visualization, C.-J.L. and S.S.-C.W.; supervision, S.-J.H.; project administration, C.-J.L. and S.-J.H.; funding acquisition, C.-J.L. and S.-J.H.; All authors have read and agreed to the published version of the manuscript.

Funding: This research received no external funding.

Institutional Review Board Statement: The project has been approved by Research Ethics Committee of the Taipei City Hospital. The approval number TCHIRB-10609119-E.

Informed Consent Statement: Informed consent was obtained from all subjects involved in the study.

Conflicts of Interest: The authors declare no conflict of interest.

References

1. Brito, G.; Flores, S. Compassion in palliative care: A review. *Curr. Opin. Support. Palliat. Care* **2018**, *12*, 472–479. [CrossRef]
2. Kellehear, A. Compassionate Cities: Global significance and meaning for palliative care. *Prog. Palliat. Care* **2020**, *28*, 115–119. [CrossRef]
3. Pfaff, K.; Markaki, A. Compassionate collaborative care: An integrative review of quality indicators in end-of-life care. *BMC Palliat. Care* **2017**, *16*, 65. [CrossRef] [PubMed]
4. Abel, J.; Kingston, H.; Scally, A.; Hartnoll, J.; Hannam, G.; Thomson-Moore, A.; Kellehear, A. Reducing emergency hospital admissions: A population health complex intervention of an enhanced model of primary care and compassionate communities. *Br. J. Gen. Pract.* **2018**, *68*, e803–e810. [CrossRef] [PubMed]
5. Sallnow, L.; Richardson, H.; Murray, S.A.; Kellehear, A. The impact of a new public health approach to end-of-life care: A systematic review. *Palliat. Med.* **2016**, *30*, 200–211. [CrossRef] [PubMed]
6. Kellehear, A. *Compassionate Cities*; Routledge: London, UK, 2012.
7. Tsouros, A.D. The WHO Healthy Cities Project: State of the art and future plans. *Health Promot. Int.* **1995**, *10*, 133–141. [CrossRef]
8. Aicher, J. *Designing Healthy Cities: Prescriptions, Principles, and Practice*; Krieger Publishing Company: Malabar, FL, USA, 1998.
9. Kellehear, A.; O'Connor, D. Health-promoting palliative care: A practice example. *Crit. Public Health* **2008**, *18*, 111–115. [CrossRef]
10. WHO. Palliative Care. Available online: https://www.who.int/health-topics/palliative-care (accessed on 26 November 2021).
11. Kellehear, A. Compassionate communities: End-of-life care as everyone's responsibility. *QJM Int. J. Med.* **2013**, *106*, 1071–1075. [CrossRef]
12. Bomba, P.A.; Orem, K. Lessons learned from New York's community approach to advance care planning and MOLST. *Ann. Palliat. Med.* **2015**, *4*, 10–21.
13. Gómez-Batiste, X.; Mateu, S.; Serra-Jofre, S.; Molas, M.; Mir-Roca, S.; Amblàs, J.; Costa, X.; Lasmarías, C.; Serrarols, M.; Solà-Serrabou, A. Compassionate Communities: Design and Preliminary Results of the Experience of Vic (Barcelona, Spain) Caring City. *Ann. Palliat. Med.* **2018**, *7* (Suppl. 2), S32–S41. [CrossRef]
14. Kelley, M.L.; Prince, H.; Nadin, S.; Brazil, K.; Crow, M.; Hanson, G.; Maki, L.; Monture, L.; Mushquash, C.J.; O'Brien, V. Developing palliative care programs in Indigenous communities using participatory action research: A Canadian application of the public health approach to palliative care. *Ann. Palliat. Med.* **2018**, *7*, S52–S72. [CrossRef]
15. Tompkins, B. Compassionate communities in Canada: It is everyone's responsibility. *Ann. Palliat. Med.* **2018**, *7*, S118–S129. [CrossRef] [PubMed]
16. Kozhikode, C. Compassionate Kozhikode. Available online: http://compassionatekozhikode.in/ (accessed on 10 September 2021).
17. Tompkins, B.; Cruz, I.; Ali, A.; Holzman, J.; Nininger, J.; Lau, J.; Johnson, K.; Johnson, W.; Candy, K.; Blackwood, P.; et al. Implementing Compassionate Communities in Canada: Emerging Approaches. Presented at the 5th International Public Health and Palliative Care Conference—IPHPC 2017, Ottawa, ON, Canada, 17–20 September 2017.
18. Chao, K.-I.; Wang, S.-C.; Huang, T.-C.; Woung, L.-C.; Lee, O.K.; Chu, D.; Chu, C.-M.; Liu, C.-J.; Huang, S.-J. The Current Status of Health Literacy Promotion in Taipei City Hospital. *Taipei City Med. J.* **2017**, *14*, 224–233. [CrossRef]
19. Huang, C.-Y.; Hsu, S.-H.; Wen-Jung, S.; Lee, Y.-H.; Ueng, R.-S.; Wu, M.-P.; Shih, C.-Y.; Huang, S.-J. Promoting Death Literacy—A High Value Health Care for Good Death at Home. *Taipei City Med. J.* **2017**, *14*, 269–278. [CrossRef]

20. Department of Budget, Accounting and Statistics, Taipei City Government. The Dependency Ratio and Aging Index. Available online: https://www-ws.gov.taipei/Download.ashx?u=LzAwMS9VcGxvYWQvMzY3L3JlbGZpbGUvMC82NDg5NC9iMjM3NmY3My1lMGQ1LTRkMGYtOTRkZS02OTAwZTE4NWFkMjcucGRm&n=MTA56Ie65YyX5biC6auY6b2h57Wx6KiI6aCF55uuLnBkZg%3d%3d&icon=..pdf (accessed on 20 November 2021).
21. Miles, L.; Corr, C.A. Death cafe: What is it and what we can learn from it. *OMEGA-J. Death Dying* **2017**, *75*, 151–165. [CrossRef]
22. McLoughlin, K.; McGilloway, S.; Lloyd, R.; O'Connor, M.; Rhatigan, J.; Shanahan, M.; Richardson, M.; Keevey, A. Walls, wisdom, worries, and wishes: Engaging communities in discussion about death, dying, loss, and care using Café Conversation. *Prog. Palliat. Care* **2016**, *24*, 9–14. [CrossRef]
23. Liu, C.-J.; Yeh, T.-C.; Wu, S.-W.; Chen, T.-H.; Hsieh, M.-H.; Wang, S.-C.; Huang, S.-J.; Woung, L.-C. Cross Generation Shared Learning in Compassionate Community. *Taipei City Med. J.* **2019**, *16*, 145–152. [CrossRef]
24. Roudometof, V. Theorizing glocalization: Three interpretations. *Eur. J. Soc. Theory* **2016**, *19*, 391–408. [CrossRef]
25. Robertson, R. Glocalization. *Int. Encycl. Anthropol.* **2018**. [CrossRef]
26. Ali, S.; Terry, L. Exploring senior nurses' understanding of compassionate leadership in the community. *Br. J. Community Nurs.* **2017**, *22*, 77–87. [CrossRef]
27. Clements, P.T.; Vigil, G.J.; Manno, M.S.; Henry, G.C.; Wilks, J.; Das, S.; Kellywood, R.; Foster, W. Cultural perspectives of death, grief, and bereavement. *J. Psychosoc. Nurs. Ment. Health Serv.* **2003**, *41*, 18–26. [CrossRef] [PubMed]
28. Brathwaite, B. *Diverse Cultural Awareness in Nursing Practice*; Sage: London, UK, 2019; p. 216.
29. Pallium Canada. Mobilizing Compassionate Communities: Take 2. Available online: http://pallium.ca/infoware/Take%202%20event%20Speaker%20approved%20online%20version.pdf (accessed on 20 November 2021).
30. Public Health Palliative Care International and Dr Julian Abel. Developing Compassionate Streets and Neighbourhoods during COVID-19. Compassionate Communities UK. Available online: https://www.compassionate-communitiesuk.co.uk/covid19-response (accessed on 20 November 2021).

healthcare MDPI

Article

The First Step to Initiate Pediatric Palliative Care: Identify Patient Needs and Cooperation of Medical Staff

Su Hyun Bae [1,2] and Yeo Hyang Kim [1,3,*]

1 Pediatric Palliative Care Center, Kyungpook National University Children's Hospital, Daegu 41404, Korea; b_suhyun@naver.com
2 Department of Social Welfare, Kyungpook National University, Daegu 41566, Korea
3 Department of Pediatrics, School of Medicine, Kyungpook National University, Daegu 41566, Korea
* Correspondence: kimyhmd@knu.ac.kr; Tel.: +82-53-200-3811

Abstract: Few Korean hospitals had experience in pediatric palliative care. Since the beginning of the national palliative care project, interest in pediatric palliative care has gradually increased, but the establishment of professional palliative care is still inadequate due to a lack of indicators. This study aimed to find considerations in the process of initiating palliative care services. The general and clinical characteristics of 181 patients aged less than 24 years who were registered at the pediatric palliative care center from January 2019 to August 2021 were evaluated. Life-limiting condition group 1 had the largest number of patients. The primary need for palliative care was psychological and emotional support, followed by information sharing and help in communication with the medical staff in decision-making processes. Seventy-two patients were technologically dependent, with one to four technical supports for each patient. The registration of patients with cancer increased with time, and the time from disease diagnosis to consultation for pediatric palliative care service was significantly reduced. In conclusion, before starting pediatric palliative care, it is necessary to understand the needs of patients and their families and to cooperate with medical staff.

Keywords: palliative care; children; life-limiting condition

Citation: Bae, S.H.; Kim, Y.H. The First Step to Initiate Pediatric Palliative Care: Identify Patient Needs and Cooperation of Medical Staff. *Healthcare* **2022**, *10*, 127. https://doi.org/10.3390/healthcare10010127

Academic Editors: Paolo Cotogni and Christian Napoli

Received: 27 November 2021
Accepted: 6 January 2022
Published: 9 January 2022

1. Introduction

Advances in medical technology have increased the survival rate of pediatric and adolescent patients affected by life-threatening diseases or life-limiting conditions (LLC) [1]. However, due to complex disabilities, instead of achieving complete recovery, many patients with these diseases depend on medical devices or require intensive medical care [2,3]. In addition, patients with such diseases experience physical, psychological, social, and spiritual distress due to long-term intensive care. Despite the increasing survival rate, the quality of life of patients and their families is significantly reduced. The United States and European countries have established and provided palliative care services on a national scale to address this issue [4,5]. South Korea has also planned a palliative care system for children and adolescents, and in July 2018, two children's hospitals in Seoul, South Korea, started pilot palliative care projects. As of 2021, nine hospitals in South Korea are participating in pilot projects (Figure 1).

In the United States, there are approximately 500,000 children and adolescents with LLC, and approximately 10% die each year [6]. In Japan, approximately 110,000 children and adolescents cope with LLC [7]. In Korea, there are approximately 130,000 children and adolescents aged less than 24 years with LLC [8]. Among them, 26.2% are patients with cancer, whereas the rest have noncancer-related diseases, such as congenital heart, genetic metabolic, neuromuscular, and degenerative diseases. While most adults who require palliative care are terminally ill, pediatric palliative care patients have various diseases.

Even if the same disease occurs, the demand for pediatric palliative care services may vary depending on the severity of the disease or stage of progression. While there is a high demand for pain control in patients with cancer, there may also be a high demand for control of neurological and respiratory symptoms in the nervous system and genetic metabolic diseases. Patients with neurological problems may require urgent physical care. Furthermore, psychosocial and spiritual care of patients and their families is essential [9]. Therefore, due to the need and specificity of pediatric palliative care, there is a limit to providing a standardized palliative care program. The guidelines for Korean pediatric palliative care projects provide recommendations for the provision of individually customized care services to patients.

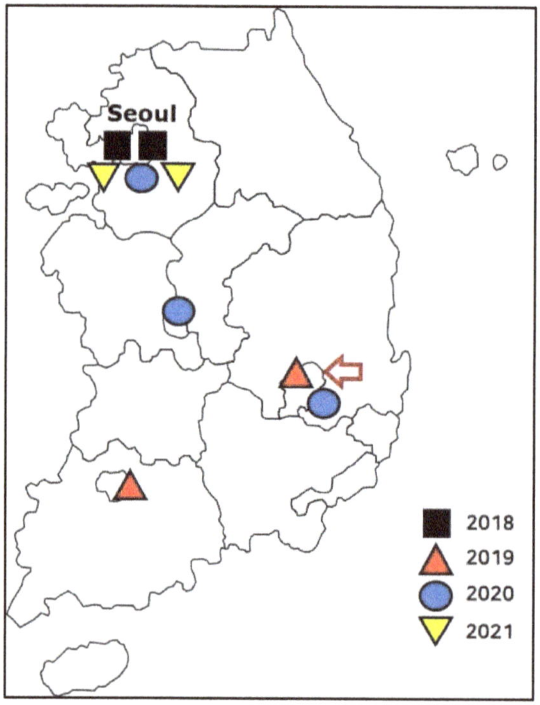

Figure 1. Pediatric palliative care centers in South Korea. Centers that opened in 2018 (■), 2019 (▲), 2020 (●), and 2021 (▽) are shown. The red arrow indicates the first local pediatric palliative care center.

Few Korean hospitals were experienced in pediatric palliative care. Except for Seoul, no other city offered pediatric palliative care services. Since the beginning of the national project, interest in pediatric palliative care has gradually increased, but the establishment of professional palliative care is still inadequate due to a lack of indicators. Therefore, it is necessary to share experiences in establishing palliative care services suitable for the region for a short period in children's hospitals that lack experience in pediatric palliative care.

This study aimed to find factors to be considered in the process of initiating palliative care services by analyzing the characteristics of patients registered at the first pediatric palliative care center established outside Seoul.

2. Materials and Methods

2.1. Participants

This study enrolled 181 patients aged less than 24 years who were registered at the Pediatric Palliative Care Center at Kyungpook National University Children's Hospital (Daegu, Korea) from January 2019 to August 2021.

The general and clinical characteristics of the patients were retrospectively reviewed from medical records, basic registration information, initial counseling records, medical progress, and withdrawal records. Patient information was classified into three categories: (1) general characteristics, such as sex, age, residence, and insurance type; (2) clinical characteristics, such as final diagnosis, date of diagnosis, and LLC classification; and (3) palliative care-related information, such as consultation date, the reason for consultation, and medical requirement.

To detect changes in the behavior of medical staff regarding pediatric palliative care consultation, the time taken from diagnosis to palliative care consultation and the number of newly registered patients with cancer and those with noncancer diseases were compared. The period was assessed by dividing it into two periods of 6 months each: 6 months from the start of the local pediatric palliative care center (January–June 2019, period 1) and the last 6 months after 3 years (January–June 2021, period 2).

2.2. Definition

In this study, LLC were classified into four categories based on the disease characteristics [10,11] as follows: group 1, life-threatening conditions for which curative treatment is feasible but can fail; group 2, conditions for which premature death is inevitable; group 3, progressive conditions without curative treatment options; and group 4, irreversible but nonprogressive conditions causing severe disability, with a high risk of premature death from an unpredictable life-threatening event or episode.

The reasons for the need for palliative care were classified into six categories as follows: (1) symptom and pain management, (2) support for decision-making processes, (3) psychological and emotional support for patients and their families, (4) socioeconomic support, (5) nursing and home care adjustment, and (6) end-of-life decision and care.

The technical supports for patients with medical complexity were classified into home ventilator application, home oxygen therapy, tracheal suction, home parenteral nutrition, and enteral nutrition through nasogastric or gastrostomy tube.

2.3. Statistical Analyses

All statistical analyses were conducted using IBM SPSS Statistics for Windows, version 26.0 (IBM Co., Armonk, NY, USA). The independent t-test and chi-square tests were used to evaluate differences between patients with cancer and noncancer diseases and between periods. A p-value of <0.05 was considered statistically significant.

3. Results

3.1. Patients' General Characteristics

Table 1 shows the general and clinical characteristics of the 181 patients registered at the pediatric palliative care center.

The patients included 100 males (55%) and 81 females (45%). The most common age group was from 1 to 5 years old. Diseases were classified into cancer and noncancer, with more patients having noncancer diseases. Eighty patients were diagnosed before the pediatric palliative care service began in January 2019, and 101 patients were diagnosed after that.

Most patients lived in the main city (Daegu), where pediatric palliative care centers are located, and in nearby areas (Gyeongsangbuk-do) (Figure 2), and 33% of patients were linked to hospitals in Seoul. All patients were supported by National Health Insurance. Among the LLC groups, groups 1 and 2 had the largest and smallest number of patients, respectively.

Table 1. General and clinical characteristics of the patients.

Characteristic	Number (%)
Sex	
Male	100 (55)
Female	81 (45)
Age (years)	
<1	10 (5)
1–5	64 (35)
6–12	54 (30)
13–18	43 (24)
19–24	10 (6)
Type of diagnosis	
Cancer	75 (41)
Noncancer	106 (59)
City of residence	
Daegu	78 (43)
Gyeongsangbuk-do	94 (52)
Others	9 (5)
Link with hospitals in the capital	59 (33)
LLC group	
group 1	111 (62)
group 2	11 (6)
group 3	24 (13)
group 4	35 (19)

Abbreviation: LLC, life-limiting condition; group 1, life-threatening conditions for which curative treatment is feasible but may fail; group 2, conditions in which premature death is inevitable; group 3, progressive conditions without curative treatment options; group 4, irreversible but nonprogressive conditions causing severe disability, with a high risk of premature death from an unpredictable fatal event or episode.

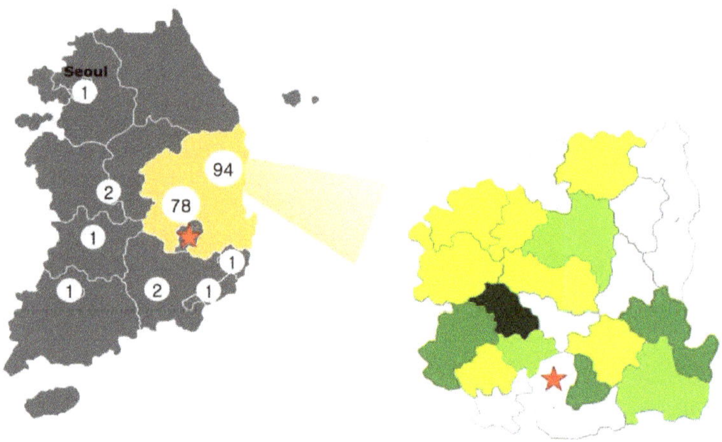

Figure 2. Patient residential areas and the number of patients. The red star indicates the main city, Daegu, with the first local pediatric palliative care center. The yellow zone indicates nearby areas (Gyeongsangbuk-do). Color severity is associated with the number of patients. Dark-green implies > 20 patients, green > 10, light-green > 5, and yellowish-green < 5. The gray zone indicates other areas where patients reside.

3.2. *Primary Reasons for the Need for Palliative Care*

Table 2 shows the reasons for the need for palliative care.

The reasons for the need for palliative care overlapped, and the highest priority was given to psychological and emotional support, followed by information sharing and communication with the medical staff in decision-making processes, such as future treatment plans. Although the National Health Insurance supported all patients, 24% of patients required additional economic support. Furthermore, approximately 10% of patients wanted to make decisions related to life-sustaining treatments, nursing homes, and end-of-life care.

These reasons for the need for palliative care did not indicate a significant difference between patients with cancer and those with noncancer diseases.

Table 2. Primary reasons for the need for palliative care.

Category	Cancer Number (%)	Noncancer Number (%)	*p*-Value
Psychological and emotional support	71 (39)	93 (51)	0.77
Decision-making process service	13 (7)	52 (29)	0.97
Socioeconomic support	9 (5)	34 (19)	0.91
Symptom and pain management	14 (8)	22 (12)	0.82
Life-sustaining treatment decision service	9 (5)	10 (6)	0.79
Nursing and home care service	2 (1)	7 (4)	0.83
Hospice care service	5 (3)	4 (2)	0.80

3.3. *Technical Support for Patients with Medical Complexity*

Technical support was required for patients with medical complexity registered at the pediatric palliative care center. Seventy-two patients had technology dependency, of which only one was cancer patient. Technical support overlapped, with one to four of the five technical supports for each patient (Figure 3).

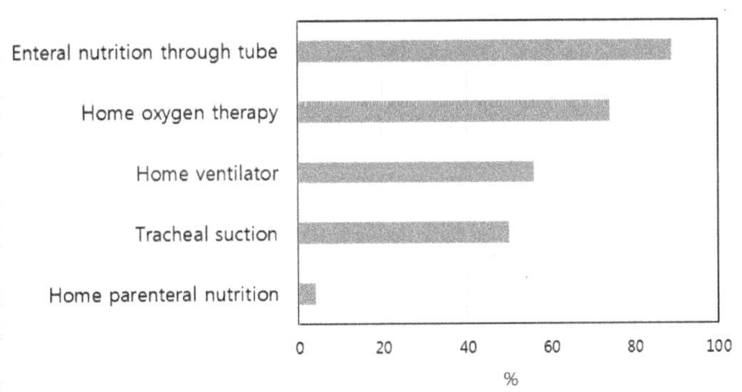

Figure 3. Technical support for patients with medical complexity.

Enteral nutrition through a nasogastric or gastrostomy tube was the most common technical support, at 89%, followed by respiratory support with simple or high flow nasal cannula at 74% and home ventilator at 56%.

3.4. *Changes in the Behavior of Medical Staff Regarding Pediatric Palliative Care*

Compared with period 1, period 2 did not show a significant difference in the number of registered patients (period 1, 32; period 2, 31). Although the proportion of patients with cancer was not significantly different between the periods (period 1, 9; period 2, 15, $p = 0.098$), the number of registered patients with cancer increased in period 2.

There were 18 newly diagnosed patients in period 1 and 20 in period 2. The time from the first disease diagnosis to consultation for pediatric palliative care service was significantly reduced from 5.2 ± 6.8 days in period 1 to 1.9 ± 1.4 days in period 2 ($p = 0.036$).

4. Discussion

This study showed that although Korea's pediatric palliative care service is still in its developing stages, the understanding of the characteristics of pediatric diseases that need palliative care and the medical staff's perception that palliative care may be considered alongside treatment is rapidly advancing.

In the 1960s, the primary focus of pediatric palliative care was within the hospice to enhance the quality of death [12]. Because hospice care is primarily intended for adult patients with terminal cancer, pediatric palliative care also has a strong perception of death. However, recently, hospice care has transitioned to palliative care, and palliative care services focus on "living" and not "dying" [5,13,14]. In other words, palliative care focuses on improving the quality of life in addition to medical care that includes a cure for patients with severe illnesses. In this study, only 5% of patients required hospice care services, and the primary reasons for the need for palliative care were psychological and emotional support, decision-making process service, and socioeconomic support.

It is important to provide psychoemotional support to patients and their families receiving pediatric palliative care [9,15,16]. The diagnosis of LLC is a significant crisis for patients and their families. Patients with LLC who have to endure pain can experience psychological difficulties such as depression and anxiety. Parents who take care of their sick children continue their daily lives tending to their children, experiencing complex emotions such as anxiety, guilt, and anger due to their children's illness; thus, they become physically and psychologically exhausted. Therefore, it is vital to manage symptoms and provide psychological support together with pediatric palliative care. This suggests that pediatric palliative care should be considered differently from adult palliative care.

Children and adolescents who require palliative care are affected by numerous diseases, so palliative care services suitable for each case profile should be made available [2,17,18]. In this study, the incidence of cancer and noncancer diseases in pediatric palliative care registered patients was 41% and 59%, respectively, similar to the incidences of 45% and 55%, respectively, reported by the National Hospice Center. Since Korean hospice palliative care services began with care for adult patients with terminal cancer, and the scope of service expanded to AIDS, cirrhosis, and chronic obstructive pulmonary disease, but there is still a lack of awareness of the need for palliative care for patients with noncancer diseases. Pediatric patients have a higher rate of noncancer diseases, such as congenital, genetic metabolic, neuromuscular, and degenerative diseases, efforts are needed to provide customized palliative care services reflecting the needs of patients and their families.

Especially, patients with noncancer diseases were found to have high technological dependence and required home care [2,19,20]. They need active care due to breathing or nutritional problems, and there are many medical demands related to technological dependence. In Korea, pediatric home care services for severely ill children started in January 2019 so that patients would be stable at home following discharge. Home care services can effectively manage pediatric and adolescent palliative care patients by educating their families on how to care for their children and periodically checking on the patient's condition, such as through phone counselling or medical staff visits to homes if necessary. This study was conducted at the pediatric palliative care center that was capable of providing home care services, and patients who need these services often wanted palliative care services.

Pediatric patients with oncological diseases were not discussed or implemented until the time of death approached despite efforts for early initiation of palliative care [21,22]. A retrospective systematic review found that from 1999 to 2016, 54.5% of pediatric patients with oncological diseases received palliative care immediately before death [23]. This study showed that as experience and understanding about pediatric palliative care increased, the number of patients receiving palliative care concurrently with a diagnosis also increased. Although the total number of registered patients did not differ among the periods, the number of patients with cancer registered in the last 6 months showed an increasing trend compared with that in the first 6 months of palliative care service. In particular, the significant reduction in the period from primary diagnosis to palliative care counseling is thought to be related to a change in the medical staff's perception that the need for palliative care needs to be combined with diagnosis and treatment.

In Korea, adult palliative care was initially started as a clinic in 1965; currently, 109 institutions provide adult palliative care. Pediatric palliative care started in 2018, and nine institutions have opened pediatric palliative care centers until 2021 [24]. Although the supply is insufficient compared with the demand for pediatric palliative care, the field has developed rapidly 3 years since the pediatric palliative care pilot project began. The Korean National Hospice Center reported that the quality of life of 781 children and adolescent patients with LLC and their families has improved with palliative care [24].

To develop pediatric palliative care services, it is necessary to improve access to services to meet the needs of patients and their families. The first local pediatric palliative care center is located in the third-largest city in Korea. Following a review of the distribution of registered patient residences, the first local pediatric palliative care center was in charge of patients residing in nearby areas and makes it easier for local patients to access services. In addition, clinical studies that conduct surveys or interviews on patients with LLC and their family needs, professionals training through customized education, and medical staff perceptions of pediatric palliative care are needed.

The limitations of this study include the fact that it was a retrospective review of medical records and that it was difficult to observe a consistent pattern of change due to the limited quantitative growth of pediatric palliative care centers as a result of the COVID-19 pandemic. It is difficult to generalize the results as this study was conducted at a single local pediatric palliative care center. Other methods such as questionnaires to investigate changes in the behavior of the medical staff were not employed. Furthermore, human and hospital internal and external factors that influenced this study were not considered.

5. Conclusions

In order for hospitals with no experience in pediatric palliative care to provide pediatric palliative care, knowledge and information related to regional background, needs of patients and families, patient technical dependence, and understanding of palliative care by medical staff are required. These will help new centers provide the most functional pediatric palliative care services as soon as possible.

Author Contributions: Conceptualization and methodology, Y.H.K.; software, S.H.B.; validation, Y.H.K.; formal analysis, S.H.B.; investigation, and data curation, S.H.B.; writing—original draft preparation, S.H.B.; writing—review and editing, Y.H.K.; supervision, Y.H.K. All authors have read and agreed to the published version of the manuscript.

Funding: This research received no external funding.

Institutional Review Board Statement: The study was conducted according to the guidelines of the Declaration of Helsinki and was approved by the Institutional Review Board (or Ethics Committee) of Kyungpook National University Chilgok Hospital (approval No. KNUCH 2021-05-030).

Informed Consent Statement: Not applicable.

Data Availability Statement: The data presented in this study are available on request from the corresponding author.

Acknowledgments: The authors would like to thank Mi Ok Ji, R.N. and Hye Eun Joh, R.N., for their contribution, cooperation, and support for pediatric palliative care.

Conflicts of Interest: The authors declare no conflict of interest.

References

1. Bogetz, J.F.; Schroeder, A.R.; Bergman, D.A.; Cohen, H.J.; Sourkes, B. Palliative Care is Critical to the Changing Face of Child Mortality and Morbidity in the United States. *Clin. Pediatr.* **2014**, *53*, 1030–1031. [CrossRef] [PubMed]
2. Cohen, E.; Kuo, D.Z.; Agrawal, R.; Berry, J.G.; Bhagat, S.K.; Simon, T.D.; Srivastava, R. Children with Medical Complexity: An Emerging Population for Clinical and Research Initiatives. *Pediatrics* **2011**, *127*, 529–538. [CrossRef]
3. Amarri, S.; Ottaviani, A.; Campagna, A.; De Panfilis, L.; Emilia Romagna Paediatric Palliative Care Working Group. Children with Medical Complexity and Paediatric Palliative Care: A Retrospective Cross-Sectional Survey of Prevalence and Needs. *Ital. J. Pediatr.* **2021**, *47*, 110. [CrossRef]
4. Sisk, B.A.; Feudtner, C.; Bluebond-Langner, M.; Sourkes, B.; Hinds, P.S.; Wolfe, J. Response to Suffering of the Seriously Ill Child: A History of Palliative Care for Children. *Pediatrics* **2020**, *145*, e20191741. [CrossRef] [PubMed]
5. Feudtner, C.; Womer, J.; Augustin, R.; Remke, S.; Wolfe, J.; Friebert, S.; Weissman, D. Pediatric Palliative Care Programs in Children's Hospitals: A Cross-Sectional National Survey. *Pediatrics* **2013**, *132*, 1063–1070. [CrossRef]
6. Himelstein, B.P.; Hilden, J.M.; Boldt, A.M.; Weissman, D. Pediatric Palliative Care. *N. Engl. J. Med.* **2004**, *350*, 1752–1762. [CrossRef]
7. MHLW. Disease Countermeasures for Children with Chronic Diseases. 2013. Available online: http://www.mhlw.go.jp/file/05-Shingikai-12601000-Seisakutoukatsukan-Sanjikanshitsu_Shakaihoshoutantou/0000022423.pdf (accessed on 11 January 2019).
8. Kim, C.H.; Song, I.G.; Kim, M.S.; Lee, J.Y.; Lim, N.G.; Shin, H.Y. Healthcare Utilization among Children and Young People with Life-Limiting Conditions: Exploring Palliative Care Needs Using National Health Insurance Claims Data. *Sci. Rep.* **2020**, *10*, 2692. [CrossRef] [PubMed]
9. Yun, H.; Hwang, A.R.; Kim, S.; Choi, E.K. Needs for Pediatric Palliative Care among Parents of Children with Complex Chronic Conditions. *Child Health Nurs. Res.* **2018**, *24*, 527–536. [CrossRef]
10. Hain, R.; Devins, M.; Hastings, R.; Noyes, J. Paediatric Palliative Care: Development and Pilot Study of a 'Directory' of Life-Limiting Conditions. *BMC Palliat. Care* **2013**, *12*, 43. [CrossRef] [PubMed]
11. Together for Short Lives, A Guide to Children's Palliative Care; Supporting Babies, Children and Young People with Life-Limiting and Life-Threatening Conditions and Their Families. Bristol: Together for Short Lives. 2018. Available online: https://www.togetherforshortlives.org.uk/wp-content/uploads/2018/03/TfSL-A-Guide-to-Children%E2%80%99s-Palliative-Care-Fourth-Edition-5.pdf (accessed on 11 January 2019).
12. Clark, D. From Margins to Centre: A Review of the History of Palliative Care in Cancer. *Lancet Oncol.* **2007**, *8*, 430–438. [CrossRef]
13. Rapoport, A.; Weingarten, K. Improving Quality of Life in Hospitalized Children. *Pediatr. Clin. N. Am.* **2014**, *61*, 749–760. [CrossRef]
14. Widger, K.; Davies, D.; Rapoport, A.; Vadeboncoeur, C.; Liben, S.; Sarpal, A.; Stenekes, S.; Cyr, C.; Daoust, L.; Grégoire, M.; et al. Pediatric Palliative Care in Canada in 2012: A Cross-sectional Descriptive Study. *CMAJ Open* **2016**, *4*, E562–E568. [CrossRef] [PubMed]
15. Levine, D.R.; Mandrell, B.N.; Sykes, A.; Pritchard, M.; Gibson, D.; Symons, H.J.; Wendler, D.; Baker, J.N. Patients' and Parents' Needs, Attitudes, and Perceptions About Early Palliative Care Integration in Pediatric Oncology. *JAMA Oncol.* **2017**, *3*, 1214–1220. [CrossRef]
16. Waldman, E.; Wolfe, J. Palliative Care for Children with Cancer. *J. Nat. Rev. Clin. Oncol.* **2013**, *10*, 100–107. [CrossRef] [PubMed]
17. Morell, E.; Moynihan, K.; Wolfe, J.; Blume, E.D. Palliative Care and Paediatric Cardiology: Current Evidence and Future Directions. *Lancet Child Adolesc. Health* **2019**, *3*, 502–510. [CrossRef]
18. Goloff, N.; Joy, B.F. A Part of the Team: The Changing Role of Palliative Care in Congenital Heart Disease. *Prog. Pediatr. Cardiol.* **2018**, *48*, 59–62. [CrossRef]
19. Rusalen, F.; Agosto, C.; Brugnano, L.; Benini, F. Impact of the Regional Pediatric Palliative Care Network on the Care of Children on Long Term Ventilation: Could the Availability of a Residential Solution into the Network Reduce the Duration of Intensive Care Unit Staying for These Patients? *J. Pediatr. Intensive Care* **2018**, *7*, 75–80. [PubMed]
20. Lazzarin, P.; Schiavon, B.; Brugnaro, L.; Benini, F. Parents Spend an Average of Nine Hours a Day Providing Palliative Care for Children at Home and Need to Maintain an Average of Five Life-Saving Devices. *Acta Paediatr.* **2018**, *107*, 289–293. [CrossRef]
21. Haines, E.R.; Frost, A.C.; Kane, H.L.; Rokoske, F.S. Barriers to Accessing Palliative Care for Pediatric Patients with Cancer: A Review of the Literature. *Cancer* **2018**, *124*, 2278–2288. [CrossRef]
22. Johnston, D.L.; Nagel, K.; Friedman, D.L.; Meza, J.L.; Hurwitz, C.A.; Friebert, S. Availability and Use of Palliative Care and End Of-Life Services for Pediatric Oncology Patients. *J. Clin. Oncol.* **2008**, *26*, 4646–4650. [CrossRef]
23. Cheng, B.T.; Rost, M.; De Clercq, E.; Arnold, L.; Elger, B.S.; Wangmo, T. Palliative Care Initiation in Pediatric Oncology Patients: A Systematic Review. *Cancer Med.* **2019**, *8*, 3–12. [CrossRef] [PubMed]
24. National Hospice Center. Hospice·Palliative Care 2019–2020 (National Hospice Center Annual Report). 2021. Available online: https://hospice.go.kr (accessed on 11 January 2019).

healthcare MDPI

Article

Play Elements as Mechanisms in Intergenerational Arts Activities to Support Community Engagement with End-of-Life Issues

Max Kleijberg [1,*], Rebecca Hilton [2], Beth Maina Ahlberg [3,4] and Carol Tishelman [1,5]

1 Department of Learning, Informatics, Management and Ethics, Karolinska Institute, 117 11 Stockholm, Sweden; carol.tishelman@ki.se
2 Research Centre, Stockholm University of the Arts, 104 50 Stockholm, Sweden; rebecca.hilton@uniarts.se
3 Skaraborg Institute for Research and Development, 541 30 Skövde, Sweden; beth.maina.ahlberg@kbh.uu.se
4 Department of Sociology, Uppsala University, 751 26 Uppsala, Sweden
5 Centre for Health Economics, Informatics and Health Care Research, Stockholm Health Care Services (SLSO), Region Stockholm, 171 11 Stockholm, Sweden
* Correspondence: max.kleijberg@ki.se

Abstract: Talking about dying, death, and loss may be difficult. Arts offer alternative ways of engaging with end-of-life (EoL) issues, but little is known about the means through which this occurs. In this article, we aim to explore mechanisms in arts activities that support community engagement with EoL issues, based on the community-based participatory action research project Studio DöBra. Studio DöBra was developed to support community engagement with EoL issues through intergenerational arts workshops involving community partners, children, and older adults. Initial analysis with community partners indicated the importance of play elements in arts activities. Continued analysis was therefore abductive, using play theory and qualitative data from Studio DöBra arts activities. Through iterative examination of theory and data, we modified play theory as we identified mechanisms supporting community engagement with EoL issues in arts activities. Findings can contribute to theory-building that can inform arts activities supporting community engagement with EoL issues.

Keywords: end-of-life; health promotion; arts activities; community-based programs; children; older people; intergenerational; play

Citation: Kleijberg, M.; Hilton, R.; Ahlberg, B.M.; Tishelman, C. Play Elements as Mechanisms in Intergenerational Arts Activities to Support Community Engagement with End-of-Life Issues. *Healthcare* **2021**, *9*, 764. https://doi.org/10.3390/healthcare9060764

Academic Editors: Georg Bollig and John Rosenberg

Received: 14 May 2021
Accepted: 17 June 2021
Published: 19 June 2021

1. Introduction and Aim

Although death and loss are all around us—in our private lives, in the news, and other media—talking about these issues may be difficult as they are often considered sensitive and involve experiences that may be difficult to put into words [1,2]. In the existing literature we found consensus that arts activities offer alternative ways of engaging with end-of-life (EoL) issues, e.g., by involving all senses and including non-verbal modes of communication [1–5].

Arts activities have been used in healthcare settings, death education, and therapies to ease communication about EoL issues [2,3,6]. They are also used for health promotion purposes to engage communities in EoL issues, helping to encourage conversation and increase the sense of social support [2,7]. Examples of arts activities include painting, music making, dance, and pottery, with generally a focus on arts processes rather than finished products [2,5].

Such arts activities are commonly facilitated by professional artists or art therapists [1,2,8]. Along with offering alternative modes of expression, arts activities have been found to support communities, patients, families, and caregivers in coping with change, meaning-making, and personal growth [2,9–12]. Furthermore, collective arts activities have been found to offer possibilities for creating relationships and supportive communities [8,9].

It is notable that research literature in this field predominantly describes arts activities developed and facilitated by institutionalized healthcare services. There appears to be a lack of research on arts activities in community settings to support the involvement of individuals and organizations outside healthcare institutions in issues related to dying, death, and loss, here referred to as community engagement with EoL issues. Furthermore, there is little literature about the specific ways, or mechanisms through which arts activities function to support engagement with EoL issues [1]. Therefore, in this article, we aim to explore mechanisms in arts activities that support community engagement with EoL issues.

Contextual Background: Studio DöBra

The arts activities underlying this investigation are part of Studio DöBra, a project within the DöBra research program in Sweden ("DöBra" is a pun which literally means dying well, but figuratively 'awesome'). The DöBra research program applies a health promotion approach to engage communities in EoL issues [13]. In Studio DöBra, we partnered with community organizations to bring together children (9 y/o) and older adults (most 80+) in a series of arts workshops to engage with issues related to dying, death, and loss [4,5]. Partnerships and development of arts workshops were informed by principles of community-based participatory research [14]. However, we refer to our process as community-based participatory *action* research (CBPAR), since learning through doing, i.e., action, is central to our approach [15,16].

Two Studio DöBra iterations were developed; Studio DöBra 1 took place in 2016 in a multi-ethnic urban area outside a large city, Studio DöBra 2 in 2018 in a mid-sized town in a more rural area. These were developed by project groups consisting of first author MK, a PhD student with a design background, and the community partners shown in Table 1. Studio DöBra 1 partnerships were initiated by MK, while Studio DöBra 2 partnerships were initiated by the municipal organization for culture, based on positive word of mouth about the first iteration. As MK was part of both project groups, he contributed with lessons learned from Studio DöBra 1 in his engagement in Studio DöBra 2. Each iteration involved eight children and eight older adults in a series of five weekly, two-hour arts workshops. Table 1 summarizes characteristics of each Studio DöBra iteration as well as demographic information about those who were involved.

In line with CBPAR principles, project groups developed arts workshops through interactive cycles of action and reflection [14,15], i.e., using lessons learned to inform following workshops. Community partners with arts backgrounds took the lead in this process in each group. In Studio DöBra 1, these partners ran an artistic organization for children in the neighborhood in which they facilitated design projects, often explicitly using play as a pedagogical tool, e.g., through games and role play. In Studio DöBra 2, these partners had backgrounds in visual and performing arts, as well as primary school arts education, working together for the first time in Studio DöBra.

Partners with arts backgrounds also facilitated the workshops, with support from the other partners. During the arts workshops, participants explored topics related to dying, death, and loss through e.g., making collages in different materials, sewing, and creating sculptures. The findings provide more details about the arts activities.

Table 1. Characteristics of the two Studio DöBra iterations and demographic information.

	Studio DöBra 1, 2016		
	Project Group Partners	**Children**	**Older Adults**
	$n = 7$ DöBra research program: MK [a,b] Artistic organization for children: • Artist manager [a,b] • Artist artistic director [a,b] • Freelance artist [a] Activity center for older adults: • Activity manager [a,b] Children's library: Librarian After-school center: Teacher	$n = 8$	$n = 8$
Invitation to participate	MK approached community organizations	Through after-school center and parents	Individually, through involved community organizations
Gender	5 women, 2 men	4 girls, 4 boys	5 women, 3 men
Age	Median 37, ages 28–65	9	Median 82 ages 65–85
	Studio DöBra 2, 2018		
	Project Group Partners	**Children**	**Older Adults**
	$n = 7$ DöBra research program: MK [a,b] Municipal organizations for culture: • Producer of cultural activities [b] • Producer of cultural activities for older adults [a,b] • Freelance artist [a,b] Municipal organization for elder care: • Activity manager [a,b] After-school center: Teacher	$n = 8$	$n = 8$
Invitation to participate	Municipal organization for culture approached MK and the other community organizations	Through after-school center and parents	As a group (independently hosting weekly creative sessions), through the municipal organization for elder care
Gender	6 women, 1 man	4 girls, 4 boys	8 women
Age	Median 33, ages 29–64	9	Median 83.5 ages 66–93

[a] Partners with an arts background. [b] Partners who participated in the participatory analysis phase. The other partners did not participate due to personal circumstances or lack of professional mandate.

2. Methods

2.1. Community-Based Data Generation

After approval by the Swedish ethical review board (2016/1517-31/5; 2018/825-32), partners, older adults, children, and their parents all signed informed consent forms. Details about the involved partners, children, and older adults, are shown in Table 1. After each workshop, partners held reflective meetings sharing their observations, reflections, and informal feedback from participants; these became the basis for developing subsequent workshops. Documentation from these reflective meetings, i.e., audio recordings and transcripts, are one form of data underlying analysis.

During the arts workshops, MK acted as participant observer, documenting observations through field notes, photographs, and audio recordings of some conversations, while also interacting with participants and partners. Within 10 weeks after each Studio DöBra iteration, follow-up interviews were conducted with partners, participating children, and older participants to inform development of future iterations as part of the CBPAR process. Interviews with the involved teachers were conducted by MK. Other partners were interviewed by researchers from the DöBra research program who were not part of the project groups. These interviews with partners (range 40–112 min, median 72 min) were held in conversational form, rather than being guided by an interview guide with predetermined questions, and focused on topics such as the experiences of developing and facilitating Studio DöBra workshops. All interviews with children and older participants were also conversation-based, focusing on their experiences of participating in Studio DöBra. In these interviews, a set of photographs from the workshops was used to support and stimulate the conversation. After Studio DöBra 1, MK interviewed children in a group (n = 6, 60 min) with the teacher present. After Studio DöBra 2, MK interviewed children individually (n = 8, range 15–37 min, median 28 min). MK interviewed older participants individually (Studio DöBra 1 n = 7, Studio DöBra 2 n = 7, range 31–118 min, median 71). All interviews were audio-recorded and transcribed.

2.2. Analysis

In an initial participatory analysis phase, partners from both project groups (indicated in Table 1) came together for two whole-day meetings to reflect on and document lessons learned. In doing so, a new insight was that elements of play, in a variety of forms, were found throughout all Studio DöBra arts activities, although partners from Studio DöBra 2 had not previously considered that they used elements of play. This led to curiosity as to whether play theory could assist in better understanding ways through which arts activities support engagement with EoL issues. In the analysis phase that followed, we therefore took an abductive approach inspired by Tavory and Timmermans [17]. This phase was university-based, led by MK in a process repeatedly discussed and reflected on with co-authors, a team of three professors in EoL/nursing research, sociology, and creative practices, external to the project groups. Community partners and MK stayed in contact concerning developments in the abductive analysis and in the community, which continued their process of learning together [14].

Abductive analysis aims to develop new theoretical ideas through the creative use of existing theory in relation to unexpected observations, it entails an iterative process of moving between empirical data and theoretical literature [17]. We chose this approach as it guided us in further investigating the hitherto unforeseen observation of play elements throughout Studio DöBra arts activities, by iteratively moving between Studio DöBra's empirical data and play theory. In doing so we developed ideas about play elements as mechanisms in arts activities that supported community engagement with EoL issues.

Hamayon describes two camps in play studies [18]; one general approach to play, originating with Huizinga's theory, first described in 1938 [19], and a second approaching play from specific contexts and disciplinary perspectives, e.g., Frissen et al. who study play in digital media [20]. Although Huizinga's ideas about how human culture evolved from play may appear outdated and even somewhat problematic today, his definition of the characteristics of play remains classic in contemporary play studies [18,20]. In our analysis we used both Huizinga's characteristics of play [19], and Frissen et al.'s critique and further development of this theory [20].

Our abductive analysis started with looking for "defamiliarized surprises" to use Tavory and Timmermans' [17] term, i.e., observations in the empirical data that do not neatly fit existing theory. Thus, MK investigated if and how play elements described in the literature were expressed in the Studio DöBra arts workshops [17]. To this end, all available empirical data from partners, children, and older adults' perspectives, were combined into one dataset for each workshop, using the qualitative analysis software NVivo. MK repeatedly read transcripts, listened to audio recordings, and examined workshop photographs. He then coded data for play elements based on the literature. Memo writing throughout this process helped to identify and reflect on surprising observations in relation to theory.

One central element of play we investigated, which then provided a basis for our continued analysis, is described by Huizinga as the "magic circle" [19]. According to Huizinga, play is distinct from "ordinary life" by taking place in temporally and spatially bounded play-spaces, e.g., playgrounds, arenas, and the boards of board games, all are "temporary worlds within the ordinary world, dedicated to the performance of an act apart" [19] (pp. 9–10). A magic circle is the temporal and spatial boundary that separates play from ordinary life [19]. Inside the magic circle, "the laws and customs of ordinary life no longer count" [19] p. 12. The term is widely adopted in play studies [21]. However, Frissen et al. argue that Huizinga's theory is contradictory as it claims that play only happens outside ordinary life while it also states that play is interwoven into many parts of our daily lives [20]. Frissen et al. therefore assert that players can be in and outside playful modes simultaneously [20].

In our data we could identify a Studio DöBra magic circle, i.e., the spatial and temporal boundaries of the arts workshops. Additionally, in line with Huizinga, the norms and customs inside the Studio DöBra magic circle deviated from ordinary life in that participants and partners interacted across generations beyond their families and engaged with EoL issues, whereas this would not occur in ordinary life in the same way, as indicated by our previous research [4,5]. However, participants and partners appeared to move in and out of playful modes within the Studio DöBra magic circle, rather than Huizinga's idea of a magic circle as a separation between play and ordinary life, or Frissen et al.'s ideas about play and ordinary life occurring simultaneously. Through iterative analysis, moving between data and theory, we can describe the functionality of the Studio DöBra magic circle in supporting engagement with EoL issues.

Other play elements we investigated are characterized by ambiguity, as pointed out by Frissen et al. [20]. They state for example that play includes both "freedom and force", because it requires voluntary participation, but also adherence to rules [19,20]. Play also relates to both "reality and appearance", as it is part of ordinary life, but also characterized by players', often unspoken, consciousness of their play as different from ordinary life, e.g., just pretending [18,20]. Furthermore, play is both an "individual and collective" activity, requiring players' individual attention [20], but often leading to "the formation of social groupings" [19].

However, during analysis we noted a friction between our empirical data and the theoretical play elements. Rather than using force, we found that partners were balancing freedoms with restrictions in the ways they facilitated arts activities. We found that participants and partners dealt with imagination and real-life experiences, rather than appearance and reality. Additionally, we found that when partners and participants moved in and out of playful modes, they did so individually, in sub-groups, or collectively. As we went back and forth between theory and data, we further developed play elements and identified ways in which they supported engagement with EoL issues in Studio DöBra arts activities.

We continued analysis by searching for variation in our modified play elements throughout the data [17]. As the use and functionality of play elements changed across and within workshops, further analysis focused on what led to these changes. Specific events within the arts activities were identified as particularly illustrative of these changes. To investigate these in detail, MK transcribed relevant parts of workshop audio recordings and drew from play theory to interpret them. He also generated illustrations from photo-documentation, which he combined with interview/workshop transcripts, to visualize different perspectives on events, as shown in the findings. Continued memo writing helped in formulating findings.

Lastly, MK met virtually (due to COVID-19-related restrictions) with the partners who participated in the initial participatory analysis to discuss tentatively formulated findings. Partners confirmed the findings from their perspectives, but also provided feedback which added nuance to the final formulation.

3. Findings

We use our modification of play elements from theory, to explain mechanisms supporting community engagement with EoL issues in arts activities. We identified four mechanisms: Creating permeable magic circles; Balancing restrictions and freedoms; Approaching dying, death, and loss through imagination and real-life experiences; and Continuing a sense of community after ending the arts workshops. In presenting our findings, we refer to examples from Studio DöBra arts activities. We chose to discuss one exemplar from each Studio DöBra iteration more in depth throughout the findings to demonstrate the diverse ways in which mechanisms acted in each iteration, and to illustrate ways in which various mechanisms acted in concert.

The Studio DöBra 1 exemplar comprises events from an arts workshop dealing with the question "Where do we end up after we die?" Participants explored this using travel as a metaphor for dying and death, creating descriptions of the afterlife as if it were a travel destination, and then building a vehicle to play-travel there. The Studio DöBra 2 exemplar consists of related events from the last three workshops of this iteration, revolving around a dead bird, brought to the workshops by a partner. Using sewing tools and fabrics of various colors and patterns, participants created images symbolizing the bird's life, death, and afterlife to decorate a large fabric sheet. During the final workshop, partners and participants held a funeral ceremony for the bird.

We use empirical data to illustrate findings. For confidentiality, partners and participants are given pseudonyms and personal information is omitted.

3.1. Creating Permeable Magic Circles

We defined the Studio DöBra magic circle as the spatial and temporal boundaries of the arts workshops. Studio DöBra 1 workshops were held in different places—a children's library, an activity center for older adults, and at the artistic organization for children. The Studio DöBra 2 workshops all took place in a project room already used for weekly creative sessions by the participating older adults. All locations were closed to the public during workshops, creating spatial and temporal boundaries from ordinary life.

The Studio DöBra magic circle provided the context for intergenerational interaction and engagement with EoL issues. Within this, partners and participants sometimes used their imagination to engage with EoL issues, and sometimes introduced elements from ordinary life by sharing EoL-related experiences, such as the death of a family member or a pet. Additionally, our earlier analyses indicated that participants created spaces in their social networks for engaging with EoL issues stimulated through Studio DöBra participation [4]. We therefore conceptualize the Studio DöBra magic circle as a permeable boundary through which participants could introduce experiences from ordinary life into Studio DöBra and introduce elements from Studio DöBra into their ordinary lives, as illustrated in Figure 1.

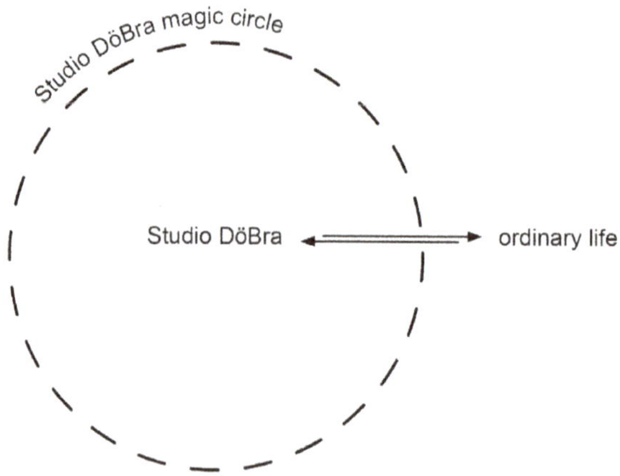

Figure 1. The Studio DöBra magic circle as a permeable boundary.

In some events, smaller groups of participants seemed to gather into their own magic sub-circles. In the Studio DöBra 2 exemplar, the whole group discussed how birds are born from eggs and how the bird at the workshop might have died, e.g., by falling as it was trying to fly. A smaller group of children began fantasizing among themselves, wondering if the bird was born from an Easter egg, killed by a meteor, and then transformed into a giant kiwi. During the reflective meeting which followed, partners discussed this:

> Sandra: *I thought it was interesting how* [I] *reacted when it got silly, because I noticed how I reacted myself* [. . .] *In my role, I thought, "oh, now maybe the older people take offense that it's not a respectful way to talk about death, but that it becomes . . . "*
>
> Anna: *I think that I took a little offense, or I thought that they weren't . . . weren't really present.*
>
> Sandra: *Yes, that they were somewhere else.*
>
> Anna: *They were in their play . . .*

Older adults reflecting on this in follow-up interviews did not appear to have taken offense, although some questioned children's understanding of the seriousness of death as illustrated by Berit (older participant):

> *They don't have the experience* [. . .] *they're still direct. You could hear it* [when they talked about] *the kiwi and everything else they came up with, which is so delightful with children.*

Thus, events in which a group of participants segregated themselves into a magic sub-circle could create tensions when outsiders perceived the participants to be "not present" or if the play was interpreted as being not serious enough in relation to EoL issues. However, segregating into magic sub-circles may be a way for participants to engage with EoL issues in their own way. An unresolved challenge for partners was therefore the degree to which they should steer participants' engagement with EoL issues in response to these tensions. They tried different approaches as described below.

3.2. Balancing Restrictions and Freedoms

Studio DöBra arts activities were guided by partners trying to balance restrictions and freedoms. This occurred in part through the use of questions and topics. In the Studio DöBra 1 exemplar, descriptions of the afterlife destinations were based on predetermined questions, e.g., What language is spoken? and what sights are worth seeing? Restricting the questions seemed to give partners a sense of control over the EoL issues raised by participants. However, partners sometimes wondered if these restrictions inhibited participants from exploring their own questions. In a follow-up interview, Charlie (partner) proposed "You might ask questions that are a little more open . . . but then maybe it becomes less playful," thus suggesting that increasing freedoms might decrease playfulness. In another Studio DöBra 1 workshop, participants were asked to create alternative ways to measure time. Partners had assumed that participants would relate the passing of time to the EoL, but later reflected that this activity did not trigger the intended discussions. Thus, narrowly defined questions could restrict participants from freely exploring, whereas more open formats risked failing to initiate engagement with EoL issues.

Based on lessons learned from Studio DöBra 1, Studio DöBra 2 partners tried to achieve balance using the first workshop for participants to freely determine the EoL issues they wanted to address. Partners met with the children and older adults in separate groups in advance. Each group made a mind-map of their thoughts about dying, death, and loss. In smaller intergenerational groups in the first joint workshop, participants compared these mind-maps and together chose words or phrases as topics for collages. By relinquishing control over the topic selection, partners also shifted the responsibility for choosing topics to participants.

Another issue concerned the artistic processes and products, which were envisioned and preplanned by partners. Some partners and participants reflected on some of the arts activities' processes as not creating enough space for self-expression. Siv (older participant) explained:

> *I wish we'd had more time to talk* [about EoL topics] *and less time to do arts and crafts. Because that took some of the focus.*

In the Studio DöBra 2 exemplar, partners envisioned that the whole fabric sheet would be filled with participants' images symbolizing the bird's life, death, and afterlife. However, they noticed that participants were creating small images that would not fill the fabric in the available time. Partners therefore told participants to create larger images, to which Alva (child) responded:

> *"But we need to have respect for the bird, it cannot become ugly."*

Alva's remark pointed out that partners' expectations did not reflect her efforts to show respect in her own way. Partners thus controlled processes and products by imposing restrictions, which in this case were not aligned with participants' processes and expectations.

In reflective meetings, partners identified such tensions, and in response adjusted planning of following arts activities to try to better balance restrictions and freedoms. Partners also adjusted approaches during arts activities, as the following excerpt from the Studio DöBra 1 exemplar illustrates. Here, Sasha (partner) adjusted freedoms and restrictions to stimulate participants to play-travel to the afterlife destinations they had described, with the vehicle they had built.

> Sasha (addressing participants): *It could be that I would decide, but* [. . .] *now you have this vehicle* [. . .] *and three* [afterlife destinations] *to travel to* [. . .] *so how are you going to travel there? Do you have any idea? This is a little bit like playing.*
>
> [Participants have a lively discussion but seem uncertain about what to do.]
>
> Sasha: *Everyone who built this, now you are going to test traveling to these three different destinations in your imagination* [. . .] *We're in a kind of airport now. How are you going to do this?*
>
> [Participants discuss but still cannot agree.]
>
> Sasha: *Shall we let each group take the others to their destination? You understand? Yes or no?*
>
> [No clear response.]
>
> Sasha: *OK, I'll make it simple. There are three groups, and each group decides how you travel to your destination. I decide that this group (points to one group) starts. You're the pilots, the others are the passengers.*
>
> [Participants get ready.]
>
> Sasha: *Everyone! Let's pretend this is a theatre or a film set, and we say 'ACTION!' so the film starts, the event of traveling to this destination.* [. . .]
>
> [Participants get ready.]
>
> Sasha: *OK!* [. . .] *ACTION!*

As participants seemed uncertain about what to do and could not agree, Sasha gradually decreased free choice by increasing restrictions. Sasha thus created a magic sub-circle by transforming the space into an imaginary airport and film set and marking temporal boundaries by saying "ACTION!" This led to children and older adults exploring different afterlife-scenarios together, as illustrated in Figure 2.

Although partners interpreted the event illustrated in Figure 2 as play, participants reflecting on this arts activity in follow-up interviews did not use this term, but rather described what they did, as illustrated by the following two excerpts:

> Nils (child): *We got to build a vehicle, and then we got to sit in it and travel* [. . .] *to different* [. . .] *after-death-places.*
>
> Bengt (older participant): *We talked about . . . up in heaven* [. . .] *we traveled up there with the spaceship . . . I said* [. . .] *it will take two hours maybe to travel there, and that's when* [. . .] *we came to the conclusion that there would be food* [. . .] *and then the little girl said that chewing gum was important.*

Sasha (partner): OK! […] ACTION!

Bengt (older pilot, holding an imaginary microphone): So then we ask, is everyone on board?

Passengers: No, not yet.

Bengt: We are departing soon.

Alex (child pilot): Is everyone on board?

Bengt: Tighten your seatbelts!

Alex: Everyone needs to have their seatbelts, does everyone have that? Is everyone sitting?!

[…]

Bengt: We depart in one minute VROOM!

Passengers are geting ready.

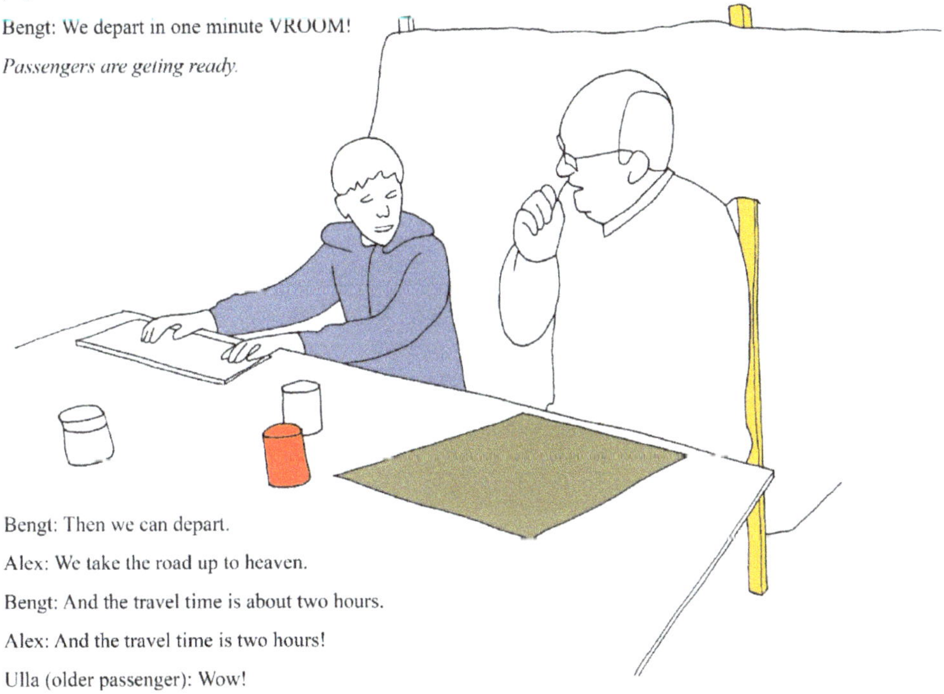

Bengt: Then we can depart.

Alex: We take the road up to heaven.

Bengt: And the travel time is about two hours.

Alex: And the travel time is two hours!

Ulla (older passenger): Wow!

Alice (child passenger): To heaven?

Maria (older passenger): I have to go home to boil potatoes!

Bengt: Haha!

Alex: I'm sure you're going to make it! OK we lift off in three, two, one, zero, we start!

Bengt: Now! Then we are on our way up to heaven, we made reservations at a cloud up there, and that will be fine, and then… we will get our first meal, some angel-food, and we get to meet a few angels.
And there we have a small football field in a cloud with a nice view.

Alex: You all can go play!

Bengt: And then we have chewing gum, a few snowflakes, and we can eat ice cream too. And we also have cloud-ball. And we have a camera so we can take photos to show where we have been. And there is cake as well. So have a nice flight, it will take two hours.

Ulla (older passenger): Thank you captain. And I'd like to have a very soft landing if that's possible.

Figure 2. Traveling to after life (illustration by author MK, based on a photograph of the workshop).

When restrictions and freedoms were well-balanced, partners reflected on participants being independent in their execution of the arts activity and engagement with EoL issues:

> Anna (partner): *We (referring to partners) all felt as if we weren't really needed, because they were so independent, both in ... that they understood, that the assignments were clear, I think, and that they worked well together, the older adults and the children, and that the material was there so they helped each other technically and theoretically. [...] and that was a nice feeling. Then it felt like ... we had prepared well, when we weren't needed.*

In conclusion, restrictions in aspects of arts activities enabled participants to explore EoL issues, but also risked diminishing both their agency and artistic freedom. Too much freedom could leave participants uncertain about both their roles and what was expected of them. Partners tried to find balance by creating a magic circle with a minimum of restrictions within which they felt in control and at the same time provided participants with enough freedoms and agency to engage with EoL issues on their own terms.

3.3. Balancing Restrictions and Freedoms

Some partners reflected on finding it challenging to approach EoL issues, as death is part of our reality but at the same time abstract and difficult to grasp. Some partners described feeling insecure about facilitating arts activities addressing questions to which they do not have answers themselves. Additionally, as EoL-related experiences and beliefs are personal, project groups aimed to create a space which could contain and foster diverse perspectives. Partners therefore approached EoL issues in arts activities through a combination of imagination and real-life experiences.

The first project group often used metaphors as a means to call on participants' imaginations to explore EoL issues, e.g., travel as a metaphor for dying and death in the Studio DöBra 1 exemplar illustrated in Figure 2. The use of metaphors could blur the line between imagination and real-life in arts activities. Participants could, for example, use metaphors to talk about personal EoL experiences, questions, and beliefs, as in the following conversation from the Studio DöBra 1 exemplar, involving a small group of participants and partners:

> Alex (child): *My mother says that my grandmother has gone on a trip, but she's dead. [...] She still says that she's gone on a trip [...] and I don't believe her.*
>
> Sasha (partner): *How long has she been gone?*
>
> Alex: [...] *since I was three.*
>
> [...]
>
> Bengt (older adult): *It's hard on kids, they ask, where did they go [...] it can be sensitive too ... She's not around anymore.*
>
> MK: *It's strange.*
>
> Bengt (older adult): *It's strange. You grow up with your family, you can think that they'll be there forever and then they're gone, that's the way of life, the same with flowers in the field, during the summer there are beautiful flowers and then they die, after that there'll be new ones, those can be their children and grandchildren, the same with trees, everything. (Addressing Alex) Your mother gave birth to you, when you grow up you'll have children, that's how we are.*

Later, a partner overheard Ulla (older participant) say to the children that she would, perhaps soon, send them a postcard from the afterlife destination they had just described together. Thus, it seemed that metaphors were used to talk about personal EoL experiences, questions, and beliefs explicitly, as in the excerpt above, or implicitly, as with Ulla who seemed to indirectly convey her awareness of nearing the end-of-her-life.

In contrast, in the Studio DöBra 2 project group chose to approach the topic head-on by introducing the dead bird. Partners recognized that as adults they had expected death to be discussed seriously and wondered how they could create space in which everyone has respect for one another's perspectives. The final Studio DöBra 2 workshop revolved around a burial ceremony for the dead bird. To create a serious and respectful atmosphere, partners changed some elements of the magic circle. A stronger sense of coming into the magic circle was created by keeping participants from entering the project room as they arrived, entering together instead. The table which usually displayed arts materials, now showcased red roses, a candle and a little box as a coffin for the dead bird. The other tables were covered with the fabric decorated with the images of the bird's life, death, and afterlife, sewn by participants. As participants came into this space, they were quiet and seemed moved, as exemplified by Siv (older participant):

> *That was very beautiful, very beautiful.* […] *The pretty fabric there and everything was so pretty.*
>
> Jenny (partner) said:
>
> *It became … very respectful,* […] *calm, and harmonious when everyone went in together,* […] *and the project starts, and then we leave other things outside.*

Partners planned the ceremony to include elements commonly found in Swedish funerals. Participants wrote farewell notes to the bird, after which they went outside to bury the bird under a tree and left flowers, as illustrated in Figure 3.

Quotes from participants in Figure 3 show that different perspectives about the funeral for the bird co-existed, but that not everyone shared their perspective openly. It seemed that some participants self-censored as they anticipated that their perspective might be deviant, as exemplified by Ida (child) and Berit (older participant). Furthermore, the line between imagination and real-life experiences became blurred, as shown by Ida (child) who seemed to perceive the group as using imagination, and Alva (child) and Berit (older participant) who described the ceremony as a real funeral. There appears to be a difference between the way imagination is used in this exemplar compared to the Studio DöBra 1 exemplar. Perhaps this is due to differences in the magic circle which in the Studio DöBra 1 exemplar was designed by partners to initiate a playful engagement with EoL issues using metaphors, whereas in the Studio DöBra 2 exemplar, partners designed the magic circle to create a serious and respectful atmosphere using elements of real-life funerals.

3.4. Continuing a Sense of Community after Ending the Arts Workshops

As noted above, according to Huizinga play is characterized by the formation of a "play-community". This community tends to "stress their difference from the common world by disguise or other means" [19] p. 13. We found examples of this in both Studio DöBra iterations as certain events became symbols only understood by participants and partners. During the first Studio DöBra 1 workshop, participants and partners created and played a new form of Bingo. 'Bingo-death' became a defining symbol for Studio DöBra 1 as it was referred to throughout the workshops and interviews, with some saying they found it hard to express its' meaning to outsiders. During the first Studio DöBra 2 workshop, Emil (child) created an image of a flying pig for a collage about dying, and explained that he believed that when he dies, a flying pig will bring him to heaven. The image of the flying pig became symbolic for Studio DöBra 2, as participants and partners referred to it throughout workshops and interviews.

The tangible products of the arts activities were another factor bonding participants. Participants brought up the question of ownership by asking whether they could take the objects home. In Studio DöBra 1, partners explained that participants were collective owners, and that products would be saved in an archive to which participants would have access. In Studio DöBra 2, products were shown at the children's school, which then discarded them without further consultation.

A group of birds in nearby trees began chirping during the funeral. Jenny (partner) wondered whether they understood that a bird was being buried, to which both children and older participants earnestly responded yes.

Ida (child) commented this retrospectively in the interview: [The birds] maybe didn't even know who it was, so I just thought, 'but hello, all birds will chirp whenever', that's what I thought.

Berit (older participant, interview): [The funeral] was beautiful and it was good, but [...] it's just because I am the way that I am when it comes to funerals [...] it's not my melody, I would say. But I... I feel so odd in my opinion, so I didn't want to say that it was wrong. No... and for the children it was clearly a natural part. They are free to take a stand on things later [in life], that's how it is for all people... I stood far in the back here (points to the photo).

Figure 3. Funeral for a bird (illustration by author MK, based on a photograph of the workshop).

During the last Studio DöBra 1 workshop, participants created an exhibition at the children's library, displaying their products accompanied by their texts and collages of workshop photographs, after which they role-played its' opening event. The day after, outsiders were invited to the formal opening of the exhibition. The funeral for the bird was also conceptualized as a goodbye to Studio DöBra 2. Alva (child) not only wrote a farewell note to the dead bird, but also to Studio DöBra, which she left in the project room:

> *"It was a lot of fun to participate* [in Studio DöBra]*! It was a pity that the bird died because it could have lived longer and done more in life!"*

After the ceremony, a group of guests were invited to an event during which participants showed what they had created. While older adults said they had no-one to invite, children invited family and friends, and partners invited colleagues and journalists. Thus, the conclusions of both Studio DöBra iterations were marked by a final collective activity, after which the magic circle was opened to outsiders.

Although the temporal and spatial structures of the Studio DöBra magic circle ended at the conclusion of each iteration, reflections in follow-up interviews suggest that a sense of community continued to exist in various forms. This is in line with Huizinga's ideas about the continuation of play-communities: "The feeling of being 'apart together' in an exceptional situation, [...] and rejecting the usual norms, retains its magic beyond the duration of the individual game" [19]. Partners and participants from both Studio DöBra iterations talked about continuing to meet in passing in the neighborhood [4]; Studio DöBra 2 participants also talked about visiting the bird's grave. The Studio DöBra 1 exhibition was later shown at the activity center for older adults, and partners organized a reunion two months later.

4. Discussion

We aimed to explore mechanisms in arts activities that support community engagement with EoL issues, through investigating Studio DöBra arts activities. Based on the partners' unexpected observation of play elements throughout the arts activities, we continued analysis with an abductive process using play theory. In doing so we modified theoretical play elements to explain mechanisms supporting engagement with EoL issues in arts activities. We found four mechanisms: (1) Creating permeable magic circles. The Studio DöBra magic circle provided the context for engagement with EoL issues, with participants sometimes segregating into magic sub-circles within which they engaged with EoL issues in their own ways. Partners struggled with the degree to which they should steer participant's engagement with EoL issues. (2) Partners aimed to balance restrictions and freedoms in arts activities to support participants' independent engagement with EoL issues and execution of arts activities, while also creating a sense of control for themselves. (3) Partners and participants approached EoL issues through both imagination and real-life experiences to deal with the potential sensitivity of the topic, but also to foster different perspectives of EoL-related experiences and beliefs. The line between imagination and real-life was not always clear in arts activities. (4) Continuing a sense of community after ending the arts workshops. We found indications of a sense of community developing through arts activities, and remaining after Studio DöBra ended, which supported continued engagement with EoL issues.

Although most literature about supporting EoL conversations through arts activities derives from healthcare, therapy, or community settings with ill or bereaved individuals [2,3,10], Studio DöBra was community-based and deliberately involved participants who were not imminently dying, in an effort to support early engagement with EoL issues. Our findings thus complement this literature with insights into mechanisms supporting engagement with EoL issues in community-based intergenerational arts activities. Our study has potential to contribute to theory-building that can inform arts activities supporting community engagement with EoL issues. One limitation of this abductive qualitative study is that it is based on play theory only. We suggest therefore that further research may not only build on our findings by critically applying mechanisms in the development and facilitation of arts activities to support community engagement in EoL issues, but might also draw on additional theories for further understanding.

In line with findings from Studio DöBra, literature points to the potential of arts initiatives and intergenerational programs to promote a sense of community [4,22–24]. It is noteworthy that the Studio DöBra magic circle shares features with McMillan's description of elements which promote a sense of community [25]. The Studio DöBra magic circle defines spatial and temporal boundaries, which McMillan points out as being essential for establishing a space in which individuals can identify as a group. McMillan contends that the community should provide a space in which members feel safe to share personal experiences [25]. This appeared to be occasionally challenging in Studio DöBra, as some participants seemed to self-censor when they felt their perspective was outside the norm.

Self-censoring on the other hand, might also point to participants' agency in modulating their engagement with EoL issues [4].

EoL experiences may be considered 'unspeakable' as they are often sensitive and difficult to put into words [1]. The Studio DöBra magic circle provided time, space, and permission for engaging with EoL issues, thereby being responsive to participants' desire for spaces in which to talk about these issues [4,26]. While talking was part of engaging with EoL issues, partners and participants also engaged through acting, doing, and making, consistently using both imagination and real-life experiences.

During the initial participatory analysis phase, partners expressed surprise at the older participants' child-like playfulness in some arts activities, as in the Studio DöBra 1 exemplar. Partners wondered whether interaction with children may have helped catalyze this; however, our data does not allow for definitive conclusions. Hamayon argues that play in Western cultures is commonly seen as restricted to childhood and adult leisure [18]. Thus, partners' interpretation of older participants' play is likely to be influenced by these cultural norms. This implies that cultural norms may constrain the kinds of play adults engage in. It may be that intergenerational interaction lowered the threshold for child-like play. This is in line with the idea of a magic circle within which norms differ from ordinary life [19]. However, it remains unclear as to whether older adults would adopt similar playful engagement with EoL issues in the absence of children. Furthermore, gender roles may also affect older adults' engagement in arts activities with play elements; however, systematic investigation of this is beyond the scope of this study. These notions also point to a need to further consider cultural and gender norms regarding play and talking about EoL issues, when considering transferability of our findings to other settings [27].

One strength of this study is that it is based on data triangulating perspectives from partners, children, and older adults [28]. It is important to reiterate that the observations regarding play elements in the arts activities were made by partners. Participants did not use the term play as they reflected on their Studio DöBra participation in follow-up interviews. Thus, rather than conceptualizing all arts activities as play, we used play theory to investigate mechanisms in arts activities that support engagement with EoL issues. As the abductive analysis phase was led by researcher/partner MK, one role of co-authors as researchers external to Studio DöBra, was to support MK in critically reflecting on his own roles as partner and researcher.

Another strength of this study is the triangulation of different types of qualitative data [28], i.e., follow-up interviews, reflective meetings, and participant observations including photographs, audio recordings of conversations, and MK's field notes. As it was not always possible to produce high-quality audio recordings during arts workshops, other types of data were also used to analyze some of the verbal interaction, e.g., MK's fieldnotes and partners' reflective meetings. However, this may risk skewing the interpretations towards partner perspectives. Prior to the start of Studio DöBra, one partner expressed concerns that MK's participant observation methods, e.g., audio-recording conversations and photographing, might disturb participants' interaction and engagement, thereby risking compromising the magic circle. MK considered himself an insider in the magic circle through his role as partner, but others may have considered him an outsider due to his research activities. On the other hand, this method itself is in line with our conceptualization of the magic circle as a permeable boundary, allowing MK to be both participant and observer simultaneously.

Our findings contribute to understanding mechanisms in arts activities supporting community engagement with EoL issues. The notion of the Studio DöBra magic circle can help to understand ways in which other health promoting initiatives can provide time, space, and permission to engage with EoL issues in community contexts. By applying our modified play elements to arts activities aiming to support community engagement with EoL issues in other contexts and with other groups, we hope that researchers and practitioners can further explore these mechanisms and build on our findings. In Studio DöBra, partners adapted their approaches in response to tensions they observed and reflections regarding their own roles. Reflective practice [14], e.g., gathering and reflecting on informal feedback from participants during arts activities, and reflective meetings in conjunction with workshops, supported partners in this process. We therefore suggest that transferring our findings to different contexts should be coupled with continuous reflective practice to adapt approaches sensitive to the local context and relevant for participants.

Author Contributions: Conceptualization, M.K., R.H., B.M.A. and C.T.; methodology, M.K., R.H., B.M.A. and C.T.; formal analysis, M.K., R.H., B.M.A. and C.T.; writing—original draft preparation, M.K.; writing—review and editing, M.K., R.H., B.M.A. and C.T.; visualization, M.K.; supervision, R.H., B.M.A. and C.T.; funding acquisition, C.T. All authors have read and agreed to the published version of the manuscript.

Funding: This work was supported by the Swedish Research Council for Health, Welfare and Working Life (FORTE) under Grant [2014-4071]; Investor AB (CT salary) under Grant [2-2314/2013]; Stockholm City Elder Care Bureau under Grant [243-662/2015]; and Karolinska Institutet's Engagement Grant 2018.

Institutional Review Board Statement: The study was conducted according to the guidelines of the Declaration of Helsinki, and approved by the Swedish ethical review board (2016/1517-31/5; 2018/825-32).

Informed Consent Statement: Informed consent was obtained from all subjects involved in the study.

Data Availability Statement: For original data, please contact the corresponding author; ethical approval does not cover making data openly accessible.

Acknowledgments: The authors thank partners, their community organizations, and the participating older adults, children and their parents for their contributions to this work. We also acknowledge the contributions of Olav Lindqvist and Malin Eneslätt to data generation. As one of MK's supervisors, Olav was a fundamental support in MK's doctoral project, but he died before the end of the second Studio DöBra iteration.

Conflicts of Interest: The authors declare no conflict of interest. The funders had no role in the design of the study; in the collection, analyses, or interpretation of data; in the writing of the manuscript, or in the decision to publish the results.

References

1. Walter, T. How people who are dying or mourning engage with the arts. *Music Arts Action* **2012**, *4*, 73–98.
2. Hartley, N.; Payne, M. *The Creative Arts in Palliative Care*; Jessica Kingsley Publishers: London, UK, 2008.
3. Tsiris, G.; Tasker, M.; Lawson, V.; Prince, G.; Dives, T.; Sands, M.; Ridley, A. Music and arts in health promotion and death education: The St Christopher's Schools Project. *Music Arts Action* **2011**, *3*, 95–119. [CrossRef]
4. Kleijberg, M.; Ahlberg, B.M.; Hilton, R.; Tishelman, C. Death, loss and community-Perspectives from children, their parents, and older adults on intergenerational community-based arts initiatives in Sweden. *Health Soc. Care Community* **2020**, *28*, 2025–2036. [CrossRef] [PubMed]
5. Kleijberg, M.; Ahlberg, B.M.; Macdonald, A.; Lindqvist, O.; Tishelman, C. Navigating power dynamics in engaging communities in end-of-life issues–Lessons learned from developing community-based intergenerational arts initiatives about death and loss. *Death Stud.* **2019**, 1–14. [CrossRef]
6. Nan, J.K.M.; Pang, K.S.Y.; Lam, K.K.F.; Szeto, M.M.L.; Sin, S.F.Y.; So, C.S.C. An expressive-arts-based life-death education program for the elderly: A qualitative study. *Death Stud.* **2018**, *44*, 131–140. [CrossRef] [PubMed]
7. Seymour, J. The impact of public health awareness campaigns on the awareness and quality of palliative care. *J. Palliat. Med.* **2018**, *21*, S30–S36. [CrossRef] [PubMed]
8. Bertman, S. Using the arts and humanities with the dying, bereaved, ... and ourselves. In *Death, Dying, and Bereavement: Contemporary Perspectives, Institutions, and Practices*; Stillion, J., Attig, T., Eds.; Springer Publishing Company: New York, NY, USA, 2015; pp. 245–259.
9. Nan, J.K.M.; Lau, B.H.-P.; Szeto, M.M.L.; Lam, K.K.F.; Man, J.C.N.; Chan, C.L.W. Competence enhancement program of expressive arts in end-of-life care for health and social care professionals: A mixed-method evaluation. *Am. J. Hosp. Palliat. Med.* **2018**, *35*, 1207–1214. [CrossRef] [PubMed]
10. la Cour, K.; Josephsson, S.; Tishelman, C.; Nygard, L. Experiences of engagement in creative activity at a palliative care facility. *Palliat. Support. Care* **2007**, *5*, 241–250. [CrossRef] [PubMed]
11. Beaumont, S.L. Art therapy for complicated grief: A focus on meaning-making approaches. *Can. Art Ther. Assoc. J.* **2013**, *26*, 1–7. [CrossRef]

12. Neimeyer, R.; Thompson, B. Meaning making and the art of grief therapy. In *Grief and the Expressive Arts: Practices for Creating Meaning*, 1st ed.; Thompson, B., Neimeyer, R., Eds.; Routledge: New York, NY, USA, 2014.
13. Lindqvist, O.; Tishelman, C. Going public: Reflections on developing the DöBra research program for health-promoting palliative care in Sweden. *Prog. Pallative Care* **2016**, *24*, 19–24. [CrossRef] [PubMed]
14. Israel, B.A.; Schulz, A.J.; Parker, E.A.; Becker, A.B.; Allen, A.J., III; Guzman, R.J.; Lichtenstein, R. Critical issues in developing and following CBPR principles. In *Community-Based Participatory Research for Health Advancing Social and Health Equity*, 3rd ed.; Wallerstein, N., Duran, B., Oetzel, J., Minkler, M., Eds.; Jossey-Bass & Pfeiffer Imprints, Wiley: Hoboken, NJ, USA, 2017; pp. 31–44.
15. Bradbury, H. Introduction: How to situate and define action research. In *The Sage Handbook of Action Research*, 3rd ed.; Bradbury, H., Ed.; Sage: Los Angeles, CA, USA, 2015; pp. 1–9.
16. Wallerstein, N.; Duran, B. Theoretical, historical, and practice roots of CBPR. In *Community-Based Participatory Research for Health Advancing Social and Health Equity*; Wallerstein, N., Duran, B., Oetzel, J., Minkler, M., Eds.; Jossey-Bass & Pfeiffer Imprints, Wiley: Hoboken, NJ, USA, 2017; pp. 17–29.
17. Tavory, I.; Timmermans, S. *Abductive Analysis*; The University of Chicago: Chicago, IL, USA, 2014.
18. Hamayon, R. *Why We Play-An Anthropological Study*; Hau Books: Chicago, IL, USA, 2016.
19. Huizinga, J. *Homo Ludens-A Study of the Play-Element in Culture [Homo Ludens. Proeve Eener Bepaling van Het Spel-Element der Cultuur, 1938]*; Angelico Press: Brooklyn, NY, USA, 1949.
20. Frissen, V.; Lammes, S.; De Lange, M.; De Mul, J.; Raessens, J. Homo ludens 2.0: Play, media, and identity. In *Playful Identities-The Ludification of Digital Media Cultures*; Frissen, V., Lammes, S., De Lange, M., De Mul, J., Raessens, J., Eds.; Amsterdam University Press: Amsterdam, The Netherlands, 2015.
21. Calleja, G. Ludic identities and the magic circle. In *Playful Identities-The Ludification of Digital Media Cultures*; Frissen, V., Lammes, S., De Lange, M., De Mul, J., Raessens, J., Eds.; Amsterdam University Press: Amsterdam, The Netherlands, 2015.
22. Gordon-Nesbitt, R.; Howarth, A. The arts and the social determinants of health: Findings from an inquiry conducted by the United Kingdom All-Party Parliamentary Group on Arts, Health and Wellbeing. *Arts Health* **2020**, *12*, 1–22. [CrossRef] [PubMed]
23. Gualano, M.R.; Voglino, G.; Bert, F.; Thomas, R.; Camussi, E.; Siliquini, R. The impact of intergenerational programs on children and older adults: A review. *Int. Psychogeriatr.* **2018**, *30*, 451–468. [CrossRef] [PubMed]
24. Fancourt, D.; Finn, S. *What Is the Evidence on the Role of the Arts in Improving Health and Well-Being? A Scoping Review*; Health Evidence Network (HEN) Synthesis Report 67; WHO Regional Office for Europe: Copenhagen, Denmark, 2019.
25. McMillan, D.W. Sense of community. *J. Community Psychol.* **1996**, *24*, 315–325. [CrossRef]
26. Westerlund, C.; Tishelman, C.; Benkel, I.; Fürst, C.J.; Molander, U.; Rasmussen, B.H.; Sauter, S.; Lindqvist, O. Public awareness of palliative care in Sweden. *Scand. J. Public Health* **2018**. [CrossRef] [PubMed]
27. Polit, D.F.; Beck, C.T. Generalization in quantitative and qualitative research: Myths and strategies. *Int. J. Nurs. Stud.* **2010**, *47*, 1451–1458. [CrossRef] [PubMed]
28. Morse, J.M. Critical analysis of strategies for determining rigor in qualitative inquiry. *Qual. Health Res.* **2015**, *25*, 1212–1222. [CrossRef] [PubMed]

healthcare MDPI

Review

Palliative and End-of-Life Care Service Models: To What Extent Are Consumer Perspectives Considered?

Bruce Rumbold [1,*] **and Samar M. Aoun** [1,2]

[1] Public Health Palliative Care Unit, School of Psychology and Public Health, La Trobe University, Melbourne, VIC 3086, Australia

[2] Perron Institute for Neurological and Translational Science, Nedlands, WA 6009, Australia

* Correspondence: b.rumbold@latrobe.edu.au

Abstract: This article presents evidence found in a search of national and international literature for patient preferences concerning settings in which to receive palliative care and the appropriateness of different models of palliative care. The purpose was to inform end-of-life care policy and service development of the Western Australian Department of Health through a rapid review of the literature. It was found that consumer experience of palliative care is investigated poorly, and consumer contribution to service and policy design is limited and selective. Most patients experience a mix of settings during their illness, and evidence found by the review has more to do with qualities and values that will contribute to good end-of-life care in any location. Models of care do not make systematic use of the consumer data that are available to them, although an increasingly common theme is the need for integration of the various sources of care supporting dying people. It is equally clear that most integration models limit their attention to end-of-life care provided by health services. Transitions between settings merit further attention. We argue that models of care should take account of consumer experience not by incorporating generalised evidence but by co-creating services with local communities using a public health approach.

Keywords: palliative care; end-of-life care; consumer preferences; models of care; hospice; hospital; residential aged care; home care; public health approach; compassionate communities

Citation: Rumbold, B.; Aoun, S.M. Palliative and End-of-Life Care Service Models: To What Extent Are Consumer Perspectives Considered? *Healthcare* **2021**, *9*, 1286. https://doi.org/10.3390/healthcare9101286

Academic Editors: Georg Bollig and John Rosenberg

Received: 23 August 2021
Accepted: 25 September 2021
Published: 28 September 2021

1. Introduction

Over the past decade, the claim that "end-of-life care is everyone's responsibility" has appeared in national and regional palliative care policies around the world. Comprehensive strategies through which this shared responsibility might be discharged are, however, far less common. In most cases, it is translated as a desire for 'community involvement' implemented through consumer consultation during policy and service development. This consultation is often individualised by involving 'representative' consumers, with little information provided as to how representative these selected consumers might be. However, more jurisdictions are beginning to draw upon a growing amount of quality assurance work on consumer experience in their policy formation.

In response to Recommendation Nine of the Western Australian (WA) Parliament Joint Select Committee on End-of-life Choices [1], the WA Department of Health commissioned an independent review of consumer perspectives of palliative care service models. The independent review comprised three phases: a literature review, a cross-sectional consumer survey and consultation forums with service providers.

The Department intended this literature review to clarify the extent to which end-of-life services address consumer needs or incorporate consumer feedback. The literature review is based on the global English language literature, but Australian studies are selected to illustrate findings where they are available.

2. Objectives

The objectives of the whole independent review, including this literature review, were to:

1. Review consumer preferences on receiving palliative care (at home; residential care; hospital; hospice; mix).
2. Describe and investigate existing models of palliative care and whether the palliative care needs of consumers are met by each model.
3. Review the appropriateness of each service model with respect to meeting the needs of consumers and care providers.

3. Methodology

Given the timeframe allocated for the review, it was necessary to develop a rapid review methodology [2]. While the debate continues around the definition of a rapid review [3], they typically include 'shortcuts' that circumvent some of the more time-consuming aspects of systematic or even scoping reviews. Rigour is to some extent sacrificed for timeliness, and the quality of the review depends upon the shortcuts taken.

Our interest here was in identifying, as far as possible, a working consensus on evidence that would inform the 3 objectives indicated above. We decided that we would focus first upon systematic reviews and that we would use a Google Scholar search to identify these. The choice of Google Scholar was based both upon this database's capacity to identify relevant, high-quality literature [4,5] and its inclusion of some grey literature. In searching for data to inform a policy review, we were interested not only in peer-reviewed literature but in data sources taken into account in other policy formation processes. The material identified in a Google Scholar search would then be checked and complemented by further targeted keyword searches of databases, principally CINAHL and PubMed [6], while further systematic reviews would be sought in the Cochrane Library and the PROSPERO International Register.

The initial Google Scholar search used keywords [systematic review] + [palliative care] + [consumer] and was limited to the previous 5 years, identifying 15,900 references. The time span of 5 years was selected because consumer perspectives have only been included routinely in policies over the past 10–15 years, and we thought it reasonable to expect that systematic reviews conducted in the past 5 years would include the literature on which these policies were based. It was hoped that a focus upon systematic reviews would enhance rigour and incorporate, through their review processes, a body of evidence prior to the search cut-off date of 2016. The search was conducted on 2 computers to check for algorithmic bias, but no significant discrepancies were found. The references were ordered according to relevance, and the first 1000 were hand-searched to identify material directly relevant to the study objectives. After the first 1000 it was clear that references were of decreasing relevance, relating principally to only 1 of the combined search terms.

To supplement this material, we searched for studies other than systematic reviews that connected consumer experiences with their settings. These searches were not limited to the previous 5 years, but our interest was principally in studies that reflected the experience of contemporary care systems. These searches in CINAHL and PubMed used keyword combinations including the following:

- [models] + [palliative care] + [delivery]
- [integrated] + [palliative care] OR [end-of-life care]
- [quality] + [evaluation] + [palliative care] OR [end-of-life care]
- [end-of-life] + [settings + home, hospice, hospital]
- [patient] + [family] + [informal] + [consumer] + [care *]
- [end-of-life] + [priorities] + [needs] + [preferences]
- [communication] + [information] + [decision-making]
- [patient] + [carer] + [reported outcomes]

Our interest here was developing insight into processes and experiences that lie behind the aggregated evidence reported in the systematic reviews.

4. Findings

The findings of the rapid review were presented in narrative form and organised according to the three objectives. A scan of articles found in the Google Scholar search showed that systematic reviews of patient and carer experiences at end-of-life do not always focus on the context in which care was provided, while systematic reviews of service models do not always attend to patient and caregiver experiences. We decided to report on these strands separately, as limiting our findings to reviews that explicitly link experiences with particular settings would have neglected a considerable amount of rich data. The references provided in this article illustrate key points of our findings: it is not possible to provide here a complete list of articles.

4.1. Consumers' Needs and Preferences at End-of-Life

Consumers of end-of-life services potentially comprise the entire population, but population-wide surveys tend to be limited to broad issues such as a preference to die at home [7] or the desirability of assisted dying legislation [8]. Studying the preferences of actual consumers of end-of-life services selects a sub-set of the population who have chosen to engage with these services. The extent to which these findings represent the whole population of dying people and carers is unclear.

Studies often investigate preferences in terms of location of care or model of care, but findings are predominantly about quality of care. The location of care and model of care may be secondary to these qualities being realized, although, of course, quality concerns may inform a preference for site and style of care.

There is reasonable consensus about the experiences and responsibilities of different participants in end-of-life care. Concerns common to patients, family, physicians and other caregivers included pain and symptom management, preparation for death, decisions about treatment management, achieving a sense of completion and being treated as a whole person. Important to patients, but less to physicians, include being mentally aware, having funeral arrangements made, not being a burden, helping others and achieving peace [9]. Within each group, differing perspectives were found concerning decision-making about life-sustaining treatments, dying at home and talking about the meaning of death.

These differences can impact the quality of care. Misalignment between the medical system and patient/family values and priorities frequently contributes to consumer dissatisfaction with care [10]. Yet, even when goals of care are aligned, information sharing can remain a problem [11], in part as a result of the increasingly varied sources of information accessed by patients and family caregivers [12].

Caregivers' effectiveness in responding to needs depended upon them knowing and adhering to patients' wishes. The extent to which health services are responsible for supporting caregivers continues to be debated, but traditionally palliative care has regarded patient and family as the unit of care. Hudson et al [13], for example, reported success with a psycho-educational program that provides information and skills to support informal caregiving in the chronic illness aspects of palliative care. A recent Cochrane review [14], however, found mixed evidence for the value of psychosocial interventions across the illness trajectory. Candy et al. [15] noted some evidence that strategies to help caregivers indirectly via patient care seemed to have some effect. Most of the other interventions that attempted to work directly with caregivers did not include practical support, although support in acquiring practical nursing skills has been shown to be important to caregivers [16]. Aoun et al. [17] used a stepped wedge cluster trial (n = 620) of a carer support intervention in community palliative care in WA, finding that priority support needs identified by caregivers included knowing what to expect in the future, having time for yourself in the day and dealing with your feelings and worries. Their intervention reduced caregiver strain before bereavement and had positive outcomes post bereavement by achieving the preferred place of death through an agreement between patients and their caregivers [18]. The authors concluded that, within palliative care, the intervention with the potential to have the greatest 'reach', and available to a wide population of carers, is the one that adopts a comprehensive, person-centred approach to carer assessment in routine practice, ensuring that carers have the opportunity to consider and express their support needs so that service providers can deliver support tailored to their individual circumstances.

A theme emerging in recent studies is the need for practitioners to give more attention to patients' experience of living with their illness, not just to providing information about the diagnosis, prognosis, treatment and symptom control, important though these remain. Wang et al. [19] identified unmet care needs as emotional support, fatigue and being informed about benefits/side effects of treatment. Sheehan et al. [20] showed how treatment burden for patients and families includes understanding the condition, juggling monitoring and adjusting treatments, engaging others for support, time and financial issues. The burden does not end with a patient's admission to hospital, hospice, or aged care [21] but transforms into a different set of responsibilities, relationships with professional caregivers, care decisions and discharge planning.

Linking illness experience with other aspects of daily living is vital for preserving quality of life. For example, in a small NSW study of older adults with terminal illness [22], participants describe their needs in the following domains: quality of life, sense of control, life on hold, need for health system support, being at home, talking about death and competent and caring health professionals. Rand et al. [23] found that patients with advanced cancer had life goals that resembled those of healthy populations and that treatment goals were separate from these life goals. A capacity to align treatment and life goals shaped the final stages of illness, and those who valued cure the highest had the worst psychological adjustment [23]. This supports the case that early palliative care intervention, introduced alongside treatment options allows better preparation and facilitates informed choice [24,25]. Collins et al. [26], however, reported that consumers' perceptions can work against early introduction of palliative care if palliative care is associated in their minds with diminished care, diminished possibility and diminished choice. Aoun [27] proposed early integration of a palliative approach in the care plans of people diagnosed with Motor Neurone Disease (MND), arguing that this can optimise their quality of life by relieving symptoms, providing emotional, psychological and spiritual support pre-bereavement, minimising barriers to a good death and supporting the family post-bereavement. Knowledge and expertise need to be extended beyond the domain of specialist palliative care services to include the full scope of health and community-based services providing care, mostly at home.

Dalal and Bruera [28] were more positive about the contribution of early palliative care intervention, in part because of the effect of palliative care in reducing costs of (futile) aggressive treatment and thus reducing financial pressure on US families. Hospice participation in care through attention to values and multidimensional needs allows care to be planned and reduces costs associated with a narrow focus on the disease, which can cause further morbidity due to harmful interventions [24]. While these studies reflect the US context, financial constraints are also found to affect treatment choices and quality of life of cancer patients in Australia's universal healthcare system [29].

Recent reviews point out that studies of needs seldom consider the full treatment pathway/cancer journey [30,31]. With advanced cancer increasingly experienced as a chronic illness [32], needs remain diverse, requiring greater attention to the illness experience of particular people. Other studies report similarly on the end-of-life needs of populations belonging to specific illness groups. Stow et al. [33] found the needs of frail people to be similar to those with advanced cancer, but that a frail person's desire for reduced interventions was not always observed. In cases where palliative care was provided to frail people, their relatives often rated it lower in comparison to the relatives of those with cancer, presumably because palliative care staff lacked familiarity with frailty and the less predictable trajectory of dying. The implication here, that end-of-life care needs to be provided by people familiar with the particular needs of a population, is reinforced for MND [27,34] and intellectual disability [35].

4.1.1. Collecting Data on Consumer Engagement

Most palliative care programs collect some form of internal consumer data, but few publish their findings. Consumer satisfaction scores are often collected by palliative care peak bodies, but this activity tends to be more a marketing measure than a focused enquiry into quality. To date, the only program that has consistently collected consumer data in granular detail across a health system is the Views Of Informal Caregivers Evaluation of Services (VOICES), commissioned by the UK Department of Health [36], and badged as the National Survey of Bereaved People (VOICES) once managed by the Office for National Statistics (ons.gov.uk). The survey investigated the quality of care delivered in the last three months of life for adults who died in England, using a sample of approximately 30% of all deaths over a four-month period selected from the death registration database.

The dataset continues to be used retrospectively [37] in various ways: identifying associations between the place of death and Advance Care Plans [38] or end-of-life experiences for particular populations such as people with intellectual disability [37]. Modified versions of the survey have also been used in comparing end-of-life care across specific settings [39].

The closest equivalent in Australia is the FAMCARE-2 tool (Family Satisfaction with Palliative Care), which measures satisfaction across four domains, management of physical symptoms and comfort, provision of information, family support and patient psychological care. The validation study [40] indicated lower levels of satisfaction in response to the subscales 'provision of information' and 'family support,' consistent with VOICES findings. FAMCARE-2 is administered periodically in selected services by Australia's Palliative Care Outcomes Collaboration (PCOC). A survey of 1592 caregivers across 49 palliative care services in 2016 [41] found generally high levels of satisfaction and positive experiences of care. Scores were higher for inpatient care on three of the four domains, provision of information being the exception. Dissatisfaction with information provision was higher for older carers, particularly around carer payments, while home carers reported that information to support them with practical caring tasks was inadequate. These findings were consistent with the Australian EOL and Bereavement Study [42].

4.1.2. End-of-Life Needs in Particular Settings

A few studies directly investigated patients' perspectives of differing end-of-life services—home care, residential care, hospital, hospice—but it is still necessary to understand what each of these services provides and how they are aligned within that particular health system in order to compare the findings of the different studies or translate them to another context. Possible confounding issues are distinguishing if a hospital setting includes the care of palliative care consult teams or if residential aged care setting accesses care from community-based palliative care programs.

Hospital

Six themes common to patients and families – expert care, effective communication and shared decision-making, respectful and compassionate care, adequate environment for care, family involvement and financial affairs – were identified by Virdun et al. [43] as important in hospital end-of-life care. Patients added the theme of maintenance of sense of self, while families added patient safety, preparation for death, care for family after death and enabling patient choice at end-of-life. A recent study [44] in five NSW hospitals confirmed these domains and suggested two more, nutritional needs and access to clinical specialists. These findings were supported by a recent review by Wong et al. [45].

Seldom, if ever, were all these areas of importance adequately addressed. While not coinciding with the eight essential elements of Australia's National Safety and Quality Health Service Standards [46] for comprehensive care at the end-of-life, the themes identified by Virdun et al. [43] were consistent with them. Bloomer et al. [47], in auditing hospitals against these national ACSQHC guidelines, found clear scope for improvement, particularly in patient-centred care, family involvement, describing and enacting goals of care and using triggers to prompt care. These are, in fact, all the essential elements for the process of end-of-life care [46] and presumably point to deficits in the underlying organisational pre-requisites. It might also be noted that the standards specify access to specialist palliative care advice as one of the requirements of any comprehensive end-of-life care plan.

Will et al. [48] conducted a review that underlined the importance of multi-disciplinary team care in patient satisfaction with care, particularly when teams comprise more than two professions (that is, include allied health practitioners) and engage the patient through more comprehensive team practice (that is, practice that involves more than a multidisciplinary ward round).

A recurring issue with hospital end-of-life care is non-beneficial treatment. Cardona-Morrell et al. [49] reviewed the treatment of older patients near end-of-life and found that on average 1/3 received non-beneficial treatments including dialysis, radiotherapy, transfusions and life support treatment and that up to 2/3 of admissions were not mandated by therapeutic need but a lack of alternative strategies for care. Taylor et al. [2], in a scoping review of initiatives to reduce inappropriate or non-beneficial hospital admissions, found a wide range of strategies being employed, but that evidence for their effectiveness was generally limited or absent.

Singotani et al. [50] pointed out that most studies of unplanned readmissions were evaluated from the hospital's perspective in terms of patients' failure in self-management or problems with integrated care. Studies differed as to which causes were preventable, nor did they take into account causes beyond the scope of the hospital. Trankle's [51] small survey of specialist physicians even questioned whether a good death was possible in Australian critical and acute care settings, noting that 70% of all deaths were in institutions, and that 15–20% of those took place in ICU where a quarter of patients were ventilated and almost 40% died in pain.

Residential Aged Care

A Cochrane review found little evidence for the effectiveness of interventions intended to improve palliative care in nursing homes [52]. Tilden et al. [53] noted the problem of high staff turnover and the high personal and economic cost that works against quality of care. They argued that investment in staff training to improve knowledge and skills and increase job satisfaction would improve staff retention and reduce transfers to hospital for conditions—including end-of-life care—that should be managed on-site. There was some indication within the New Zealand context [54] that the nature and quality of end-of-life care can be contingent upon a General Practitioner's engagement with a residential aged care facility. This finding is confirmed in studies of rural RACFs in the Monaro region of Australia, where monthly Needs Rounds involving RAC staff and local GPs increased capacity to provide end-of-life care [55].

Milte et al. [56] surveyed 17 nursing homes across four Australian states to ascertain the characteristics most valued by residents and family members. While residents receiving palliative care were excluded, these values have important implications for understanding the context with which palliative care ideally might articulate. Belonging (feeling at home) is of primary importance to residents, as is flexibility in the care routines provided by staff.

Residential Hospice

There are surprisingly few systematic reviews of the quality of residential hospice care. Weerakkody et al. [57], in a study involving 100 bereaved caregivers of people who died in a Toronto (Canada) hospice, found that quality (measured by the Quality of Dying and Death- QODD) was average to above average and that higher scores were reported by those whose relative had been admitted for more than one week. A possible explanation can be inferred from the evaluation by Lucey et al. [58] of patients admitted to Milford Hospice, Limerick, Eire. They found nearly half were unstable on admission, and it took three days for 70% of these patients to be stabilised. That is, longer admissions were needed to be of clinical benefit, let alone to access other forms of support provided in the hospice.

Home

Reviews by Stajduhar et al. [59] and Funk et al. [60] highlighted the need for a systematic study of home-based family caregiving at the end-of-life. Their findings identified the ways caregiver experience can be disrupted as demands change and different services become involved, outlined forms of support required, discussed barriers to receiving that support (often the reluctance of caregivers to articulate their own needs) and explored caregivers' role in decision-making. A further theme identified was the rewards of caregiving as a source of comfort, strength and meaning alongside the stress and challenges involved. A Cochrane review found that home palliative care more than doubles the chances of dying at home and reduced symptom burden without increasing grief for family caregivers after the patient died [61]. Another Cochrane review of the impact of hospital at home programs (Shepperd et al. [62]) made similar findings.

A small Dutch study [63] identified medical proficiency in the primary care team, including clarity about procedures and pro-active approach, as essential elements of high-quality palliative care at home. Barriers to dying at home identified by O'Brien and Jack [64] were, from a service perspective, poor discharge planning, difficulty in accessing equipment and services and inadequate out-of-hours service provision.

Debate continues as to whether death at home should be an outcome measure [65]. While well-being may be greater at home, preference alone is not enough to ensure death at home and instead is influenced by other factors such as extended family support, availability of home care and affluence [66]. People who have had a stroke or people with dementia are less likely to die in their preferred place [67]. A longitudinal study to elicit the end-of-life preferences of terminally ill people who live alone was undertaken in community palliative care in WA [68]. Congruence between the preferred and actual place of death shifted from 53% based on preferences at baseline to 41% based on preferences at follow-up. For nearly half of the patients in this study, home was not their preferred location for dying. The authors suggested that the ability to die in the place of choice (rather than home) needs to be looked at as a possible indicator of meeting patient needs or as a quality measure in end-of-life care.

The critical role of the GP in supporting care in the home through linkage with specialist palliative care services is shown in the review by Carmont et al. [69]. A nationwide integrated information network for primary end-of-life care in Australia was designed and piloted, and early findings show that palliative care training for GPs improves the uptake of ACP in general practice [70].

4.1.3. Comparative Studies of Care in Different Settings

The English National Bereavement Survey [71] reviewed care in the last three months of life and consistently found the overall quality of care in hospitals to be worse than any other setting, with 30% rating hospital care as fair or poor. Care in care homes, hospices or own homes was rated highly (80% as outstanding, excellent, or good). The overall quality of care ratings did not vary significantly for different illnesses, except that those responding on behalf of cancer patients gave more outstanding ratings (nearly 50%) than for cardiovascular patients (less than 40%). In 2015, but not 2014, females were perceived by respondents as receiving better care than males. Excellent ratings for quality of care were highest for hospices (76%) and lowest for urgent care services (26%). The majority of informal caregivers agreed that their information and communication needs were met.

About 20% said that decisions were made about the patient's care that the patient would not have wanted. An overwhelming majority felt the person had died in the right place, even if at times that place had not been the person's expressed preference.

Sandsdalen et al. [72] conducted a study using the Quality from the Patients' Perspective for Palliative Care (QPP-PC) measure of 191 Norwegian palliative patients in hospice inpatient care, hospice day care, palliative care units in nursing homes and home care. Perceptions of care quality were higher for hospice inpatient care than other settings, although perceptions of subjective importance did not vary across settings. In all settings, the prime area for improvement related to receiving information.

The Australian End-of-life and Bereavement Survey found significant differences in the quality of palliative care received between the three settings: community, inpatient/hospice and nursing home. More respondents rated inpatient settings as excellent/good (93%) than care in the community (81%) or care in nursing homes (73%) [42]. This, to some degree, contrasts with de Boer et al. (2017), who found relatives more positive about care received from palliative care teams at home or in hospice than in the hospital setting. Their study drew upon data from 14 European countries for deaths from a wide range of causes. They noted that the psychosocial support provided in the hospital or aged care was less than at the home or hospice and that the level of satisfaction with a setting also varied according to the illness from which a person had died. In the Australian study, most in the palliative care group had died from cancer, and the higher rating for inpatient care may reflect both the complexity of managing symptoms in this group and the wide availability of hospital palliative care consult teams.

This review of the evidence related to consumer preferences suggests that best practice is defined more by the qualities and values embedded in the care provided, not a particular program structure or setting. The most appropriate model of care will be one that is able to respond flexibly to this variety of needs across the illness journey, with that flexibility extending to end-of-life experiences.

4.2. Models of Care

Many health systems have over the past decade reviewed and revised their end-of-life care strategies, usually in an attempt to better integrate palliative care with the overall health system. The majority of these revised end-of-life service models are based on practitioners' perceptions of patients' needs. That is, although patients' responses may be considered in revising services and in evaluating the effectiveness of the revisions, service design has tended to give priority to solving health service problems more than patients' perspectives of their need of preference for care. A rich variety of reports and reviews is available from selected health services and peak bodies within their jurisdiction. Peer-reviewed studies more often focus on a single aspect of the multi-faceted end-of-life care system. Models draw upon such studies in the hope that the sum will be greater than the parts.

A theme common to the recent literature on models of care is the need for integration. It is equally clear that most integration models being put forward limit their attention to end-of-life care provided by health services.

Integrated Palliative Care

Luckett et al. [73], in a rapid review, concluded that effective palliative care models integrated specialist expertise with primary and community care services and enabled transitions across settings, including residential aged care. Their focus was on elements relevant to the Australian health system—that is, the terminology was aligned with Australian definitions. They also noted that:

- The use of volunteers has potential when other informal caregivers are lacking, but that this raises governance issues.
- GPs lack capacity due to workload and inadequate remuneration.

- Effective models such as the Gold Standards Framework [74] are not readily transferable to Australia.
- Case management is important, but also problematic given the multiple jurisdictions and care settings in Australia.
- Population-based models of palliative care should support case management via integration of Specialist Palliative Care (SPC) with primary and community care services. That is, they advocate a model of care that provides continuity through the illness course.

Reviews of palliative care integration in Europe have also been carried out [75,76]. The definition of integrated palliative care (IPC) developed by van Beek et al. [76] is:

"Integrated palliative care involves bringing together administrative, organisational, clinical and service aspects in order to realise the continuity of care between all actors involved in the care network of patients receiving palliative care. It aims to achieve quality of life and a well-supported dying process for the patient and the family in collaboration with all the caregivers (paid and unpaid)" [76] (p2).

For the purposes of their review, they used Emanuel et al.'s [77] IPC criteria.

The same research team identified 14 empirically tested integrative models [75] that showed the benefits of involving a multidisciplinary palliative care team, namely better symptom control, less caregiver burden, improved continuity and coordination of care, fewer admissions, cost effectiveness and patients dying in their preferred place. On this basis, they proposed a generic framework for integrated palliative care in cancer and chronic disease. Interestingly, however, the framework they propose pays no attention to engaging primary and community care, or informal caregivers, although these contributors are an integral part of both their own definition of ICP above [76] and Emanuel et al.'s [77] criteria.

Other reviews considered integration of care at particular points of the illness trajectory or for specific illness journeys. For example, Gardiner et al. [78] reviewed effective collaborative partnerships between generalist and specialist palliative care services, identified by good communication between providers, clear delineation of roles and responsibilities, opportunities for shared learning and coordination shown in timely access to specialist services. These same conditions are endorsed, albeit by identifying barriers to integrating primary and specialist cancer care, by Dossett et al. [79]. Gardiner et al. [78] did not, however, find any distinctive model of collaborative working undergirding these partnerships. The same team reviewed the transition from curative care to palliative care [78], and again found multidisciplinary collaboration to be a key requirement for navigating this complex transition. Other studies considered integration of respiratory and palliative care [80] and oncology and palliative care [81]. Again, communication and multidisciplinary practice were found to be core elements of successful practice.

A variety of triage tools to assist clinicians in monitoring transitions is being developed. El Mokhallati et al. [82] reviewed 10 screening tools, noting the disparity between those that focus primarily on prognosis and functional decline and those that anticipate palliative needs. They found the predictive ability of all tools to be limited. The recently validated Responding to Urgency of Need in Palliative Care (RUN-PC) triage tool is an important step in making triage more transparent and evidence-based [83]. While these tools support clinical judgement, the pre-conditions of collaborative stance and multidisciplinary practice are essential for their effective use.

The published literature overwhelmingly addresses integration issues that involve health services, with little or no attention paid to integration of these services with informal care. Schulz et al. [84], through a review of family caregiving literature, provided some useful insights into the impact health services can have upon family caregivers as illness progresses and service delivery responds to increasing demand. They found that family caregivers, while still a major source of support to the seriously ill patient, are often marginalised by healthcare systems and procedures. Familiar routines of home care are often now supplemented, or replaced, by further medical and hospital appointments or admissions, additional decision-making about treatment and support and new care issues to be managed at home. The family caregiver also becomes a major source of information for a number of new specialist providers. These additional responsibilities require new knowledge and skills that would ideally be provided by the specialised health service partners being brought into the expanded care network. This introduces a further range of responsibilities that most specialist providers do not recognise and for which they are often not equipped. Yet facilitating partnerships between formal and informal caregivers includes formal caregivers being able to identify and assess the capacity of informal caregivers, support them and equip them to engage with the new challenges.

4.3. *Appropriateness of Different Models of Palliative Care*

The research literature tends to report palliative care outcomes in terms of the setting in which care is received, but both within and across those settings, a range of organisational models can be found [73,85]. Comparisons of models based on such studies can only be performed in general descriptive terms because of the different outcome and process measures used in various studies and different health jurisdictions. As reported above, criteria for evaluating the effectiveness of services usually focus on symptom control and the delivery of clinical care: attention to consumer engagement has been minimal. Brereton et al. [85] note that the majority of evaluation studies demonstrate the overall benefit of providing palliative care compared with other forms of care available in that palliative care service's health system. There is seldom any information about the components of the palliative intervention or the comparators against which benefit is shown. They conclude:

"Irrespective of setting or patient characteristics, models of palliative care appear to show benefits and some models of palliative care may reduce total healthcare costs. However, much more detailed and systematic reporting of components and agreement about outcome measures is essential to understand the key components and successfully replicate effective organisational models" [85], p. 781.

While there is no consensus about organisational models, there is agreement that certain quality standards for care should be the goal of care in any setting. The Australian National Consensus Statement on essentials of end-of-life care [86] applies to all end-of-life care programs, although how care should be provided is not prescribed. The NICE guidelines [87] address what are effectively the same quality standards but do this in ways that make implementation clear and provide links to explore further the rationale for each guideline and the evidence supporting it. Impact findings for the guidelines are also provided [88].

Cost-effectiveness is clearly an important consideration in developing palliative care services. Unfortunately, comparisons of the costs of different palliative care models, as Groeneveld et al. [89] show, encounter problems similar to those identified by Brereton et al. [85]. Funding mechanisms are country-specific and often tenuously aligned with overall health policy [89,90]. It can be shown that palliative care is cost-effective, with savings improved by earlier palliative interventions in cases of multi-morbidity and the use of palliative care strategies that reduce or avoid hospitalisation. For example, in Australia, elderly cancer cohorts incur greater costs at the end-of-life, primarily through hospitalization—those who die in residential aged care incur half the costs of those who die in hospital [91]—although it might also be noted that the survey undertaken for this review indicates a lower quality of care for residents of aged care. Groeneveld et al. [89] suggest six 'desirable features' for palliative care funding models:

1. Support early access to palliative care.
2. Provide an appropriate mix of palliative and curative services.
3. Provide services in the most appropriate location.
4. Avoid financial hardship for service users and families.
5. Provide stable and predictable funding that allows coherent planning and development of services.
6. Ensure clarity concerning entitlement to services and ways services can be navigated.

Duckett [90] argues that, for these features to be realised, palliative care funding needs to move toward an activity-based funding model with agreed classification.

It is also notable that these features point toward the integration of specialist and generalist services. As noted in our review, the most recent literature shows a move from comparing settings toward integrating services across the illness journey. This integration seeks to extend the effectiveness and reach of palliative care by better connecting generalist and specialist palliative care in ways that are appropriate to each person's illness journey. A key component of integration, Luckett et al. [73] suggested, was case management, which is the service element most common to models of care that are effective. It cannot, however, be assumed that providing case management will of itself achieve integration: case management is usually present as part of quite complex and diverse interventions. But it does appear that case management allows consumers to make the best use of the resources available to them.

4.3.1. Involving the Community: Public Health Approaches to End-of-Life Care

It is clear from the evidence concerning end-of-life need that any comprehensive model of care must take very seriously the intersection between health service provision and social network support. Yet, while integrated palliative care guidelines acknowledge the need to involve communities and unpaid caregivers, in practice most service models continue to be designed within the boundaries of the health system.

Over the past decade in particular, palliative care service guidelines have increasingly sought to take consumer experience into account. This has been attempted, for the most part, by collecting data from consumers on their experience, or involving a representative consumer in a reference group, then proceeding to design a health service response to the consumer needs that are of central interest to palliative care practitioners. Public health approaches have a different strategy that focuses less upon identifying patient and family perspectives to which services should develop a response, more upon building systems of care that allow active participation of people and their social networks in the care provided at end-of-life. That is, public health approaches to palliative care pay attention not only to integrating care within health services but also to connecting informal care—a patient's existing social networks and local community assets—with the care provided by the formal services. By doing this, a public health approach extends issues such as management, accreditation and governance beyond the health sector alone.

A comprehensive public health approach sees people at the centre of care [92]. Rather than individual care, public health approaches give focus and substance to clinical palliative care's notion of 'patient-and-family' as the unit of care, an approach represented in the circles of care model [93]. End-of-life care systems, to be effective, must not only recognise this 'patient and social network' context but ensure that professional care, service delivery and policy enhance the care provided by the person's social network. The unfortunate reality of most health service programs is that they can actively disrupt rather than support that network [94].

Evidence for the effectiveness of this public health approach to care is accumulating rapidly. The scoping review by Daryll Archibald and colleagues [95] is nearing publication. Another overview of relevant evidence and resources is in the report by Nous "Compassionate communities: implementation guide for community approaches to end-of-life care" [96].

4.3.2. Building Community Capacity to Care

Most public health initiatives in palliative care began with identifying community members interested in end-of-life care and building upon their knowledge and skills to communicate these to family, friends and neighbours. Often, although not always, these people were already connected as volunteers with community palliative care services, and through their wider community engagement were able to connect these services with other community groups. One early program, funded by the Victorian Department of Health through the "Strengthening Palliative Care through Health Promotion 2004–2007" program, is outlined in Salau et al. [97].

Around that time, Australian efforts tended to be initiated by palliative care services through their volunteer programs. However, such a strategy has limited community engagement, largely due to the way services have managed volunteer programs. Volunteers have extended the reach of the services more than developed community capacity [98]. Some services in the UK took a different approach, in effect building community capacity with no expectation of ongoing management. Cronin [99] reported on a 2010 experiment to assist local communities by training free-standing volunteer networks to support the most frail and vulnerable in their midst. Their focus was on improving social connection, but they found that consistently after hours call-outs to GP services or trips to EDs declined significantly in the areas where these trained volunteers operated.

The most systematic development of this finding to date has been the connectors project [100] in Frome, Somerset. The sole GP practice in Frome cares for a population of around 28,000 people. The intervention involved rigorous identification of all those in need, not limited by age or diagnosis, followed by care planning and referral to a community development service for goal setting and social network enhancement. This service, Health Connections Mendip (HCM), was established as part of the project. Participants were selected by 'clinical impression'. Palliative patients are thus part of the mix, not treated as a separate cohort. The GP clinic works in partnership with Health Connections Mendip, which is operated by community development workers known as health connectors. HCM generates and maintains a comprehensive Mendip Directory, offers one-on-one care planning, and trains and then supports volunteer Community Connectors. Health connectors are the bridge between clinic and community; community connectors are conversation partners/promoters of the program. The research team was able to demonstrate over a three-year period a 14% reduction of unplanned admissions to Emergency Departments, compared with a 28.5% increase in the remainder of Somerset.

The Frome project combined capacity building with social network enhancement, informed by work carried out by the Western Sydney University Care at End-of-Life Research Group. Rather than extend the reach of community palliative care services as earlier capacity-building approaches had carried out, the latter group identified social networks in the community that had already cared for a dying friend or relative and explored the experiences of members in the networks [94,101–107]. They found that effective networks had at least one person with previous experience of dying (not necessarily at home); comprised family, friends and work colleagues; and were most likely to exist when the dying person or primary carer was already embedded in a community with well-established networks (hence the emphasis on enhancing social networks in subsequent public health interventions). Service providers, while essential, were part of the outer network, together with employers and people who worked in local businesses, schools, clubs and community groups (as illustrated in the circles of care diagram).

Wegleitner et al. [108,109] implemented a social networks enhancement project in Landgren, Austria, a town of 8000 people with a strong reputation for civic action but lacking a specialised palliative care service. As part of a large-scale community research project they used a participatory action method first to investigate, and then enhance, the networks through which elderly people were supported in the final years of their lives. They identified 'ingredients' of these webs of caring relationships as a focus on relationships and social systems; creating reflective spaces; strengthening social capital; and addressing inequalities in care. All these ingredients, they noted, needed to be cultivated through a process of co-creation. The social networks created a 'third social space' between private households and institutional care, but maintaining this space involved resisting the privatisation of care that splits care between commercial and private provision.

Compassionate communities are the descriptor used to capture much of this community development work [108,110,111]. The concept reflects the priority public health gives to settings: if compassion—recognition of our fundamental human connectedness—

characterises our communities, then they should be settings in which living and dying can be healthy. The concept has been operationalised in the Compassionate City Charter (https://www.phpci.org/tools, accessed on 28 September 2021) to which a number of UK cities, and increasingly cities in other places, including Australia, have subscribed.

The Compassion Charter is one strategy for developing civic engagement around end-of-life issues. Sallnow and Paul [112] showed how community engagement could range from services providing information to a community through to active co-design of services with a community. The latter is the stance that best reflects a public health approach. Models for citizen-led approaches to health and care include the Wigan local government project [113] and citizens' juries for health policy decision-making [114]. Co-design has been shown to be effective in developing programs with vulnerable communities [115,116]. End-of-life care applications have been explored by Chung et al. [117] and McCarron et al. [118].

4.3.3. Integrated Public Health Palliative Care

To build a system of end-of-life care that connects health services with community services, and formal care with informal care, further development of palliative care linkages with primary care and aged care, and with civic programs that mobilise and nurture compassionate care in local communities is needed. Tools and resources to create compassionate communities or, more specifically, to create, support and maintain social networks with capacity to care for each other at the end-of-life, have been developed in a variety of jurisdictions. The principal resources are available through Public Health Palliative Care International (https://www.phpci.org/tools accessed on 28 September 2021). This site also provides links to projects where particular tools are being implemented.

Evidence is being produced but, as with many community-development projects, larger-scale implementation requires longer time scales to produce sustainable change. The core empirical evidence supporting the compassionate communities approach continues to be the social networks studies outlined above, together with case study collections [109,119]. Specific Australian resources include End-of-life Care at Home [104], Compassionate Communities: An implementation guide for community approaches to end-of-life care [96], Greater Choice for At Home Palliative Care Evaluation [120] and the Healthy End-of-life Project [121]. Examples of Australian projects that can contribute to an Essentials Model of Palliative Care [122] include The South West Compassionate Communities Connector Project [123] and The Australian End-of-life and Bereavement Survey [17,18,42,124]. This body of work, innovative in content, conceptual model and recruitment approach, has challenged the existing bereavement support structure and provision and influenced practice and policy in the UK and Ireland [125].

5. Discussion

This review, which has an Australian focus, draws upon national and international literature to gather evidence concerning patient preferences for settings in which to receive palliative care (home, residential care, hospital, hospice or a mix) and to review the usefulness of different models of palliative care.

The findings require us to qualify the objectives of the review, which assume that the locus of care—hospital, home, hospice, residential aged care—could lead to different experiences of care and levels of satisfaction with care. In practice, most patients experience a mix of settings during their illness, but the findings of the review have more to do with qualities and values that will contribute to good end-of-life care in any location, not a choice of setting as such. Of course, specific needs may be best met in particular settings, but preferences are based on needs being met at that stage in the illness journey. The hierarchy of need will vary from person to person, and consumers should be involved in negotiating transitions between different locations, recognising that giving priority to one need (for example, hospital admission to adjust medications) may inevitably reduce the extent to which another need is met (security provided by home care). The finding that good care can be achieved in a variety of locations is encouraging, but issues raised by transitions between settings merit further attention.

Evidence for the benefit of extending a palliative approach to all at end-of-life is strong. There is no compelling evidence that points to a preferred organisational model. End-of-life needs of particular groups incorporate the needs associated with their illness or condition. Thus, end-of-life care should be provided collaboratively, led as much as possible by primary care providers with expertise in a person's illness experience, enhanced by care from those with end-of-life expertise.

There appears to be overall a preference for receiving care at home, but this does not mean that patients or family members are dissatisfied with care in other contexts. While the literature increasingly supports an illness journey perspective, there are insufficient data concerning patients' overall illness journeys to draw any conclusions about a preferred mix of sites of care. An illness journey perspective is, however, linked with early palliative care referral, perhaps because palliative care can then perform a case management role through the illness course.

Consumer experience of palliative care is investigated poorly, and consumer contribution to service and policy design is limited and selective. It is important that a strategy for receiving consistent and regular consumer feedback, such as FAMCARE-2 or a Palliative Care Experience survey, be introduced into the sector's Continuous Quality Improvement processes.

The literature examined here agrees on core relational values that should undergird treatment, and that patients' and families' needs around information sharing require further practical attention. These needs appear to be independent of setting and to be more related to consumers' capacity to engage with the process of care, that is, consumers need guidance on how they can contribute, particularly during transitions in care, not merely information about treatment being provided. The literature calls for a person-centred approach from health services but the lack of clarity surrounding this phrase requires more detailed description of what this might involve.

Current literature is less interested in comparing models of care, more interested in the integration of existing approaches to palliative care. Thus the NICE service delivery guidelines for end-of-life care for adults [87], the most recent and comprehensive available, provide evidence and recommend strategy, but emphasise that translation of the guidelines into particular settings requires professional judgement exercised in consultation with the individual and family or carers. The integrated models being put forward in the past few years tend to focus more upon the potential role of primary care in facilitating integration, although there is reference to the place of informal caregivers and community support in meeting consumer need. In the Australian context this suggests the need for Primary Health Networks (PHNs) to be equipped as hubs that connect community services with aged care and palliative care services, and for GPs to be seen as an integral part of end-of-life care. In terms of costs, it seems clear that any palliative care strategy that reduces hospitalisation is likely to be cost-effective. It also seems imperative that aged care services have a greater capacity for end-of-life care on-site and can thus reduce costly non-beneficial hospital admissions. While inappropriate end-of-life care in hospital settings can be addressed to a certain degree by Advance Care Plans that include refusal of non-beneficial treatment, non-beneficial admissions remain a systemic issue that must be addressed beyond the acute care setting.

Some models for integrating different aspects of health services are available. There are fewer models that consider the integration of health services with other social and community services, and fewer again that explore collaboration and integration of formal services with informal networks of care. Despite their rhetoric about community engagement and involvement of informal caregivers, most current models of IPC fall short because their integration is limited to formal health services and consumers are involved as clients to be consulted rather than partners in the co-design of services. Effective integration must include the multiple systems that provide care for a dying person, their family and immediate social network. This raises some largely unexplored questions about the reciprocal contributions of formal and informal care providers, including the mutual recognition of those contributions through role sharing and referral. Formal service providers, while expressing goodwill toward informal networks, do little to establish, support or maintain them.

Public health approaches to end-of-life care have the potential to enhance the integration of services and provide a comprehensive approach that engages the assets of local communities. They also offer frameworks in which partnerships can be developed with communities that have distinctive end-of-life needs, and thus provide a more inclusive approach to end-of-life care. However, it needs to be noted that quite complex governance issues can be involved in collaborations between formal services and informal networks of care. These issues need to be identified and explored in depth so that risks can be mitigated, and the potential of such collaborations be realised. Clearly such approaches resonate with that of community-controlled health organisations that lead indigenous healthcare in Australia [126]. This is of particular relevance to Western Australia, but considerable further work is needed to develop community-controlled partnerships in end-of-life care [127].

6. Limitations

As indicated in the methodology section, this rapid review was intended to identify national or international consensus on patient preferences for settings in which to receive palliative care and the appropriateness of different models of palliative care in order to inform end-of-life care policy and service development for the Western Australian Department of Health. Consensus is based on systematic reviews available in English. These findings were supplemented by studies selected to provide further insights into experiences of care or the process of providing care not available in the evidence provided by systematic reviews. The studies were selected for their relevance to gaps in knowledge. There was no formal attempt to assess quality or risk of bias in the studies found through these supplementary searches, but only reasonably robust studies were included in the review, and a note included in several instances where sample size or specific location could be an issue.

In this article, we have not given specific attention to studies in a rural setting or involving indigenous perspectives, both of which have particular relevance to Western Australian policy priorities. Nor have we included studies of under-served populations that are of particular interest in public health approaches. The lack of access to palliative care by Aboriginal and Torres Strait Islanders, rural and regional people, CALD communities, 'condition-specific' groups such as dementia or mental illness, and 'marginalised groups' such as homeless, refugees, members of the LGBTIQ+ community, has been acknowledged in many WA Health documents across the years. While these population groups have been the subject of a more recent tailored national review into their needs [128], further efforts are needed to document and incorporate consumer feedback from these groups in prospective frameworks on end-of-life care.

We are aware that we have undertaken substantial interpretation in our thematic organisation of the studies included here but given the breadth of the question and the need to cover consumer characteristics, experiences and existing service model studies, we believe this to be justified.

7. Conclusions

Evidence gathered through the review points toward a consensus that an optimal end-of-life care system will integrate formal services and informal networks of care along the illness pathway. The stumbling block for such integration continues to be the gulf established by contemporary policy and funding constraints that distinguish between professional and informal care—the former regulated, the latter recognised for the most part only when under professional surveillance. Several localised models that bridge this gulf by creating conditions under which active collaboration can flourish have been developed but are not easily scaled-up under current forms of healthcare governance. The key common element appears to be enabling local communities to negotiate with and adapt service delivery programs that have been established at a national or regional level. That is, good models of care take account of consumer experience not by incorporating generalised evidence but by co-creating services with local communities. While it is important to gather feedback on the consumer experience of end-of-life services through continuous quality assessment, we should put an end to approaches that study consumer experience in order that professionals can design organisational responses. Consumer experience should be incorporated in policy and service design through co-design that enhances the social network supporting dying people and their carers and puts this at the centre of a comprehensive, integrated care model.

Author Contributions: The two authors have made substantial contributions to the conception and design of the work; the acquisition, analysis, or interpretation of data; have drafted the work or substantively revised it; have approved the submitted version; and agree to be personally accountable for their own contributions and for ensuring that questions related to the accuracy or integrity of any part of the work are appropriately investigated, resolved and documented in the literature. All authors have read and agreed to the published version of the manuscript.

Funding: This review was funded by the End-of-life and Palliative Care Program, Department of Health Western Australia.

Institutional Review Board Statement: The study was conducted according to the guidelines of the Declaration of Helsinki, and approved by La Trobe University research ethics committee, approval number HEC20232.

Acknowledgments: This review was funded by the End-of-life and Palliative Care Program, Department of Health Western Australia. Thanks to Robyn Richmond for assistance in formatting the references.

Conflicts of Interest: The authors declare no conflict of interest.

References

1. Joint Select Committee on End of Life Choices. *My Life, My Choice: The Report of the Joint Select Committee on End of Life Choices*; Government of Western Australia: Perth, Australia, 2018; p. 248.
2. Taylor, R.; Ellis, J.; Gao, W.; Searle, L.; Heaps, K.; Davies, R.; Hawksworth, C.; Garcia-Perez, A.; Colclough, G.; Walker, S.; et al. A scoping review of initiatives to reduce inappropriate or non-beneficial hospital admissions and bed days in people nearing the end of their life: Much innovation, but limited supporting evidence. *BMC Palliat. Care* **2020**, *19*, 24. [CrossRef]
3. Hamel, C.; Michaud, A.; Thuku, M.; Skidmore, B.; Stevens, A.; Nussbaumer-Streit, B.; Garritty, C. Defining Rapid Reviews: A systematic scoping review and thematic analysis of definitions and defining characteristics of rapid reviews. *J. Clin. Epidemiol.* **2021**, *129*, 74–85. [CrossRef]
4. Halevi, G.; Moed, H.; Bar-Ilan, J. Suitability of Google Scholar as a source of scientific information and as a source of data for scientific evaluation—Review of the literature. *J. Informetr.* **2017**, *11*, 823–834. [CrossRef]
5. Nourbakhsh, E.; Nugent, R.; Wang, H.; Cevik, C.; Nugent, K. Medical literature searches: A comparison of PubMed and Google Scholar. *Health Inf. Libr. J.* **2012**, *29*, 214–222. [CrossRef] [PubMed]
6. Bramer, W.M.; Rethlefsen, M.L.; Kleijnen, J.; Franco, O.H. Optimal database combinations for literature searches in systematic reviews: A prospective exploratory study. *Syst. Rev.* **2017**, *6*, 245. [CrossRef] [PubMed]
7. Gomes, B.; Calanzani, N.; Gysels, M.; Hall, S.; Higginson, I.J. Heterogeneity and changes in preferences for dying at home: A systematic review. *BMC Palliat. Care* **2013**, *12*, 7. [CrossRef]
8. Grove, G.L.; Hughes, I.; Lovell, M.; Best, M. A Content Analysis of Euthanasia Polls in Australia and New Zealand—Words Do Matter. *Intern. Med. J.* **2021**. [CrossRef]
9. Steinhauser, K.E.; Christakis, N.A.; Clipp, E.C.; McNeilly, M.; McIntyre, L.; Tulsky, J.A. Factors considered important at the end of life by patients, family, physicians, and other care providers. *JAMA* **2000**, *284*, 2476–2482. [CrossRef] [PubMed]
10. Hirshberg, E.L.; Butler, J.; Francis, M.; Davis, F.A.; Lee, D.; Tavake-Pasi, F.; Napia, E.; Villalta, J.; Mukundente, V.; Coulter, H.; et al. Persistence of patient and family experiences of critical illness. *BMJ Open* **2020**, *10*, e035213. [CrossRef]
11. Heins, M.; Hofstede, J.; Rijken, M.; Korevaar, J.; Donker, G.; Francke, A. Palliative care for patients with cancer: Do patients receive the care they consider important? A survey study. *BMC Palliat. Care* **2018**, *17*, 61. [CrossRef] [PubMed]
12. Jo, H.S.; Park, K.; Jung, S.M. A scoping review of consumer needs for cancer information. *Patient Educ. Couns.* **2019**, *102*, 1237–1250. [CrossRef] [PubMed]

13. Hudson, P.; Aranda, S. The Melbourne Family Support Program: Evidence-based strategies that prepare family caregivers for supporting palliative care patients. *BMJ Support. Palliat. Care* **2014**, *4*, 231–237. [CrossRef] [PubMed]
14. Treanor, C.J.; Santin, O.; Prue, G.; Coleman, H.; Cardwell, C.R.; O'Halloran, P.; Donnelly, M. Psychosocial interventions for informal caregivers of people living with cancer. *Cochrane Database Syst. Rev.* **2019**, *6*, CD009912. [CrossRef] [PubMed]
15. Candy, B.; Jones, L.; Drake, R.; Leurent, B.; King, M. Interventions for supporting informal caregivers of patients in the terminal phase of a disease. *Cochrane Database Syst. Rev.* **2011**, *6*, CD007617. [CrossRef] [PubMed]
16. Bee, P.E.; Barnes, P.; Luker, K.A. A systematic review of informal caregivers' needs in providing home-based end-of-life care to people with cancer. *J. Clin. Nurs.* **2009**, *18*, 1379–1393. [CrossRef] [PubMed]
17. Aoun, S.M.; Breen, L.J.; Howting, D.A.; Rumbold, B.; McNamara, B.; Hegney, D. Who needs bereavement support? A population based survey of bereavement risk and support need. *PLoS ONE* **2015**, *10*, e0121101. [CrossRef] [PubMed]
18. Aoun, S.M.; Ewing, G.; Grande, G.; Toye, C.; Bear, N. The Impact of Supporting Family Caregivers Before Bereavement on Outcomes After Bereavement: Adequacy of End-of-Life Support and Achievement of Preferred Place of Death. *J. Pain Symptom Manag.* **2018**, *55*, 368–378. [CrossRef]
19. Wang, T.; Molassiotis, A.; Chung, B.P.M.; Tan, J.Y. Unmet care needs of advanced cancer patients and their informal caregivers: A systematic review. *BMC Palliat. Care* **2018**, *17*, 96. [CrossRef]
20. Sheehan, O.C.; Leff, B.; Ritchie, C.S.; Garrigues, S.K.; Li, L.; Saliba, D.; Fathi, R.; Boyd, C.M. A systematic literature review of the assessment of treatment burden experienced by patients and their caregivers. *BMC Geriatr.* **2019**, *19*, 262. [CrossRef]
21. Digby, R.; Bloomer, M.J. Families and caregivers of older people: Expectations, communication and care decisions. *Collegian* **2014**, *21*, 345–351. [CrossRef]
22. Lewis, E.T.; Harrison, R.; Hanly, L.; Psirides, A.; Zammit, A.; McFarland, K.; Dawson, A.; Hillman, K.; Barr, M.; Cardona, M. End-of-life priorities of older adults with terminal illness and caregivers: A qualitative consultation. *Health Expect.* **2019**, *22*, 405–414. [CrossRef] [PubMed]
23. Rand, K.L.; Banno, D.A.; Shea, A.M.; Cripe, L.D. Life and treatment goals of patients with advanced, incurable cancer. *Support. Care Cancer* **2016**, *24*, 2953–2962. [CrossRef] [PubMed]
24. Khan, S.A.; Gomes, B.; Higginson, I.J. End-of-life care—What do cancer patients want? *Nat. Rev. Clin. Oncol.* **2014**, *11*, 100–108. [CrossRef] [PubMed]
25. Haun, M.W.; Estel, S.; Rucker, G.; Friederich, H.C.; Villalobos, M.; Thomas, M.; Hartmann, M. Early palliative care for adults with advanced cancer. *Cochrane Database Syst. Rev.* **2017**, *6*, CD011129. [CrossRef] [PubMed]
26. Collins, A.; McLachlan, S.A.; Philip, J. Initial perceptions of palliative care: An exploratory qualitative study of patients with advanced cancer and their family caregivers. *Palliat. Med.* **2017**, *31*, 825–832. [CrossRef]
27. Aoun, S. The palliative approach to caring for motor neurone disease: From diagnosis to bereavement. *Eur. J. Pers. Cent. Healthc.* **2018**, *6*, 675. [CrossRef]
28. Dalal, S.; Bruera, E. End-of-Life Care Matters: Palliative Cancer Care Results in Better Care and Lower Costs. *Oncologist* **2017**, *22*, 361–368. [CrossRef]
29. McLean, L.; Hong, W.; McLachlan, S. Financial toxicity in patients with cancer attending a public Australian tertiary hospital: A pilot study. *Asia-Pac. J. Clin. Oncol.* **2021**, *17*, 245–252. [CrossRef]
30. Sanson-Fisher, R.; Fakes, K.; Waller, A.; Mackenzie, L.; Bryant, J.; Herrmann, A. Assessing patients' experiences of cancer care across the treatment pathway: A mapping review of recent psychosocial cancer care publications. *Support. Care Cancer* **2019**, *27*, 1997–2006. [CrossRef]
31. Sercu, M.; Beyens, I.; Cosyns, M.; Mertens, F.; Deveugele, M.; Pype, P. Rethinking End-of-Life Care and Palliative Care: Learning From the Illness Trajectories and Lived Experiences of Terminally Ill Patients and Their Family Carers. *Qual. Health Res.* **2018**, *28*, 2220–2238. [CrossRef]
32. Moghaddam, N.; Coxon, H.; Nabarro, S.; Hardy, B.; Cox, K. Unmet care needs in people living with advanced cancer: A systematic review. *Support. Care Cancer* **2016**, *24*, 3609–3622. [CrossRef] [PubMed]
33. Stow, D.; Spiers, G.; Matthews, F.E.; Hanratty, B. What is the evidence that people with frailty have needs for palliative care at the end of life? A systematic review and narrative synthesis. *Palliat. Med.* **2019**, *33*, 399–414. [CrossRef]
34. Aoun, S.M.; Cafarella, P.A.; Hogden, A.; Thomas, G.; Jiang, L.; Edis, R. Why and how the work of Motor Neurone Disease Associations matters before and during bereavement: A consumer perspective. *Palliat. Care Soc. Pr.* **2021**, *15*, 26323524211009537. [CrossRef]
35. Grindrod, A.; Rumbold, B. Providing end-of-life care in disability community living services: An organizational capacity-building model using a public health approach. *J. Appl. Res. Intellect. Disabil.* **2017**, *30*, 1125–1137. [CrossRef]
36. Hunt, K.; Shlomo, N.; Richardson, A.; Addington-Hall, J. VOICES redesign and testing to inform a national end of life care survey. 2011. Available online: https://www.gov.uk/government/publications/voices-redesign-and-testing-to-inform-a-national-end-of-life-care-survey (accessed on 28 September 2021).
37. Hunt, K.J.; Richardson, A.; Darlington, A.E.; Addington-Hall, J.M. Developing the methods and questionnaire (VOICES-SF) for a national retrospective mortality follow-back survey of palliative and end-of-life care in England. *BMJ Support. Palliat. Care* **2019**, *9*, e5. [CrossRef]
38. Dixon, J.; King, D.; Knapp, M. Advance care planning in England: Is there an association with place of death? Secondary analysis of data from the National Survey of Bereaved People. *BMJ Support. Palliat. Care* **2019**, *9*, 316–325. [CrossRef]

39. Donnelly, S.; Prizeman, G.; Coimin, D.O.; Korn, B.; Hynes, G. Voices that matter: End-of-life care in two acute hospitals from the perspective of bereaved relatives. *BMC Palliat. Care* **2018**, *17*, 117. [CrossRef]
40. Aoun, S.; Bird, S.; Kristjanson, L.J.; Currow, D. Reliability testing of the FAMCARE-2 scale: Measuring family carer satisfaction with palliative care. *Palliat. Med.* **2010**, *24*, 674–681. [CrossRef]
41. Pidgeon, T.M.; Johnson, C.E.; Lester, L.; Currow, D.; Yates, P.; Allingham, S.F.; Bird, S.; Eagar, K. Perceptions of the care received from Australian palliative care services: A caregiver perspective. *Palliat. Support. Care* **2018**, *16*, 198–208. [CrossRef]
42. Aoun, S.M.; Rumbold, B.; Howting, D.; Bolleter, A.; Breen, L.J. Bereavement support for family caregivers: The gap between guidelines and practice in palliative care. *PLoS ONE* **2017**, *12*, e0184750. [CrossRef]
43. Virdun, C.; Luckett, T.; Lorenz, K.; Davidson, P.M.; Phillips, J. Dying in the hospital setting: A meta-synthesis identifying the elements of end-of-life care that patients and their families describe as being important. *Palliat. Med.* **2017**, *31*, 587–601. [CrossRef]
44. Virdun, C.; Luckett, T.; Lorenz, K.; Davidson, P.M.; Phillips, J. Hospital patients' perspectives on what is essential to enable optimal palliative care: A qualitative study. *Palliat. Med.* **2020**, *34*, 1402–1415. [CrossRef]
45. Wong, E.; Mavondo, F.; Fisher, J. Patient feedback to improve quality of patient-centred care in public hospitals: A systematic review of the evidence. *BMC Health Serv. Res.* **2020**, *20*, 530. [CrossRef]
46. ACSQHC. National Safety and Quality Health Service Standards. 2nd ed. Available online: https://www.safetyandquality.gov.au/sites/default/files/migrated/National-Safety-and-Quality-Health-Service-Standards-second-edition.pdf (accessed on 28 September 2021).
47. Bloomer, M.J.; Hutchinson, A.M.; Botti, M. End-of-life care in hospital: An audit of care against Australian national guidelines. *Aust. Health Rev.* **2019**, *43*, 578–584. [CrossRef]
48. Will, K.K.; Johnson, M.L.; Lamb, G. Team-Based Care and Patient Satisfaction in the Hospital Setting: A Systematic Review. *J. Patient Cent. Res. Rev.* **2019**, *6*, 158–171. [CrossRef] [PubMed]
49. Cardona-Morrell, M.; Kim, J.; Turner, R.M.; Anstey, M.; Mitchell, I.A.; Hillman, K. Non-beneficial treatments in hospital at the end of life: A systematic review on extent of the problem. *Int. J. Qual. Health Care* **2016**, *28*, 456–469. [CrossRef]
50. Singotani, R.G.; Karapinar, F.; Brouwers, C.; Wagner, C.; de Bruijne, M.C. Towards a patient journey perspective on causes of unplanned readmissions using a classification framework: Results of a systematic review with narrative synthesis. *BMC Med. Res. Methodol.* **2019**, *19*, 189. [CrossRef]
51. Trankle, S.A. Is a good death possible in Australian critical and acute settings?: Physician experiences with end-of-life care. *BMC Palliat. Care* **2014**, *13*, 41. [CrossRef] [PubMed]
52. Hall, S.; Kolliakou, A.; Petkova, H.; Froggatt, K.; Higginson, I.J. Interventions for improving palliative care for older people living in nursing care homes. *Cochrane Database Syst. Rev.* **2011**, *3*, CD007132. [CrossRef]
53. Tilden, V.P.; Thompson, S.A.; Gajewski, B.J.; Bott, M.J. End-of-life care in nursing homes: The high cost of staff turnover. *Nurs. Econ.* **2012**, *30*, 163–166.
54. Balmer, D.; Frey, R.; Gott, M.; Robinson, J.; Boyd, M. Provision of palliative and end-of-life care in New Zealand residential aged care facilities: General practitioners' perspectives. *Aust. J. Prim. Health* **2020**, *26*, 124–131. [CrossRef] [PubMed]
55. Rainsford, S.; Johnston, N.; Liu, W.-M.; Glasgow, N.; Forbat, L. Palliative care Needs Rounds in rural residential aged care: A mixed-methods study exploring experiences and perceptions of staff and general practitioners. *Prog. Palliat. Care* **2020**, *28*, 308–317. [CrossRef]
56. Milte, R.; Ratcliffe, J.; Chen, G.; Crotty, M. What Characteristics of Nursing Homes Are Most Valued by Consumers? A Discrete Choice Experiment with Residents and Family Members. *Value Health* **2018**, *21*, 843–849. [CrossRef] [PubMed]
57. Weerakkody, I.; Hales, S.; Fernandes, S.; Emmerson, D.; O'Neill, W.; Zimmermann, C.; Rodin, G. The Quality of Dying and Death in a Residential Hospice. *J. Pain Symptom Manag.* **2018**, *56*, 567–574. [CrossRef] [PubMed]
58. Lucey, M.; O'Reilly, M.; Currow, D.; Eagar, K.; Walsh, D.; Conroy, M.; Twomey, F.; O'Reilly, V.; Doherty, M.; Coffey, S.; et al. Is Inpatient Hospice Care Clinically Effective? Using Phase of Illness to Evaluate Care Outcomes for Patients Admitted to a Specialist Palliative Care Unit in Ireland. *J. Palliat. Med.* **2020**, *23*, 535–541. [CrossRef] [PubMed]
59. Stajduhar, K.; Funk, L.; Toye, C.; Grande, G.; Aoun, S.; Todd, C. Part 1: Home-based family caregiving at the end of life: A comprehensive review of published quantitative research (1998–2008). *Palliat. Med.* **2010**, *24*, 573–593. [CrossRef]
60. Funk, L.; Stajduhar, K.; Toye, C.; Aoun, S.; Grande, G.; Todd, C. Part 2: Home-based family caregiving at the end of life: A comprehensive review of published qualitative research (1998–2008). *Palliat. Med.* **2010**, *24*, 594–607. [CrossRef] [PubMed]
61. Gomes, B.; Calanzani, N.; Curiale, V.; McCrone, P.; Higginson, I.J. Effectiveness and cost-effectiveness of home palliative care services for adults with advanced illness and their caregivers. *Cochrane Database Syst. Rev.* **2013**. [CrossRef]
62. Shepperd, S.; Gonçalves-Bradley, D.C.; Straus, S.E.; Wee, B. Hospital at home: Home-based end-of-life care. *Cochrane Database Syst. Rev.* **2016**, *2*, CD009231. [CrossRef]
63. Oosterveld-Vlug, M.G.; Custers, B.; Hofstede, J.; Donker, G.A.; Rijken, P.M.; Korevaar, J.C.; Francke, A.L. What are essential elements of high-quality palliative care at home? An interview study among patients and relatives faced with advanced cancer. *BMC Palliat. Care* **2019**, *18*, 96. [CrossRef]
64. O'Brien, M.; Jack, B. Barriers to dying at home: The impact of poor co-ordination of community service provision for patients with cancer. *Health Soc. Care Community* **2010**, *18*, 337–345. [CrossRef]
65. Higginson, I.J.; Sarmento, V.P.; Calanzani, N.; Benalia, H.; Gomes, B. Dying at home–is it better: A narrative appraisal of the state of the science. *Palliat. Med.* **2013**, *27*, 918–924. [CrossRef] [PubMed]

66. Murray, M.A.; Fiset, V.; Young, S.; Kryworuchko, J. Where the dying live: A systematic review of determinants of place of end-of-life cancer care. *Oncol. Nurs. Forum* **2009**, *36*, 69–77. [CrossRef] [PubMed]
67. De Boer, D.; Hofstede, J.M.; de Veer, A.J.E.; Raijmakers, N.J.H.; Francke, A.L. Relatives' perceived quality of palliative care: Comparisons between care settings in which patients die. *BMC Palliat. Care* **2017**, *16*, 41. [CrossRef] [PubMed]
68. Aoun, S.M.; Skett, K. A longitudinal study of end-of-life preferences of terminally-ill people who live alone. *Health Soc. Care Community* **2013**, *21*, 530–535. [CrossRef] [PubMed]
69. Carmont, S.A.; Mitchell, G.; Senior, H.; Foster, M. Systematic review of the effectiveness, barriers and facilitators to general practitioner engagement with specialist secondary services in integrated palliative care. *BMJ Support. Palliat. Care* **2018**, *8*, 385–399. [CrossRef]
70. Ding, J.; Cook, A.; Saunders, C.; Chua, D.; Licqurish, S.; Mitchell, G.; Johnson, C.E. Uptake of advance care planning and its circumstances: An nationwide survey in Australian general practice. *Health Soc. Care Community* **2021**. [CrossRef]
71. National Survey of Bereaved People (VOICES): England, 2015. Available online: https://www.ons.gov.uk/peoplepopulationandcommunity/healthandsocialcare/healthcaresystem/bulletins/nationalsurveyofbereavedpeoplevoices/england2015 (accessed on 18 August 2021).
72. Sandsdalen, T.; Grondahl, V.A.; Hov, R.; Hoye, S.; Rystedt, I.; Wilde-Larsson, B. Patients' perceptions of palliative care quality in hospice inpatient care, hospice day care, palliative units in nursing homes, and home care: A cross-sectional study. *BMC Palliat. Care* **2016**, *15*, 79. [CrossRef]
73. Luckett, T.; Phillips, J.; Agar, M.; Virdun, C.; Green, A.; Davidson, P.M. Elements of effective palliative care models: A rapid review. *BMC Health Serv. Res.* **2014**, *14*, 136. [CrossRef]
74. Hansford, P.; Meehan, H.P. Gold Standards Framework: Improving community care. *End Life Care* **2007**, *1*, 56–61.
75. Siouta, N.; Van Beek, K.; van der Eerden, M.E.; Preston, N.; Hasselaar, J.G.; Hughes, S.; Garralda, E.; Centeno, C.; Csikos, A.; Groot, M.; et al. Integrated palliative care in Europe: A qualitative systematic literature review of empirically-tested models in cancer and chronic disease. *BMC Palliat. Care* **2016**, *15*, 56. [CrossRef]
76. Van Beek, K.; Siouta, N.; Preston, N.; Hasselaar, J.; Hughes, S.; Payne, S.; Radbruch, L.; Centeno, C.; Csikos, A.; Garralda, E.; et al. To what degree is palliative care integrated in guidelines and pathways for adult cancer patients in Europe: A systematic literature review. *BMC Palliat. Care* **2016**, *15*, 26. [CrossRef] [PubMed]
77. Emanuel, L.; Alexander, C.; Arnold, R.M.; Bernstein, R.; Dart, R.; Dellasantina, C.; Dykstra, L.; Tulsky, J.; Palliative Care Guidelines Group of the American Hospice Foundation. Integrating palliative care into disease management guidelines. *J. Palliat. Med.* **2004**, *7*, 774–783. [CrossRef]
78. Gardiner, C.; Ingleton, C.; Gott, M.; Ryan, T. Exploring the transition from curative care to palliative care: A systematic review of the literature. *BMJ Support. Palliat. Care* **2015**, *5*, 335–342. [CrossRef] [PubMed]
79. Dossett, L.A.; Hudson, J.N.; Morris, A.M.; Lee, M.C.; Roetzheim, R.G.; Fetters, M.D.; Quinn, G.P. The primary care provider (PCP)-cancer specialist relationship: A systematic review and mixed-methods meta-synthesis. *CA Cancer J. Clin.* **2017**, *67*, 156–169. [CrossRef]
80. Smallwood, N.; Moran, T.; Thompson, M.; Eastman, P.; Le, B.; Philip, J. Integrated respiratory and palliative care leads to high levels of satisfaction: A survey of patients and carers. *BMC Palliat. Care* **2019**, *18*, 7. [CrossRef]
81. Kaufmann, T.L.; Kamal, A.H. Oncology and Palliative Care Integration: Cocreating Quality and Value in the Era of Health Care Reform. *J. Oncol. Pract.* **2017**, *13*, 580–588. [CrossRef]
82. ElMokhallalati, Y.; Bradley, S.H.; Chapman, E.; Ziegler, L.; Murtagh, F.E.; Johnson, M.J.; Bennett, M.I. Identification of patients with potential palliative care needs: A systematic review of screening tools in primary care. *Palliat. Med.* **2020**, *34*, 989–1005. [CrossRef]
83. Russell, B.; Vogrin, S.; Philip, J.; Hennessy-Anderson, N.; Collins, A.; Burchell, J.; Le, B.; Brand, C.; Hudson, P.; Sundararajan, V. Triaging the Terminally Ill-Development of the Responding to Urgency of Need in Palliative Care (RUN-PC) Triage Tool. *J. Pain Symptom Manag.* **2020**, *59*, 95–104.e111. [CrossRef]
84. Schulz, R.; Beach, S.R.; Friedman, E.M.; Martsolf, G.R.; Rodakowski, J.; James, A.E., 3rd. Changing Structures and Processes to Support Family Caregivers of Seriously Ill Patients. *J. Palliat. Med.* **2018**, *21*, S36–S42. [CrossRef] [PubMed]
85. Brereton, L.; Clark, J.; Ingleton, C.; Gardiner, C.; Preston, L.; Ryan, T.; Goyder, E. What do we know about different models of providing palliative care? Findings from a systematic review of reviews. *Palliat. Med.* **2017**, *31*, 781–797. [CrossRef] [PubMed]
86. ACSQHC. National Consensus Statement: Essential Elements for Safe and High-Quality End-of-Life Care. Available online: https://www.safetyandquality.gov.au/publications-and-resources/resource-library/national-consensus-statement-essential-elements-safe-and-high-quality-end-life-care (accessed on 28 September 2021).
87. NICE. End of Life Care for Adults. Available online: https://www.nice.org.uk/guidance/qs13/resources/end-of-life-care-for-adults-pdf-2098483631557 (accessed on 18 August 2021).
88. NICE. NICE Impact End of Life Care for Adults. Available online: https://www.nice.org.uk/Media/Default/About/what-we-do/Into-practice/measuring-uptake/End-of-life-care-impact-report/nice-impact-end-of-life-care.pdf (accessed on 18 August 2021).
89. Groeneveld, E.I.; Cassel, J.B.; Bausewein, C.; Csikos, A.; Krajnik, M.; Ryan, K.; Haugen, D.F.; Eychmueller, S.; Gudat Keller, H.; Allan, S.; et al. Funding models in palliative care: Lessons from international experience. *Palliat. Med.* **2017**, *31*, 296–305. [CrossRef] [PubMed]
90. Duckett, S. Aligning policy objectives and payment design in palliative care. *BMC Palliat. Care* **2018**, *17*, 42. [CrossRef] [PubMed]

91. Reeve, R.; Srasuebkul, P.; Langton, J.M.; Haas, M.; Viney, R.; Pearson, S.A. Health care use and costs at the end of life: A comparison of elderly Australian decedents with and without a cancer history. *BMC Palliat. Care* **2017**, *17*, 1. [CrossRef]
92. People-Centred Health Care: A Policy Framework. Available online: https://www.who.int/publications/i/item/9789290613176 (accessed on 23 August 2021).
93. Abel, J.; Walter, T.; Carey, L.B.; Rosenberg, J.; Noonan, K.; Horsfall, D.; Leonard, R.; Rumbold, B.; Morris, D. Circles of care: Should community development redefine the practice of palliative care? *BMJ Support. Palliat. Care* **2013**, *3*, 383–388. [CrossRef]
94. Horsfall, D.; Leonard, R.; Rosenberg, J.P.; Noonan, K. Home as a place of caring and wellbeing? A qualitative study of informal carers and caring networks lived experiences of providing in-home end-of-life care. *Health Place* **2017**, *46*, 58–64. [CrossRef]
95. Archibald, D.; Patterson, R.; Haraldsdottir, E.; Hazelwood, M.; Fife, S.; Murray, S.A. Mapping the progress and impacts of public health approaches to palliative care: A scoping review protocol. *BMJ Open* **2016**, *6*, e012058. [CrossRef]
96. Nous. Compassionate Communities: An Implementation Guide for Community Approaches to End of Life Care. Available online: https://palliativecare.org.au/wp-content/uploads/dlm_uploads/2018/09/An-implementation-guide-for-community.pdf (accessed on 18 August 2021).
97. Salau, S.; Rumbold, B.; Young, B. From concept to care: Enabling community care through a health promoting palliative care approach. *Contemp. Nurse* **2007**, *27*, 132–140. [CrossRef]
98. Vanderstichelen, S.; Cohen, J.; Van Wesemael, Y.; Deliens, L.; Chambaere, K. The involvement of volunteers in palliative care and their collaboration with healthcare professionals: A cross-sectional volunteer survey across the Flemish healthcare system (Belgium). *Health Soc. Care Community* **2020**, *28*, 747–761. [CrossRef]
99. Cronin, P. Compassionate Communities in Shropshire, West Midlands, England. In *Compassionate Communities: Case Studies from Britain and Europe*, 1st ed.; Wegleitner, K.H., Kellehear, K.A., Eds.; Routledge: London, UK, 2015; p. 16.
100. Abel, J.; Kingston, H.; Scally, A.; Hartnoll, J.; Hannam, G.; Thomson-Moore, A.; Kellehear, A. Reducing emergency hospital admissions: A population health complex intervention of an enhanced model of primary care and compassionate communities. *Br. J. Gen. Pract.* **2018**, *68*, e803–e810. [CrossRef]
101. Horsfall, D. Developing compassionate communities in Australia through collective caregiving: A qualitative study exploring network-centred care and the role of the end of life sector. *Ann. Palliat. Med.* **2018**, *7*, S42–S51. [CrossRef] [PubMed]
102. Horsfall, D.; Leonard, R.; Noonan, K.; Rosenberg, J. Working together–apart: Exploring the relationships between formal and informal care networks for people dying at home. *Prog. Palliat. Care* **2013**, *21*. [CrossRef]
103. Horsfall, D.; Noonan, K.; Leonard, R. Bringing our Dying Home: How caring for someone at end of life builds social capital and develops compassionate communities. *Health Sociol. Rev.* **2013**, *21*, 373–382. [CrossRef]
104. Horsfall, D.; Yardley, A.; Leonard, R.; Noonan, K.; Rosenberg, J. *End of Life at Home: Co-Creating an Ecology of Care*; Western Sydney University: Penrith, NSW, Australia, 2015. [CrossRef]
105. Leonard, R.; Horsfall, D.; Noonan, K. Identifying changes in the support networks of end-of-life carers using social network analysis. *BMJ Support. Palliat. Care* **2015**, *5*, 153–159. [CrossRef]
106. Leonard, R.; Horsfall, D.; Rosenberg, J.; Noonan, K. Carer experience of end-of-life service provision: A social network analysis. *BMJ Support. Palliat. Care* **2020**, *10*, e20. [CrossRef] [PubMed]
107. Rosenberg, J.P.; Horsfall, D.; Leonard, R.; Noonan, K. Informal caring networks for people at end of life: Building social capital in Australian communities. *Health Sociol. Rev.* **2015**, *24*, 29–37. [CrossRef]
108. Wegleitner, K.; Schuchter, P.; Prieth, S. 'Ingredients' of a supportive web of caring relationships at the end of life: Findings from a community research project in Austria. *Sociol. Health Illn.* **2020**, *42*, 987–1000. [CrossRef]
109. Wegleitner, K.; Heimerl, K.; Kellehear, A. *Compassionate Communities. Case Studies from Britain and Europe*; Routledge: London, UK, 2015. [CrossRef]
110. Kellehear, A. Compassionate cities: Public health and end-of-life care. In *Compassionate Cities: Public Health End—Life Care*; Routledge: London, UK, 2012; pp. 1–179. [CrossRef]
111. Abel, J. Compassionate communities and end-of-life care. *Clin. Med.* **2018**, *18*, 6–8. [CrossRef]
112. Sallnow, L.; Paul, S. Understanding community engagement in end-of-life care: Developing conceptual clarity. *Crit. Public Health* **2015**, *25*, 231–238. [CrossRef]
113. Naylor, C.; Wllingd, D. *A Citizen-Led Approach to Health and Care: Lessons from the Wigan Deal*; The Kings Fund: London, UK, 2019.
114. Street, J.; Duszynski, K.; Krawczyk, S.; Braunack-Mayer, A. The use of citizens' juries in health policy decision-making: A systematic review. *Soc. Sci. Med.* **2014**, *109*, 1–9. [CrossRef]
115. Dietrich, T.; Trischler, J.; Schuster, L.; Rundle-Thiele, S. Co-designing services with vulnerable consumers. *J. Serv. Theory Pract.* **2017**, *27*, 663–688. [CrossRef]
116. Johns, R.; Davey, J. Introducing the transformative service mediator: Value creation with vulnerable consumers. *J. Serv. Mark.* **2019**, *33*, 5–15. [CrossRef]
117. Chung, A.; Collier, A.; Gott, M. Community-led and/or focused initiatives to support family carers within a palliative care context: An integrative review. *Palliat. Med.* **2019**, *33*, 250–256. [CrossRef] [PubMed]
118. McCarron, T.L.; Moffat, K.; Wilkinson, G.; Zelinsky, S.; Boyd, J.M.; White, D.; Hassay, D.; Lorenzetti, D.L.; Marlett, N.J.; Noseworthy, T. Understanding patient engagement in health system decision-making: A co-designed scoping review. *Syst. Rev.* **2019**, *8*, 97. [CrossRef]

119. Barry, V.; Patel, M. *An Overview of Compassionate Communities in England*; Murray Hall Community Trust: London, UK; National Council for Palliative Care Dying Matters: Tipton, UK, 2013.
120. Department of Health. Greater Choice for at Home Palliative Care. Available online: https://www.health.gov.au/initiatives-and-programs/greater-choice-for-at-home-palliative-care-measure (accessed on 18 August 2021).
121. Grindrod, A.; Rumbold, B. Healthy End of Life Project (HELP): A progress report on implementing community guidance on public health palliative care initiatives in Australia. *Ann. Palliat. Med.* **2018**, *7*, S73–S83. [CrossRef] [PubMed]
122. Abel, J.; Kellehear, A.; Karapliagou, A. Palliative care-the new essentials. *Ann. Palliat. Med.* **2018**, *7*, S3–S14. [CrossRef]
123. Aoun, S.M.; Abel, J.; Rumbold, B.; Cross, K.; Moore, J.; Skeers, P.; Deliens, L. The Compassionate Communities Connectors model for end-of-life care: A community and health service partnership in Western Australia. *Palliat. Care Soc. Pract.* **2020**, *14*, 2632352420935130. [CrossRef]
124. Aoun, S.M.; Breen, L.J.; White, I.; Rumbold, B.; Kellehear, A. What sources of bereavement support are perceived helpful by bereaved people and why? Empirical evidence for the compassionate communities approach. *Palliat. Med.* **2018**, *32*, 1378–1388. [CrossRef]
125. Aoun, S.M.; Keegan, O.; Roberts, A.; Breen, L.J. The impact of bereavement support on wellbeing: A comparative study between Australia and Ireland. *Palliat. Care Soc. Pract.* **2020**, *14*, 2632352420935132. [CrossRef]
126. NACCHO. National Aboriginal Community Controlled Health Organisation. Available online: https://www.naccho.org.au (accessed on 23 September 2021).
127. Australian Indigenous HealthInfoNet. Palliative Care and End-of-Life Care. Available online: https://healthinfonet.ecu.edu.au/learn/health-system/palliative-care/ (accessed on 23 September 2021).
128. *Australian Government Department of Health Exploratory Analysis of Barriers to Palliative Care Summary Policy Paper*; Australian Healthcare Associates: Melbourne, Australia, 2020.

MDPI
St. Alban-Anlage 66
4052 Basel
Switzerland
www.mdpi.com

Healthcare Editorial Office
E-mail: healthcare@mdpi.com
www.mdpi.com/journal/healthcare

www.ingramcontent.com/pod-product-compliance
Lightning Source LLC
Chambersburg PA
CBHW041950260926
51850CB00019B/2281
* 9 7 8 3 0 3 6 5 9 0 4 7 9 *